D1535237

WITHDRAWN

INTERNATIONAL ORGANIZATIONS SERIES
Edited by Jon Woronoff

1. *European Community,* by Desmond Dinan. 1993
2. *International Monetary Fund,* by Norman K. Humphreys. 1993
3. *International Organizations in Sub-Saharan Africa,* by Mark W. DeLancey and Terry M. Mays. 1994
4. *European Organizations,* by Derek W. Urwin. 1994
5. *International Tribunals,* by Boleslaw Adam Boczek. 1994
6. *International Food Agencies: FAO, WFP, WFC, IFAD,* by Ross B. Talbot. 1994
7. *Refugee and Disaster Relief Organizations,* by Robert F. Gorman. 1994
8. *United Nations,* by A. LeRoy Bennett. 1995
9. *Multinational Peacekeeping,* by Terry Mays. 1995

HISTORICAL DICTIONARY of the UNITED NATIONS

by
A. LeRoy Bennett

International Organizations Series, No. 8

The Scarecrow Press, Inc.
Lanham, Md., & London

SCARECROW PRESS, INC.

Published in the United States of America
by Scarecrow Press, Inc.
4720 Boston Way, Lanham, Maryland 20706

4 Pleydell Gardens, Folkestone
Kent CT20 2DN, England

British Cataloging in Publication Information Available

Library of Congress Cataloging-in-Publication Data

Bennett, A. LeRoy (Alvin LeRoy), 1914–
Historical dictionary of the United Nations / by A. LeRoy Bennett.
p. cm. — (International organizations series ; no. 8)
Includes bibliographical references.
1. United Nations—History. I. Title. II. Series: International
organizations series ; no. 8.
JX1976.B395 1995 341.23—dc20 95–1505

ISBN 0–8108–2992–4 (cloth : alk. paper)

Printed in the United States of America

 The paper used in this publication meets the minimum requirements of
American National Standard for Information Sciences—Permanence
of Paper for Printed Library Materials, ANSI Z39.48–1984.

DEDICATION

Dedicated to my family whose unity, cohesion, empathy, and tolerance might well serve as a microcosmic model for a not always harmonious United Nations

CONTENTS

List of Photographs   vii

Editor's Foreword   ix

Abbreviations and Acronyms   xi

Chronology   xvii

INTRODUCTION   1

THE DICTIONARY   25

BIBLIOGRAPHY   152
    Official Publications   152
    Other Basic General Sources   153
    Reference Works   154
    Background   155
    Structure of the UN   157
    Membership Issues   159
    Peace and Security Activities   160
    Arms Control and Disarmament   166
    Legal Activities   167
    Economic and Social Development   169
    Human Rights Activities   172
    Independence and Self-Government   173
    UN Leadership and the Secretary-General   175
    Evaluation and Prospects   178
    Specialized Agencies and Other Bodies   182

Appendices
    1. Charter of the United Nations   189
    2. The Universal Declaration of Human Rights 226

3. Members of the United Nations:
   Date of Membership and Assessment   235
4. Presidents of the General Assembly   241
5. Secretaries-General of the United Nations   243

About the Author   245

LIST OF PHOTOGRAPHS

Secretaries-General Dag Hammarskjöld and Trygve Lie   xxxiii
Secretary-General U Thant   xxxiv
Secretary-General Kurt Waldheim   xxxv
Secretary-General Javier Pérez de Cuéllar   xxxvi
Secretary-General Boutros Boutros-Ghali   xxxvii
United Nations Headquarters, New York   xxxviii
Security Council in Session   xxix
General Assembly in Session   xl
United Nations European Headquarters, Geneva   xli
International Court of Justice in Session   xlii

(All of these photos were provided by the United Nations Information Service, Geneva, Switzerland, whose kind assistance we gratefully acknowledge.)

EDITOR'S FOREWORD

This is a particularly good time to review the evolution of the United Nations. For half a century, it has been laboring to achieve almost unachievable tasks laid down optimistically and idealistically in its Charter. And, despite all the carping and criticizing, despite all the insufficiencies, setbacks and concessions to political realities, it has done an amazingly good job. It has pursued activities—alone or with specialized agencies—in a vast range of fields: agriculture, economic development, environment, health, peacekeeping and many, many more. And it has had its successes, resolving or at least attenuating conflicts and making this world better than it would otherwise be.

This is also a particularly good time to look toward the future. Not only because the United Nations will continue all these activities as in the past and make further progress, but because it can move in completely new directions with greater chances of success. The end of the Cold War, which forced the UN time and again to focus on the chilling possibility of a hot war between the Great Powers, allows it to devise new forms of cooperation between all countries, larger and smaller. What will come of this, nobody knows exactly. Still, based on our knowledge of the past, we can get a better feel for the future.

Such knowledge is provided very amply in this *Historical Dictionary of the United Nations*. It includes concise but informative entries on dozens of bodies in the UN family, dozens of topics and issues the UN has dealt with, and dozens of persons who have contributed to its growth. To keep track of the many bodies, issues and players, there is an extremely useful chronology. And, since such a book cannot begin to cover everything, there is a comprehensive bibliography, including significant works which, informative as they may be, also tell only part of the story. This book is thus a starting point, and a very helpful one.

It is written by someone in an uncommonly good position to

ix

describe the past and hint at the future, A. LeRoy Bennett. Dr. Bennett has been teaching international relations and international organizations for some 40 years, at Michigan State University, Drake University and the University of Delaware, of which he is now Professor Emeritus. He was at the United Nations headquarters on a Ford Foundation fellowship in 1951–52 and has been active in the United Nations Association. Dr. Bennett has written widely, including articles in learned journals, and is the author of the leading textbook on international organization, *International Organizations: Principles and Issues.* This may explain the ease with which he leads us through the complicated maze of UN organizations.

Jon Woronoff
Series Editor

ABBREVIATIONS AND ACRONYMS

AIDS	Acquired Immune Deficiency Syndrome
CBR	Chemical, Bacteriological, and Radiological Weapons
CSDHA	United Nations Center for Social Development and Humanitarian Affairs
ECA	Economic Commission for Africa
ECAFE	Economic Commission for Asia and the Far East
ECE	Economic Commission for Europe
ECLA	Economic Commission for Latin America
ECLAC	Economic Commission for Latin America and the Caribbean
ECOSOC	Economic and Social Council
ECWA	Economic Commission for Western Asia
EPTA	Expanded Program of Technical Assistance
ESCAP	Economic and Social Council for Asia and the Pacific
ESCWA	Economic and Social Commission for Western Asia
FAO	Food and Agriculture Organization
GATT	General Agreement on Tariffs and Trade
GEMS	Global Environmental Monitoring Service
GNP	Gross National Product
HABITAT	United Nations Conference on Human Settlements
IAEA	International Atomic Energy Agency
IBRD	International Bank for Reconstruction and Development

ICAO	International Civil Aviation Organization
ICJ	International Court of Justice
IDA	International Development Association
IFAD	International Fund for Agricultural Development
IFC	International Finance Corporation
ILC	International Law Commission
ILO	International Labour Organisation
IMF	International Monetary Fund
IMO	International Maritime Organization
INSTRAW	International Research and Training Institute for the Advancement of Women
IRO	International Refugee Organization
ITU	International Telecommunication Union
MIGA	Multilateral Investment Guarantee Agency
MINURSO	United Nations Mission for the Referendum in Western Sahara
MNCs	Multinational Corporations
NATO	North Atlantic Treaty Organization
NGOs	Nongovernmental Organizations
NIEO	New International Economic Order
OAS	Organization of American States
OAU	Organization of African Unity
OECD	Organization for Economic Cooperation and Development
OEEC	Organization for European Economic Cooperation
ONOGIL	United Nations Observer Group in Lebanon
ONUC	United Nations Operation in the Congo
ONUCA	United Nations Observer Group in Central America
ONUMOZ	United Nations Operation in Mozambique
ONUSAL	United Nations Observer Mission in El Salvador
ONUVEN	United Nations Observation Mission for the Verification of Elections in Nicaragua
OPEC	Organization of Petroleum Exporting Countries
OPEX	Operational Executive and Administrative Personnel Services

PLO	Palestine Liberation Organization
SDRs	Special Drawing Rights
TNCs	Transnational Corporations
UN	United Nations
UNAMIR	United Nations Assistance Mission to Rwanda
UNAVEM	United Nations Angola Verification Mission
UNAVEM II	United Nations Angola Verification Mission—Second Version
UNCED	United Nations Conference on Environment and Development
UNCI	United Nations Commission for Indonesia
UNCITRAL	United Nations Commission for International Trade Law
UNCTAD	United Nations Conference on Trade and Development
UNDOF	United Nations Disengagement Observer Force (Golan Heights)
UNDP	United Nations Development Program
UNDRO	Office of United Nations Disaster Relief Coordinator
UNEF	United Nations Emergency Force (Sinai)
UNEF II	United Nations Emergency Force—Second Version
UNEP	United Nations Environmental Program
UNESCO	United Nations Educational, Scientific and Cultural Organization
UNFICYP	United Nations Peacekeeping Force in Cyprus
UNFPA	United Nations Fund for Population Activities
UNGOMAP	United Nations Good Offices Mission in Afghanistan and Pakistan
UNHCR	United Nations High Commissioner for Refugees
UNICEF	United Nations Children's Fund
UNIDO	United Nations Industrial Development Organization
UNIDR	United Nations Institute for Disarmament Research
UNIFEM	United Nations Development Fund for Women

UNIFIL	United Nations Interim Force in Lebanon
UNIIMOG	United Nations Iran-Iraq Observer Group
UNIKOM	United Nations Iraq-Kuwait Observation Mission
UNIPOM	United Nations India-Pakistan Observation Mission
UNITAF	Unified Task Force (Somalia)
UNITAR	United Nations Institute for Training and Research
UNMOGIP	United Nations Military Observer Group in India and Pakistan
UNOGIL	United Nations Observer Group in Lebanon
UNOMIG	United Nations Observer Mission in Georgia
UNOMIL	United Nations Observer Mission in Liberia
UNOMSA	United Nations Observer Mission in South Africa
UNOMUR	United Nations Observer Mission Uganda-Rwanda
UNOSOM	United Nations Operation in Somalia
UNOSOM II	United Nations Operation in Somalia—Second Enlarged Version
UNPROFOR	United Nations Protection Force (Yugoslavia)
UNRRA	United Nations Relief and Rehabilitation Administration
UNRWA	United Nations Relief and Works Agency for Palestine Refugees in the Near East
UNSCOB	United Nations Special Committee on the Balkans
UNSF	United Nations Security Force (West Irian)
UNTAC	United Nations Transitional Authority in Cambodia
UNTAG	United Nations Transition Assistance Group (Namibia)
UNTEA	United Nations Temporary Executive Authority (West Irian)
UNTSO	United Nations Truce Supervision Organization (Middle East)
UNYOM	United Nations Yemen Observation Mission
UPU	Universal Postal Union

WFP	World Food Programme
WHO	World Health Organization
WIPO	World Intellectual Property Organization
WMO	World Meteorological Organization
WTO	World Trade Organization

CHRONOLOGY

1865   International Telegraph Union (ITU, later renamed the International Telecommunication Union) established. In October 1947 it became a specialized agency of the UN system.

1873   World Meteorological Organization (WMO) began operation as a nongovernmental organization. In December 1951 it entered into UN relationship as a specialized agency after a four-year process of conversion to an intergovernmental organization.

1874   General Postal Union formed with title changed to Universal Postal Union (UPU) in 1878. In July 1948 it entered into specialized agency status within the UN system.

1883   World Intellectual Property Organization (WIPO) created, operating under various related titles until, in 1974, it completed the process of becoming a UN-affiliated specialized agency.

April 28, 1919   Text of League of Nations Covenant unanimously approved by Paris Peace Conference.

1919   International Labour Organisation (ILO) established as an autonomous part of League of Nations. Relationship served as model for UN specialized agency system and ILO became the first such agency in 1946.

January 10, 1920   League of Nations began official operations. This was the first general purpose international organization open to universal membership. Weakened by U.S. failure to join.

1939   Planning for a postwar international organization begun by private groups in the United States and United Kingdom, followed in 1940 by initial official government planning.

January 1942   Twenty-six nations in Washington, D.C. signed Declaration by United Nations stating war and peace aims.

May 1943   United Nations Conference on Food and Agriculture at Hot Springs, Virginia, laid basis for UN Food and Agriculture Organization (FAO).

October 1943   Representatives of USSR, U.S.A., United Kingdom, and China issued Moscow Declaration pledging cooperation for establishment of a "general international organization."

November 1943   Allies established United Nations Relief and Rehabilitation Administration (UNRRA) for rebuilding war-torn economies and care for refugees.

July 1944   Bretton Woods Conference developed plans for International Bank for Reconstruction and Development (IBRD) and International Monetary Fund (IMF).

August– October 1944   Dumbarton Oaks Conference of Big Four governments produced plans for peace and security provisions of UN Charter.

February 1945   Yalta Conference, attended by Roosevelt, Churchill, and Stalin, and their foreign ministers agreed on voting formula in Security Council and on date for convening San Francisco Conference.

April–June 1945   San Francisco Conference, attended by delegates of 50 states, produced United Nations Charter.

October 24, 1945   United Nations Charter took effect on receipt of certificates of ratification of a majority of signatories including five permanent members of Security Council. October 24th subsequently celebrated as United Nations Day.

December 1945   All 51 original members completed Charter ratification.

January 10, 1946   First meeting of UN General Assembly.

January 1946   Security Council considered, as its first dispute, the withdrawal of Soviet forces from northern Iran.

1946   United Nations Children's Fund (UNICEF) established and International Labour Organisation (ILO), International Bank for Reconstruction and Development (IBRD), International Monetary Fund (IMF), Food and Agriculture Organization (FAO), and United Nations Educational, Scientific and Cultural Organization (UNESCO) began operations as UN specialized agencies.

April 1946   League of Nations dissolved and turned over assets to United Nations.

April 1946   International Court of Justice convened for first time.

March 1947	Trusteeship Council held its first session.
April 28–May 15, 1947	General Assembly Special Session on Palestine.
Fall 1947	Economic Commission for Europe (ECE) and Economic Commission for Asia and the Far East (ECAFE, later ESCAP) established.
November 29, 1947	General Assembly adopted plan to establish the state of Israel.
April 16–May 14, 1948	General Assembly Special Session on Palestine.
May 20, 1948	General Assembly appointed Count Folke Bernadotte as Palestine Mediator.
August 1948	International Refugee Organization (IRO) began operations.
Fall 1948	Economic Commission for Latin America (ECLA, later ECLAC) established.
December 10, 1948	General Assembly adopted Universal Declaration of Human Rights. December 10th annually observed as Human Rights Day.
August 1949	Security Council created United Nations Truce Supervision Organization (UNTSO) as observers in the Middle East.
December 1949	General Assembly created United Nations Relief and Works Agency for Palestine Refugees in the Near East (UNRWA).
June 1950	Expanded Program of Technical Assistance (EPTA) became operative.

June–July 1950   Security Council, in voluntary absence of Soviet delegates, legitimized military action to repel North Korean military attack on South Korea.

November 3, 1950   General Assembly adopted Uniting for Peace Resolution providing for calling of emergency sessions of General Assembly when Security Council is deadlocked.

January 1, 1951   Office of United Nations High Commissioner for Refugees (UNHCR) began operations.

January 12, 1951   Convention on the Prevention and Punishment of the Crime of Genocide came into force.

February 1, 1951   General Assembly condemned China as an aggressor in Korea.

February 1952   International Refugee Organization (IRO) turned over its responsibilities to United Nations High Commissioner for Refugees (UNHCR).

Fall 1952   General Assembly began consideration of Apartheid in South Africa as a major issue until 1993.

April 10, 1953   Dag Hammarskjöld assumed office as Secretary General.

August–
September 1954   World Population Conference in Rome.

December 1955   East-West "package deal" provided for simultaneous admission to UN membership of 16 states, breaking ten-year deadlock.

July 1956	International Finance Corporation (IFC) created as affiliate of World Bank to stimulate private investment in developing countries.
November 1956	General Assembly Emergency Special Session on the Suez crisis.
November 1956	General Assembly Emergency Special Session on the Hungarian crisis.
November 1956–February 1957	First large-scale United Nations peacekeeping force, the United Nations Emergency Force (UNEF), dispatched to the Sinai.
October 1957	International Atomic Energy Agency (IAEA) began operations.
April 1958	Economic Commission for Africa (ECA) established.
August 1958	General Assembly Emergency Special Session on Lebanon and Jordan.
Fall 1959	United Nations Special Fund began operations to provide large-scale preinvestment surveys and feasibility studies on development projects.
1959	Security Council reached nadir of activity with only five meetings during 1959.
July 1960–June 1964	United Nations Operation in the Congo (ONUC) involving 20,000 peacekeeping personnel.
September 1960	General Assembly Emergency Special Session on the Congo Crisis.
September 1960	International Development Association (IDA) created as World Bank affiliate to make soft loans to poorest countries.

September–October 1960	Seventeen new member states admitted to the United Nations.
December 1960	General Assembly adopted historic, sweeping Declaration on the Granting of Independence to Colonial Countries and Peoples.
August 1961	General Assembly Special Session on Tunisia.
September 17, 1961	Death of Dag Hammarskjöld in plane crash in Northern Rhodesia (now Zambia).
November 3, 1961	U Thant appointed acting Secretary-General. Later made permanent Secretary-General with service until December 31, 1971.
December 1962	General Assembly authorized creation of United Nations Conference on Trade and Development (UNCTAD) with Secretariat in Geneva.
January 1963	World Food Programme began operations.
May–June 1963	General Assembly Special Session on Financial and Budgetary Problems.
July 1963	Partial Test-Ban Treaty negotiated.
March 1964	United Nations peacekeeping force (UNFICYP) deployed in Cyprus.
March–June 1964	First session of United Nations Conference on Trade and Development (UNCTAD).
August 1965	Amendments to UN Charter came into force enlarging membership of Security Council and Economic and Social Council.
August–September 1965	World Population Conference in Belgrade.

November 1965   Expanded Program of Technical Assistance (EPTA) and United Nations Special Fund combined into United Nations Development Program (UNDP).

December 1965   Convention on the Elimination of All Forms of Racial Discrimination opened for ratification. Came into force in 1969.

November 1966   United Nations Industrial Development Organization (UNIDO) established by General Assembly.

December 1966   General Assembly unanimously approved the International Covenant on Civil and Political Rights and the International Covenant on Economic, Social, and Cultural Rights.

April–June 1967   General Assembly Special Session on Review of Peacekeeping Operations and Southwest Africa.

June–
September 1967   General Assembly Emergency Special Session on the Middle East Crisis.

July 1967   Secretary-General U Thant initiated the United Nations Fund for Population Activities (UNFPA).

June 1968   Treaty on the Non-Proliferation of Nuclear Weapons opened for signature and ratification.

October 1971   Nationalist Chinese representatives at UN replaced by those of Communist China.

Fall 1971   General Assembly established Office of United Nations Disaster Relief Coordinator (UNDRO).

January 1, 1972   Kurt Waldheim assumed office as Secretary-General.

April 10, 1972   Convention on the Prohibition of the Development, Production and Stockpiling of Bacteriological and Toxin Weapons opened for signature and ratification.

June 1972   United Nations Conference on the Human Environment in Stockholm.

December 1972   General Assembly approved the creation of the United Nations Environment Program (UNEP) with headquarters in Nairobi, Kenya.

August 1973   Economic Commission for Western Asia (ECWA), later Economic and Social Commission for Western Asia (ESCWA), established by Economic and Social Council.

September 1973   West and East Germany became UN members.

December 1973–   Law of the Sea Conference worked out comprehensive treaty on all aspects of ocean access and usage.
December 1982

Spring 1974   General Assembly Special Session on Raw Materials and Development adopted Declaration and Program of Action on the Establishment of a New International Economic Order (NIEO).

May 31, 1974   Security Council authorized peacekeeping force for Golan Heights (UNDOF).

August 1974   World Population Conference in Bucharest.

November 1974	World Food Conference in Rome.
December 1974	General Assembly adopted Charter of Economic Rights and Duties of States.
June 1975	First international conference on women's issues held in Mexico City.
September 1975	General Assembly Special Session on Development and International Economic Cooperation.
December 1975– June 1977	Conference on International Economic Cooperation in Paris.
May 1976	International Research and Training Institute for the Advancement of Women (INSTRAW) established by Economic and Social Council.
June 1976	United Nations Conference on Human Settlements (HABITAT) in Vancouver.
March 1977	United Nations Water Conference in Mar del Plata, Argentina.
August– September 1977	United Nations Conference on Desertification in Nairobi, Kenya.
November 1977	International Fund for Agricultural Development (IFAD) began operations.
March 1978	United Nations Interim Force in Lebanon (UNIFIL) established.
April 1978	General Assembly Special Session on Financing of United Nations Interim Force in Lebanon.

April–May 1978	General Assembly Special Session on Namibia.
May–June 1978	General Assembly Special Session on Disarmament.
August 1978	World Conference to Combat Racism and Racial Discrimination in Geneva.
August–September 1978	Conference on Technical Cooperation among Developing Countries in Buenos Aires.
July 1979	Conference on Agrarian Reform and Rural Development in Rome.
August–September 1979	United Nations Conference on Science and Technology for Development in Vienna.
January 1980	General Assembly Emergency Special Session on Afghanistan.
May 24, 1980	International Court of Justice ruled that Iran had violated international law in seizing the U.S. embassy and personnel.
July 1980	General Assembly Emergency Special Session on Palestine.
August–September 1980	General Assembly Special Session on International Economic Cooperation.
June 19, 1981	Security Council condemned Israeli attack on Iraqi nuclear facility.
August 1981	United Nations Conference on New and Renewable Sources of Energy in Nairobi, Kenya.

September 1981   General Assembly Emergency Special Session on Namibia.

January 1, 1982   Javier Peréz de Cuéllar assumed office as UN Secretary-General.

January–   General Assembly Emergency Special Session on the Occupied Arab Territories.
February 1982

June 6, 1982   Security Council unanimously demanded withdrawal of Israeli forces from Lebanon.

August 1983   Second World Conference to Combat Racism and Racial Discrimination in Geneva.

August 1984   World Population Conference in Mexico City.

1984–85   United States, United Kingdom, and Singapore withdraw from UNESCO membership.

July 1985   Conference to Review and Appraise the Achievements of the United Nations Decade for Women in Nairobi, Kenya.

1986   U.S. Congress appropriated less than half of U.S. assessed amount for the regular UN budget as well as shortages in peacekeeping assessments, thus exacerbating ongoing UN financial crisis.

May–June 1986   General Assembly Special Session on the Critical Economic Situation in Africa.

September 1986   General Assembly Special Session on Namibia.

March–April 1987   United Nations Conference for the Promotion of International Cooperation in the Peaceful Uses of Nuclear Energy in Geneva.

August 1987   World Commission on Environment and Development issued report stressing "sustainable development."

August–
September 1987   International Conference on the Relationship between Disarmament and Development in New York.

April 1988   Multilateral Investment Guarantee Agency (MIGA) established as subsidiary of World Bank.

May–June 1988   General Assembly Special Session on Disarmament.

April 1989–
March 1990   United Nations Transition Assistance Group (UNTAG) of 8,000 personnel assisted Namibia's transition to self-rule.

September 1989   General Assembly Special Session on Apartheid.

February 1990   General Assembly Special Session on Drug Problems.

April 1990   General Assembly Special Session on International Economic Cooperation.

August 6–
November 29, 1990   Security Council adopted 12 resolutions relating to Iraq's invasion of Kuwait. Final resolution (678) authorized use of "all necessary means" to ensure compliance with resolutions and set January 15, 1991 as deadline for Iraqi compliance.

April 3, 1991   Security Council in resolution 687 set terms for Iraq in aftermath of Persian Gulf War including destruction of chemical and biological weapons and long-range missiles.

April 6, 1991   Iraq accepted terms of Security Council resolution 687.

April 9, 1991   Security Council established UN Iraq-Kuwait Observation Mission (UNIKOM) to monitor Iraq-Kuwait border.

April 1991   UN Mission for the Referendum in Western Sahara (MINURSO) established.

May 1991   UN Observer Mission in El Salvador (ONUSAL) established to monitor cease-fire and the human rights situation there.

May 1991   UN Angola Verification Mission (UNIVEM II) established to verify compliance with peace accords.

January 1, 1992   Boutros Boutros-Ghali assumed office as UN Secretary-General.

January 1992   Security Council held historic meeting at level of Heads of State and Government.

February 1992   UN Protection Force (UNPROFOR) established to ensure security in Yugoslavia pending overall settlement.

March 1992   UN Transitional Authority in Cambodia (UNTAC) of 22,000 personnel dispatched to Cambodia to oversee elections and transition to new government.

April 1992   UN Operation in Somalia (UNISOM) established to obtain and maintain cease-fire and provide humanitarian assistance.

June 1992   World's largest conference, United Nations Conference on Environment and Development (UNCED), held in Rio de Janeiro.

December 1992   UN Operation in Mozambique (ONUMOZ) established to monitor cease-fire and electoral process and coordinate humanitarian aid.

Spring 1993   UN Conference on Disarmament completed a Chemical Weapons Treaty.

April 1993   Second UN Operation in Somalia (UNOSOM II) of more than 30,000 personnel dispatched to Somalia to assist in rebuilding that country's government and economy. Authorized to use force if necessary.

May 25, 1993   Security Council established International Tribunal for Crimes in the former Yugoslavia.

June 1993   Security Council established UN Observer Mission Uganda-Rwanda (UNOMUR) to prevent military assistance from crossing border.

June 1993   World Conference on Human Rights in Vienna.

August 1993   Security Council established first peacekeeping operation in former territory of Soviet Union-UN Observer Mission in Georgia (UNOMIG).

Fall 1993   UN membership reached 184.

Fall 1993   Security Council imposed sanctions against Haiti and demanded departure of Haitian Armed Forces Commander-in-Chief.

October 1993   General Assembly lifted all previous sanctions against South Africa.

October 1993   Security Council established UN Assistance Mission for Rwanda (UNAMIR) to monitor the security situation in Rwanda and coordinate humanitarian aid.

December 1993   General Assembly created position of UN High Commissioner for Human Rights.

February 1994   Security council rescinded authority of UN Operation in Somalia (UNOSOM II) to use "coercive measures."

April–May 1994   Global Conference on the Sustainable Development of Small Island Developing States in Bridgetown, Barbados.

May 1994   World Conference on Natural Disaster Reduction in Yokohama.

September 1994   World Population Conference in Cairo.

Secretaries-General Dag Hammarskjöld and Trygve Lie

Secretary-General U Thant

Secretary-General Kurt Waldheim

Secretary-General Javier Pérez de Cuéllar

Secretary-General Boutros Boutros-Ghali

United Nations Headquarters, New York

Security Council in Session

General Assembly in Session

United Nations European Headquarters, Geneva

International Court of Justice in Session

INTRODUCTION

Background

Since the philosophy and practice of international relations usually evolve slowly, it should be expected that the United Nations was the product of a series of precedents gradually developing within the context of the modern interstate system. The state system itself was not clearly established until the 17th century, after numerous challenges to the earlier feudal order in such forms as contests for power between church and state, the rise of monarchs and subsequent questioning of the divine right of kings, the age of exploration, and emerging age of science, and the philosophical underpinnings of the Enlightenment. A period of relative peace and security was maintained in Europe from 1815 to 1914, bolstered in part by the Concert of Europe and The Hague Peace Conferences of 1899 and 1907. During the 19th century the first international organizations were established; they were either of a regional type, such as the European Commission for the Control of the Danube, or a potentially universal type, such as the Universal Postal Union. These were all specific, limited-purpose organizations, two of which, the Universal Postal Union and the International Telegraph Union (later renamed the International Telecommunication Union), eventually became specialized agencies of the United Nations system of agencies.

The first general-purpose international organization open to universal membership was the League of Nations. It was established in 1919 by the victorious powers in World War I, in the hope that it could be an instrument for peace. The means to enforce peace was the principle of collective security exercised by sovereign states through voluntary cooperation. The member states assumed commitments not to resort to war, to respect treaty obligations and the provisions of international law, to settle

1

disputes by a variety of peaceful settlement procedures, and to take collective action against violators of these principles. The League also instituted a Mandate System whereby the territories detached from the losing powers as a result of the war were assigned to the supervision of the major victorious states. Finally, the League undertook the coordination of efforts for international cooperation in several important social and economic areas.

The League, after some minor successes in the 1920s, failed to meet the challenges of states bent on aggression in the 1930s. It was severely weakened by the failure of the United States to become a member, by the defection of other states from membership, by the difficulties of agreeing on and effectively enforcing collective security measures, and by hopes that appeasing some of the ambitions of aggressor states would avoid war. The League was more effective in its social and economic cooperative efforts than in maintaining peace.

With regard to its principles and basic organizational pattern, the United Nations is substantially a mirror image of the League. Because of residual negative attitudes toward the League in the United States, references to this heritage of ideas were carefully avoided in promoting support for the United Nations among the American public. However, all the essential principles are the same; the League Council with permanent and non-permanent members was replaced by a similar UN Security Council, the League Assembly became the UN General Assembly, the two Secretariats were nearly identical, the Permanent Court of International Justice created by the League was absorbed intact into the UN structure, and the League's Mandate System became a modified Trusteeship System. The UN Charter is much more detailed than the League Covenant, but even the creation of a new Economic and Social Council as a major UN organ had its precedent in a 1939 recommendation of a League committee for a new, similar body to coordinate work of this nature.

The United States government led the way in planning for a postwar general-purpose international organization and it was bolstered by the input of nongovernmental organizations from academia, the professions, business, labor, religion, and foreign policy associations. Private groups in Great Britain and Canada made contributions, and gradually the British, Soviet, and Chinese governments became involved in the process. Some postwar planning activities were begun in the U.S. Department of State in 1940, but these were greatly expanded during 1942. After an initial impetus toward a regional or decentralized system of organizations, the tide turned toward a global approach. After a series of meetings of heads of states or foreign ministers of the United States, the United Kingdom, the Soviet Union, and China, in which general postwar planning was a part of the agenda, the United States government invited the other major powers to send representatives to Dumbarton Oaks in Washington, D.C. in August 1944 to thresh out major elements of a plan for a postwar international organization. After seven weeks they published a set of proposals to be used as the basic working document for the subsequent conference to draft the Charter of United Nations. The Dumbarton Oaks Proposals, which concentrated primarily on security provisions, were circulated to all governments invited to the San Francisco Conference the following year, and its basic provisions were incorporated, without major modification, into the Charter.

At a conference at Yalta in February 1945, Roosevelt, Churchill, and Stalin and their foreign ministers included in the broad agenda some unfinished business of the Dumbarton Oaks Conference. Stalin finally accepted the voting formula in the Security Council, proposed by the United States, which conferred veto power on each of the permanent members over any substantive matter, but not over procedural questions. Stalin, in exchange, received a promise of separate UN membership for the Ukraine and Byelorussia. Some broad understandings were reached concerning the Trusteeship System. Finally the date was set for a conference in San Francisco to produce a finished Charter, with the United States issuing the invitations on behalf of the Sponsoring States, which included China.

The San Francisco Conference was convened on April 25, 1945 with representatives of 50 states in attendance. During the next two months the delegates worked through an elaborate committee structure to put together a coherent treaty establishing a general-purpose international organization. The middle and small states attacked the privileged position of the United States, Britain, the Soviet Union, China, and France, which were accorded permanent membership in the Security Council with the power of veto. The Big Powers refused to budge on this issue and the other states had to settle for a statement from the Sponsoring States explaining some of the specifics of the use and limitations on use of the veto. In other than security matters most of the detailed provisions of the Charter had to be developed during the Conference. These provisions included: (1) the working relationships between regional organizations and the United Nations; (2) the provisions for the Trusteeship System; (3) elaborate provisions for economic and social programs under the aegis of the Economic and Social Council; (4) an expanded role for the General Assembly; (5) the conferring of major organ status upon the Economic and Social Council, the Trusteeship Council, and the International Court of Justice; and (6) a "Declaration Regarding Non-Self-Governing Territories" which subsequently became an instrument for hastening the end of the colonial system.

The first state to ratify the Charter was the United States, with Senate approval by an 89–2 vote. All required ratifications were deposited with the United States government by October 24, 1945, and October 24 is celebrated annually as United Nations Day. The first meeting of the General Assembly was held in London on January 10, 1946, and subsequently headquarters for the United Nations were established in New York City.

Structure of the United Nations

The United Nations is structured around six major organs and a large number of subsidiary bodies in varying relationships to the major organs. The Security Council originally had 11 members— five permanent and six elective—but four additional elective members were added in 1965 to accommodate the growing number of members from Africa and Asia. Nine affirmative votes are required for the adoption of any measure, with the five permanent members accorded veto power to block any substantive decision. The Security Council is assigned "primary responsibility for the maintenance of international peace and security" and its decisions are, in theory, legally binding on all member states. Except for the creation of ad hoc bodies for specific assignments, the Security Council operates without a complex auxiliary set of agencies.

In many respects the General Assembly is the central organ of the United Nations. It is a world forum on the entire spectrum of United Nations concerns. It meets annually for at least three months commencing on the third Tuesday in September. All member states participate in its sessions. It may convene in special sessions or in emergency special sessions for specific purposes. Emergency sessions are used when the Security Council is stalemated on a crisis situation. The General Assembly controls the budget and the rates of assessment of the member states. All other major organs report to the Assembly. It carries on its work through seven main committees. The General Assembly elects the rotating members of the Security Council, all members of the Economic and Social Council, and, as necessary in the past, some members of the Trusteeship Council. It shares with the Security Council the choice of judges on the International Court of Justice and the selection of the Secretary-General. It admits new members to the United Nations upon the recommendation of the Security Council. The General Assembly has created a large number of subsidiary bodies, and has authorized the agreements for working relationships with the 17 autonomous specialized agencies. The Assembly has instigated numerous treaties and acts to give final approval of treaties before submitting them to states for ratification.

The third major UN organ is the Economic and Social Council (ECOSOC). It was assigned major organ status at the San Francisco Conference at the insistence of the smaller states. It was originally composed of representatives of 18 members, but this was raised in 1965 to a membership of 27, and again in 1973 to 54. Its size is one of its impediments to efficiency and a series of committees and studies since 1974 has recommended methods to increase its effectiveness. In 1992 its former pattern of two sessions per year was changed to a single session. The ECOSOC attempts to coordinate the work of a complex array of agencies. Directly under its supervision are functional commissions, such as the Commission on Human Rights and the Commission for Social Development, five regional commissions, and a changing group of five or six standing and ad hoc committees. The ECOSOC also attempts to provide a degree of coordination for a dozen agencies created by the General Assembly but not subject to the ECOSOC's direct jurisdiction, such as the United Nations Development Program and the World Food Programme. The ECOSOC also reviews the work and makes suggestions to the 17 autonomous specialized agencies of the UN system, such as the World Health Organization and the Food and Agriculture Organization. In addition to its coordinative responsibilities, the ECOSOC directs research projects, generates reports, and issues recommendations.

Another major UN organ is the Secretariat. This is not a deliberative body, but a corps of international civil servants under the direction of the Secretary-General. The Secretariat must provide all the support services necessary to carry out the directives of the delegate bodies and the smooth conduct of hundreds of meetings annually. The total staff is about 20,000, divided among New York, Geneva, Vienna, and field assignments throughout the world.

A fifth major UN organ is the International Court of Justice, seated in The Hague. Its 15 judges are elected for nine-year terms by concurrent majorities of all members of the Security Council and of the General Assembly. No two justices may be of the same nationality. The Court has two major functions: (1) to hear cases submitted to it and render decisions on them, and (2) to issue advisory opinions on legal questions submitted by the various UN agencies authorized by the General Assembly. By 1993 the Court had rendered 31 judgments and issued 20 advisory opinions.

The remaining major UN organ is the Trusteeship Council, which was the successor organ to the League of Nations' Mandates Commission. Eleven trust territories, mostly former League-mandated territories, were placed under its jurisdictional review. The membership of the Council included automatic membership of the permanent members of the Security Council and of the administering states, and an equal balance between administering and non-administering states. The General Assembly chose the necessary number of elected members. The peak membership was 14; it then diminished by the mid-1970s to only the five Security Council permanent members. Also, after 1975 only one of the 11 trust territories, the Trust Territory of the Pacific Islands administered by the United States, remained for Trusteeship Council surveillance.

Membership Issues

Two groups of states compose the membership of the United Nations—original members and admitted members. The 51 original members had only to file certificates of Charter ratification to become members, and all eligible states did so before the end of 1945. States are admitted by a two-thirds vote of the General Assembly upon the recommendation of the Security Council, but the Security Council decision can be blocked by the negative vote of one or more of the permanent members. The advent of the Cold War prevented the admission of a number of clearly eligible states during the first ten years of the United Nations. Finally, in 1955, in spite of an advisory opinion of the International Court of Justice that each state's eligibility should be judged on its own merits without regard to any other state, a "package deal" was agreed upon to admit 16 states, including candidates previously blocked by Soviet vetoes of non-Communist states and Western collective opposition to Soviet satellite states. East and West Germany did not apply for admission until 1973, Vietnam was not admitted until 1977, and the two Koreas became members in 1991. Otherwise, there has been no real impediment to admissions since 1955.

The other membership concern is the admission of ministates with full equality of voting rights in the General Assembly. In spite of questions concerning the ability of ministates to contribute significantly to the responsibilities of UN members, and suggestions for a more limited associate member status, the practice of admitting all sovereign states that apply has been the rule. The result is a total membership of 184, of which eight have populations of 24,000 to 100,000, and another 27 have less than one million.

Financial Problems

Aside from the budgets of the specialized agencies and the UN programs supported by voluntary contributions, the United Nations has two other budgets whose costs are assessed—a regular budget roughly based on ability to pay, and peacekeeping expenses shared by all members but with heavier assessments on the more affluent states. The first UN financial crisis occurred in funding the costs of the Congo peacekeeping operation (1960–64), which cost $400 million and for which the Soviet Union and France refused to pay. This annual deficit has plagued the United Nations since the 1960s. An additional problem has been the practice of members of not paying their assessments for both the regular budget and the peacekeeping budget until late in the fiscal year.

Beginning in 1985 the financial crisis was exacerbated by the decision of the U.S. Congress to withhold 20 percent of its regular assessment until the United Nations modified its budgetary procedures and made administrative reforms. In 1986 Congress actually appropriated money to pay less than 50 percent of the United States assessment. By the 1990s Congress had agreed to pay the arrears over a five-year period, but the goals were not always met.

A further factor in the financial crisis was the doubling since 1988 of the number of UN peacekeeping missions, several of which were very large and expensive. The peacekeeping budget for 1991 operations of $600 million skyrocketed in 1992 to $2.8 billion, with further increases anticipated. Because of all the above factors, the total deficits owed by member states in April 1993 amounted to more than $2.3 billion, of which $1.2 billion was for the regular budget and $1.1 billion was for the peacekeeping budget. United States arrearages totalled $923 million and the Russian Federation owed $473 million, with other substantial amounts owed by South Africa, Brazil, and Ukraine. In 1992 the Ford Foundation, in cooperation with the UN, formed an international advisory group of eminent persons to study the financial problems of the UN. Their report included a proposal for the creation of a $400 million revolving reserve fund for peacekeeping. However, the UN exists on the brink of insolvency from year to year.

Peace and Security Efforts

The first purpose stated in the UN Charter is "to maintain international peace and security," and all members pledge to "settle their international disputes by peaceful means" and to "refrain . . . from the threat or use of force against the territorial integrity or political independence of any state." Chapter VI deals with peaceful settlement procedures in which states promise, as a first step, to "seek a solution [of any dispute] by negotiation, enquiry, mediation, conciliation, arbitration, judicial settlement, resort to regional agencies or arrangements, or other peaceful means of their own choice." In practice the Security Council and General Assembly have also utilized good offices and cease-fires as "other peaceful means."

Altogether more than 200 disputes have been on the agendas of the Security Council and General Assembly. Of these, approximately 20 remain under active consideration by these organs, most of them of recent origin. A few long-range disputes, such as the Kashmir dispute between India and Pakistan, the Middle East problem, and the Cyprus question, have never been resolved, but the UN's perennial preoccupation with the South African situation has largely subsided. Of course, dozens of other disputes, for a variety of reasons, are either not submitted to the United Nations, or not adopted as agenda items by the Security Council or General Assembly. Also, the United Nations cannot take major credit for the resolution of every dispute that has disappeared from its agendas. Some, such as the independence of Indonesia (1946–49) and the transition from white to black majority rule in Zimbabwe (1962–80), were resolved by negotiation among the disputing parties. Others involved complaints concerning a single incident, and, after discussion in the UN, were allowed to expire. A few, such as the Hungarian situation in 1956 and the Grenada question in 1983, were dropped in recognition of the powerlessness of the United Nations to override a military fait accompli by either of the superpowers.

Although the Charter confers on the Security Council "primary responsibility for the maintenance of international security," and provides that the General Assembly shall not make recommendations regarding a dispute under consideration by the Security Council, the Assembly has assumed a larger role in conflict resolution than originally anticipated. Nearly one-fifth of all disputes considered by the United Nations were handled solely by the General Assembly, and more than 20 percent have been simultaneously on the agendas of the General Assembly and the

Security Council. One of the reasons for an enhanced role for the Assembly was the frequent impasse in the Council resulting from issues with Cold War overtones. Hence such issues as the Austrian Peace Treaty in 1952, the Question of Tibet in 1959, and Human Rights in South Vietnam in 1963 appeared only on the General Assembly agenda. Since 1986 nearly all new disputes have been referred solely to the Security Council, and the General Assembly deals mainly with unsettled situations of long duration. The Security Council has always been the more appropriate and efficient organ for conflict resolution, but the end of the Cold War also engendered a new climate of big power cooperation in that body.

When nations, in spite of their Charter commitments, resort to the use of force, the United Nations is supposed to apply principles of collective security. These provisions are contained in Chapter VII of the Charter, entitled "Action with Respect to Threats to the Peace, Breaches of the Peace, and Acts of Aggression." The theory of collective security involves the obligation of all members to take collective measures against an aggressor state. This could require the application of political, economic, or military sanctions to put down the aggression. Several difficulties exist in the application of the theory. These include (1) disagreement over what constitutes aggression, (2) the difficulty of determining which state committed aggression, (3) the reluctance of member states to cooperate in applying sanctions, (4) the precedence of other national interests over the desire to restore peace, and (5) the failure of the major powers to carry out Article 43 of the Charter, which anticipated prompt agreements setting up armed forces subject to call by the Security Council under the command of the Military Staff Committee.

Since the United Nations is not a supergovernment but depends on the voluntary cooperation of sovereign states, the record of collective security through Chapter VII is a meager one. In a few cases military arms embargoes or economic sanctions have been requested by the Security Council or General Assembly against Southern Rhodesia (now Zimbabwe), South Africa, and China, but these had little impact. Beginning in 1990 the Security Council has imposed stringent economic sanctions against Iraq, ordered the destruction of its major armaments, and held it liable for war damages. Also, since 1990, various embargoes have been invoked against Yugoslavia, Libya, Liberia, and Haiti. True military collective measures of the kind envisaged in Article 43 of the Charter have never been applied. The closest approaches were in Korea in 1950 and against Iraq in 1990. However, instead of a collective military force under United Nations command, the Security Council adopted resolutions authorizing and legitimizing military action by states using the UN flag and other symbols, but organized under United States military command and direction with the aid of supplementary forces from a limited number of states.

The third aspect of peace and security measures is peacekeeping—a unique technique not anticipated by the architects of the Charter. Although utilized in a limited sense before 1956, its principles became fully developed in that year in the establishment of the United Nations Emergency Force (UNEF) deployed in the Sinai. A true peacekeeping operation requires (1) a ceasefire and the establishment of a buffer zone, (2) the deployment of a lightly-armed international force into the buffer zone, (3) absolute neutrality of the peacekeeping personnel, (4) the insulation of the operation from major power direct involvement, and (5) the obligation of the peacekeeping force to observe and report, and to fire only in self-defense. These principles, with minor exceptions, were generally adhered to before 1990.

Since that time the number of peacekeeping operations has doubled, the major powers have furnished forces in such operations as Somalia and Yugoslavia, and the missions have been assigned new tasks, some of which impair the obligations of neutrality and non-use of force. The mandates of recent peacekeeping missions have included overseeing the creation of stable governments, the delivery of humanitarian aid, the protection of refugees, the supervision of elections, the training of police forces, oversight of the demobilization of rebel forces, and even the use of force against contending armed contingents. Although the label "peacekeeping missions" is still applied by the Security Council to these operations, their new roles sometimes become those of peacemaking or peace-enforcing rather than following the original principles of peacekeeping. Many of these recent missions also involve intervention in the internal affairs of a single state rather than a dispute between states. Finally, the enormous expense of numerous, large operations in Namibia,

Cambodia, Yugoslavia, and Somalia have raised questions concerning the future willingness of states to furnish forces and to fund other similar large-scale operations.

Economic and Social Development Programs

The most diverse, costly, and widespread activities of the United Nations are in the economic and social development area. At least three-fourths of all personnel are engaged in these programs. An elaborate network of commissions, programs, and other agencies has been established under the direction of the Economic and Social Council and the General Assembly to carry on this work, and a dozen of the autonomous specialized agencies affiliated with the United Nations engage, almost exclusively, in development activities. Large loans and expenditures are involved, including those of the World Bank family of agencies, a major share of the regular budget of the United Nations, the United Nations Development Program, several other programs supported by voluntary funding, and the bulk of the budgets of the UN specialized agencies other than the Bank group. To the substantial majority of UN member states which are classified as developing nations, these activities represent the most important programs of the United Nations. They see the United Nations as the agency which should promote activities for narrowing the gap between rich and poor, between the privileged and the disadvantaged segments of the world.

The original members of the United Nations were mainly the more industrialized nations of the world. Even though the Charter declared a commitment ''to promote social progress and better standards of life in larger freedom,'' and the Economic and Social Council was declared to be a major UN organ, the early programs for economic and social development were modest. In those years a majority of the later UN members were still under colonial rule. By 1948 the Economic and Social Council had established regional commissions for Asia and Latin America and functional commissions on population and social concerns. Also, the specialized agencies dealing with health, education, food and agriculture, and labor were providing limited technical assistance services to some economically and socially disadvantaged areas. War-torn countries of Europe and Asia were given aid by the United Nations Relief and Rehabilitation Administration (UNRRA) during 1945–46, but this was a temporary program to help restore the economies mostly of industrialized states.

The first enlargement of UN technical assistance funds came in 1950 with a United States-led initiative for an Expanded Program of Technical Assistance (EPTA). The costs, still nominal, were covered by voluntary contributions ranging from $14 million to $54 million annually. Direct bilateral aid programs have always been much larger than multilaterally-distributed funds. In 1959 a United Nations Special Fund, with somewhat more generous financial support than for the EPTA, was created to provide pre-investment funding, including some equipment, for development projects. In 1965 the Special Fund and the EPTA were merged into a single United Nations Development Program (UNDP). This is now the largest UN source of development grant funds, with recent annual budgets reaching $1.5 billion. Development loans far exceed grants, with the agencies affiliated with the World Bank and International Monetary Fund now furnishing approximately $30 billion annually.

By the 1960s the influx of newly-independent developing states into UN membership gave these third-world nations a working majority in the General Assembly, and, by 1973, a similar majority in the Economic and Social Council. Pressure for new programs, increased funding, and concessions from the affluent states multiplied. The General Assembly declared the 1960s as the United Nations Development Decade and renewed this emphasis in each subsequent decade. In planning for each decade, targets were set for such matters as (1) rates of economic growth of the developing states, (2) increased trade of these states, (3) increased domestic savings for investment in domestic production, (4) increased agricultural production, (5) increased manufacturing production, and (6) an annual rate of resource transfer of one percent of their GNP from developed to developing countries, with 0.7 percent of this from the public sector.

In 1962 the General Assembly authorized the formation of the United Nations Conference on Trade and Development (UNCTAD). The first Conference met for nearly three months in Geneva in 1964 and created an elaborate new system of conferences, boards, committees, and a special new section of the Secretariat with headquarters in Geneva. In fact, a large new wing soon had to be added to the Geneva UN headquarters, primarily to accommodate UNCTAD activities. Subsequent conferences were planned for three-year intervals but have actually met at three- to five-year periods with UNTAD VIII meeting in Cartagena, Colombia in 1992. From the beginning, UNCTAD has been controlled by the developing nations and has acted as "the poor man's lobby" within the UN. Each conference session has produced demands for extensive concessions by the developed countries to the developing ones, but, since implementation depends on actions by the affluent states, which have been largely resisted or ignored by those states, the aspirations of the developing countries have been frustrated.

Since industrialization in developing countries was an important goal in the development process, these countries proposed a new organization, the United Nations Industrial Development Organization (UNIDO), which was approved by the General Assembly in 1965 and began operations, with headquarters in Vienna, in 1967. Its independent status and special secretariat, with control by the developing countries, followed the example of UNCTAD. In 1985, after years of planning, UNIDO was converted to UN specialized agency status with its own state membership, constitution, and budget.

Perhaps the most radical set of demands of the developing states emerged from a special session of the General Assembly in 1974 on the topic of raw materials and development. Emanating from this session was a demand for a New International Economic Order (NIEO) which incorporated but expanded the principles and requested concessions previously developed by UNCTAD. The NIEO doctrines attacked the "unfair" operation of the existing economic order which was perceived to impair the economic growth of poor states. In the subsequent 1974 General Assembly regular session, the proponents of the NIEO pushed through a Charter of Economic Rights and Duties of States which declared that states not only have exclusive sovereignty over their wealth and resources, but also the right to nationalize, expropriate, or transfer ownership of foreign-held property. All the developed market economy representatives denounced this aspect of the resolution. By the 1990s the militant demands of the NIEO doctrines were muted as the resistance of the affluent states continued to frustrate any meaningful North-South dialogue. Attitudes on each side softened and were reflected in a greater assumption of self-help by the developing nations and a merging of interests around a doctrine of "sustainable development" in the forums of UNCTAD VIII in February 1992 and the Earth Summit or United Nations Conference on Environment and Development (UNCED) in Rio de Janeiro in June 1992.

In addition to the broad-brush approach to economic and social development discussed above, the United Nations has, from its earliest days, carried on sectoral activities through its own agencies and the programs of its affiliated autonomous specialized agencies. Even before the United Nations, the International Labour Organisation (ILO) had been gradually building an International Labour Code of treaties and recommendations for the protection of workers in both developed and developing countries. The ILO also conducts technical assistance projects in economically disadvantaged nations. One of its concerns is the role of women in development.

The Food and Agriculture Organization (FAO), with headquarters in Rome, has been involved with both the problem of food supply and the improvement of agricultural production in developing countries. Its limited resources have been supplemented by funds from the United Nations Development Program (UNDP), UNICEF, and other public and private sources. Its program has been augmented by the World Food Conference (1974), a World Food Council, a World Food Programme, and an International Fund for Agricultural Development—another UN specialized agency.

A major problem in developing countries is health, and the World Health Organization (WHO) is the key UN agency working to eliminate disease, to improve sanitary conditions, and to increase the longevity of peoples throughout the world. It also administers funds supplied by the UNDP and UNICEF. Its programs have succeeded in eliminating smallpox, reducing the incidence of several tropical diseases, and inoculating 80 percent of the world's children against the most common and threatening childhood diseases.

The developing countries have more than three-fourths of the world's population and the proportion increases with each successive decade. In the early years the UN population efforts were limited to research and publication of statistical data by the UN Secretariat under the guidance of the Economic and Social Council and its Population Commission. In 1967 Secretary-General U Thant initiated a United Nations Fund for Population Activities (UNFPA), supported by voluntary contributions; its initial annual budget was barely over $1 million but this has gradually swelled to $225 million. World Population Conferences, held every ten years since 1954, have, in recent sessions, emphasized the necessity to limit rates of population growth in most developing countries as an essential element in overcoming the spread of poverty.

Another necessity for developmental progress in a country is the provision of appropriate education programs and facilities for a large segment of the nation's people. The United Nations Educational, Scientific and Cultural Organization (UNESCO) has, among its goals, the elimination of illiteracy, the development of functional literacy education, and the promotion of education for an increasing number of persons in developing countries at levels of higher education. UNESCO has concentrated on projects for improving school buildings and equipment, the provision of textbooks, curriculum development, and teacher training. It carries out projects financed by the UNDP and UNICEF. Of course, UNESCO can only be a catalyst for the bulk of the efforts in support of domestic agencies. UNESCO came under fire in the 1980s for administrative inefficiencies and for scattering its resources over too many small projects. By 1985 the withdrawal of the United States, the United Kingdom, and Singapore from membership meant a loss of 30 percent of its budget. In spite of administrative and program reforms, these countries had not rejoined by 1994 and UNESCO's effectiveness has been proportionately diminished.

Before the 1972 World Conference on the Human Environment in Stockholm, the common attitude in the developing countries was that environmental problems were mainly caused by the industrialized states and were of little concern to the nonindustrialized world. However, they did participate in the conference and since that time have increased their involvement in environmental matters. As a result of the conference a United Nations Environment Program (UNEP) was established with headquarters in

Nairobi, Kenya, a location intended to further woo developing countries' support. In 1976 the United Nations Conference on Human Settlements (HABITAT) focused on the role of shelter in human welfare, an issue of particular concern in poor countries. The United Nations Water Conference in 1977 highlighted problems of supplies of safe drinking water, drought, soil erosion, and floods. Also in 1977 the United Nations Conference on Desertification sought to foster methods for halting the spread of deserts and reclaiming land at their margins. Large-scale tree planting and finding energy sources to replace a diminishing wood fuel supply are of special concern to many developing countries.

Finally, after more than five years of preparatory work, the issues of the environment and of development were linked in the United Nations Conference on Environment and Development (UNCED) in Rio de Janeiro in June 1992. This was the most publicized and largest international conference to date, with more than 100 heads of state and government participating. The Rio Declaration adopted by the conference prescribed 27 principles for "sustainable development." Another document was a statement of principles for protecting the world's forests, and a treaty on biodiversity was opened for signature and ratification. The climate of cooperation between affluent and developing states seemed to be improving, but the proof is in the measures taken by individual governments in carrying out the "spirit of Rio."

Most of the efforts of the United Nations Children's Fund (UNICEF) on behalf of child welfare have been concentrated in the poorer countries. More than 25 percent of UNICEF funds come from private sources. UNICEF supplies funds for health, education, nutrition, and family welfare projects and requires recipient governments to more than match these funds and to furnish personnel. External experts are supplied through cooperation with WHO, UNESCO, and FAO. Improving children's welfare generally evokes emotional and financial support.

After the refugees of World War II were repatriated or resettled, the major new refugee problems were in Africa, Asia, and the Middle East. In 1951 the Office of the United Nations High Commissioner for Refugees (UNHCR) was established. This office, with limited funds, has to depend on other sources for most refugee aid. The Office acts, however, as a coordinating agency to stimulate refugee aid and to provide legal protection to refugees.

Prior to 1990 the largest number of refugees was in Africa, but a major temporary crisis also occurred in 1971 by the movement of seven million refugees into India from East Pakistan. By 1994 the total number of refugees and internally displaced persons world-wide was approximately 45 million persons. In addition to substantial numbers from the African states of Somalia, Mozambique, Rwanda, Sudan, Ethiopia, and Liberia, there were at least 3.5 million from the former state of Yugoslavia, more than two million Palestinian refugees, and a very large number from Afghanistan.

The Palestinian refugees' needs are under the jurisdiction of a special UN agency, the United Nations Relief and Works Agency for Palestine Refugees in the Near East (UNRWA), created in 1950 to assume relief functions for Palestinians displaced by the Arab-Israeli conflict of 1948. In addition to providing food supplies for Palestinian refugees living in camps in Lebanon, the West Bank, the Gaza Strip, Jordan, and Syria, the greatest efforts of UNRWA are in the areas of education and health. UNRWA employs more than 9,000 teachers, most of whom are refugees.

This brief summary of economic and social development programs of the United Nations system of agencies suggests the broad scope of these activities. The dictionary which follows contains dozens of items which collectively spell out in greater detail the diverse projects carried out by the UN to foster economic and social development for the three-fourths of the world's population that aspire to improved living standards and well-being.

The Impetus Toward Political Independence

In 1945 one-third of the world's people were not self-governing. However, in the next five years the most populous of the former colonies—India, Pakistan, Indonesia, and the Philippines— attained self-rule, leaving about 200 million people in dozens of territories under the political control of colonial powers. The UN Charter incorporated provisions promising progress toward the attainment of political independence and self-rule for all subjugated peoples. These provisions fell into two categories: (1) a trusteeship system whose supervision was extended by 1950 to about 20 million people, living in 11 territories, under the jurisdiction of seven administering countries; and (2) guarantees for all other non-self-governing peoples of the promotion of their well-being and of progress toward self-government.

The UN trusteeship system was an improved version of the League of Nations mandate system. The membership of the Trusteeship Council was composed of government representatives rather than the private experts of the former Mandates Commission. The previous reporting requirements and the right of petition were strengthened and visiting missions to the territories were introduced to provide on-the-spot verification of conditions. All administering states and all permanent members of the Security Council had automatic Trusteeship Council representation, with the General Assembly electing enough member states to provide an equal balance between administering and nonadministering states. Ten of the 11 trust territories had been mandates under the League system and Somaliland had been an Italian protectorate prior to World War II. Progress toward independence for the trust territories was fairly rapid, with eight of them gaining self-rule between 1957 and 1962, another in 1968, and New Guinea in 1975. After that date only the Trust Territory of the Pacific Islands, which had been accorded special status as a strategic trust territory under United States' jurisdiction, remained for Trusteeship Council supervision. In 1986 this territory was divided into four units associated with the United States, but not until 1994 were the final details for one of these units, Palau, settled, allowing the Trusteeship Council to terminate its functions.

Chapter XI of the Charter outlined the obligations of colonial powers toward the indigenous peoples of their colonies. These included the promotion of "their political, economic, social, and educational advancement" and "to develop self-government." The right of independence was not specifically stated but the metropolitan powers were required to submit regular reports "to the Secretary-General for information purposes . . . [including] statistical and other information of a technical nature relating to economic, social, and educational conditions in the territories." These unprecedented obligations were seized upon and expanded to hasten the demise of the old political colonial system.

In 1960, the year of the admission to UN membership of 17 newly-independent former colonies, the General Assembly adopted a Declaration on the Granting of Independence to Colonial Countries and Peoples by a vote of 90–0, on which nine abstentions included those of the colonial states. The gist of the declaration was that all peoples have the right to self-government, without delay, and without regard to political, economic, social, or educational preparedness. In order to monitor progress toward self-government, the General Assembly created special committees which were active and vocal in their demands for speeding up the process. Although the old colonial system was probably eventually doomed because it carried the seeds of its own destruction, the UN was used as a vehicle for pressuring the colonial powers to accelerate the schedule for granting self-rule. By 1990 the old colonial system was virtually dead.

The Leadership Role of the Secretary-General

Although the primary responsibility of the UN Secretary-General is an administrative one in organizing and supervising the Secretariat to carry out the directives of the deliberative bodies of the organization and to provide necessary support functions, some leadership qualities are also desirable. The introduction to the annual report of the Secretary-General to the General Assembly serves as an instrument for expressing his philosophy, assessment of needs, and suggestions for improving the role of the United Nations in world affairs. He is frequently requested by the deliberative bodies to make studies and prepare reports for those bodies and can influence the underlying principles of these documents. In the political arena, Article 99 of the Charter confers on him the authority to bring to the Security Council's attention any matter which in his judgment may threaten international peace and security. The Security Council must, of necessity, leave to the Secretary-General the details of raising, deploying, and providing the principles and directives for the numerous peacekeeping forces authorized by the Council. On many occasions the Secretary-General or his special representatives have acted as mediators in disputes. In cases in which directives of the

Security Council or General Assembly are lacking in specific detail for handling a complex situation, the Secretary-General with his advisers must fill these gaps, relying on Charter principles and personal judgment. When reforms of an administrative nature are demanded, the Secretary-General must determine how to reorganize the Secretariat to foster the desired goals.

Some Secretaries-General have contributed more to developing effective leadership than others. The first Secretary-General, Trygve Lie of Norway, tried to express his strong stance on issues by being vocally aggressive in press conferences, by taking a strong posture on issues, and by lecturing the major powers on their responsibilities. He authored a Twenty-Year Program for Peace and successively alienated each of the Cold War adversaries by his position on such issues as Chinese representation and the Korean War.

The second Secretary-General, Dag Hammarskjöld of Sweden, developed the theory of the leadership position of the Secretary-General in situations in which his instructions from the delegate bodies were vague or lacking in detail. He believed in quiet and preventive diplomacy. He established the principles underlying peacekeeping. When Khrushchev, in resentment of his Congo policies, demanded his resignation and replacement with a troika or triumvirate of administrative heads, which would have emasculated the leadership possibilities of the office, he refused to resign and appealed for the support of the UN members to save the integrity and effectiveness of the institution.

The next three Secretaries-General, U Thant of Burma, Kurt Waldheim of Austria, and Javier Pérez de Cuéllar of Peru, were able administrators who maintained the support of the major powers, and who judiciously preserved and practiced the established prerogatives of the Secretary-General, but added no innovative dimensions to the leadership role. Each incumbent was personally involved in crisis management and dispute settlement processes. The end of the Cold War, by enlarging the possibilities for United Nations contributions to conflict resolution, opened opportunities for Pérez de Cuéllar to practice his considerable diplomatic and management abilities. He also responded well to pressures for budgetary and administrative reform.

The sixth Secretary-General, Boutros Boutros-Ghali of Egypt, took office in January 1992. The challenges testing his leadership include (1) the need for further administrative reform and (2) raising, deploying, and financing major new peacekeeping operations including large and costly missions in Somalia and the former Yugoslavia. He has demonstrated some frustration with the reluctance and delays of the major powers in approving prompt and effective measures for containing conflicts, but he has maintained general respect and support of the UN members.

Conclusions

In 1995 the United Nations celebrates its 50th anniversary. In spite of the adverse climate of a 40-year Cold War, it has demonstrated much more vitality in contributing to world peace and security than did its predecessor, the League of Nations, during 1919–39. Its multiplex programs in economic and social development have acted as catalysts for the development efforts in nonindustrial countries. Although these programs are insufficient to narrow the world's rich-poor gap, they have contributed to some improvements in human welfare, and have alleviated many potential human disasters. The United Nations furthered the cause of bringing an end to colonialism by keeping the spotlight on the processes of decolonization. The organization has fostered human rights through comprehensive treaties and by publicizing violations of human rights. It has produced some key treaties in the field of arms control. It has contributed to the development of international law through the principles laid down in multilateral treaties as well as in landmark resolutions of the General Assembly. The United Nations provides the only forum for discussing and publicizing the spectrum of world problems that challenge humankind.

On the other hand, the United Nations provides no panaceas. It is a confederation of sovereign states dependent on the voluntary cooperation of its members for its utility. Their cooperation determines whether policies can be adopted, implemented, and financed. A single permanent member of the Security Council can still obstruct action by the majority of states. Debate goes on concerning the wisdom of involving the UN in large, complex, and expensive civil disorders. The problem of near-bankruptcy of the organization is a perennial one. Administrative reorganization and efficiency need further attention.

In spite of the above difficulties there is little doubt in world public opinion and government attitudes that the United Nations is an indispensable instrument for fostering international cooperation. In an interdependent world it provides multiple avenues for confronting and attempting to alleviate international problems. Its survival and improved utility are linked to the long-range national interests of each of its member states.

THE DICTIONARY

ACHESON-LILIENTHAL PLAN (also known as THE BAR-
UCH PLAN). This was a set of proposals submitted by the
United States in 1946 to the United Nations **Atomic Energy
Commission*** for the control and destruction of atomic
weapons and the sharing of information on the peaceful uses
of atomic energy. Serious disagreements over details in
implementing the plan led to its rejection by the Soviet
Union.

ACQUIRED IMMUNE DEFICIENCY SYNDROME (AIDS).
Although the principal expenditures and programs for fighting the growing AIDS threat to life and health are concentrated at the national level, the **World Health Organization
(WHO)** acts as a central coordinating agency for the collec-
tion, analysis, and dissemination of information on the
control of AIDS, and operates a special program of research
and professional training in combatting the disease.

ADJUDICATION *see* INTERNATIONAL COURT OF JUS-
TICE; PEACEFUL SETTLEMENT OF DISPUTES

ADMINISTRATIVE COMMITTEE ON COORDINATION. In
order to overcome some of the disadvantages of a decentralized system of specialized agencies affiliated with the United
Nations, the **Economic and Social Council** authorized the
formation of this committee. The United Nations **Secretary-
General** is its chairman and the administrative heads of the
specialized agencies are its other members. Its object is to

---

*Items in entries which are in bold type indicate that there are separate entries for
these items.

25

prevent duplication of effort, to allocate responsibilities, and to harmonize the purposes of the various agencies.

ADVISORY OPINIONS. The **International Court of Justice (ICJ)** may be requested to give advisory opinions by the **General Assembly,** the **Security Council** and such other United Nations organs or **specialized agencies** as authorized by the General Assembly. Although not binding, such opinions are authoritative interpretations applying **international law** to the questions specified in the request. Weaknesses in the system include the infrequency of Security Council requests for such advice on appropriate legal questions, and the failure of some nations to abide by the obligations specified by the Court. However, the General Assembly has sought and received advice on several important matters involving interpretation of obligations arising from the **Charter of the United Nations.** (See also INTERNATIONAL COURT OF JUSTICE.)

AFGHANISTAN SITUATION. In late December 1979 Soviet forces entered Afghanistan. The **Security Council** discussed the situation but was deadlocked on producing any recommendation. The **General Assembly** was then called into emergency special session, and, in a resolution adopted on January 14, 1980, deplored the intervention and called for the withdrawal of Soviet troops from Afghanistan. In February 1981 Secretary-General **Kurt Waldheim** appointed Under-Secretary-General **Javier Pérez de Cuéllar** as his personal representative on the situation in Afghanistan. When Pérez de Cuéllar became UN Secretary-General in January 1982 he appointed Diego Cordovez as his personal representative. Cordovez engaged in protracted negotiations with all parties in **Geneva,** and, after Moscow announced its intention to withdraw its forces from Afghanistan, the Geneva Accords were signed in April 1988. These accords, signed by Afghanistan and Pakistan and witnessed by the USSR and the United States, provided for: (1) non-interference by the parties in each other's affairs; (2) the withdrawal of Soviet troops; and (3) the voluntary return of refugees.

In order to supervise the carrying out of the terms of the

Geneva Accords, the Secretary-General's personal representative was to be assisted by a United Nations **peacekeeping** force. The Security Council approved the Secretary-General's request for a 50-member United Nations Good Offices Mission in Afghanistan and Pakistan (UNGOMAP). By late April 1988 these peacekeeping forces had established headquarters in Kabul and Islamabad and had entered upon their assigned duties. UNGOMAP was officially terminated on March 15, 1990, with any further responsibilities in carrying out the terms of the Geneva Accords assigned to the Secretary-General's personal representative assisted by ten military advisers.

AFRICAN ECONOMIC CONDITIONS. In May 1986 the **General Assembly,** prompted by crisis economic conditions in a majority of African countries, met in special session and unanimously adopted a five-year United Nations Programme of Action for African Economic Recovery. However, in most of the countries involved, economic conditions continued to worsen during the five-year period due primarily to a failure of the non-African states to carry out their commitments to furnish 35 percent of the costs of the Programme. In 1991 the General Assembly adopted a United Nations New Agenda for the Development of Africa. The **Secretary-General** formed a Panel of High-Level Personalities to advise him on implementing the New Agenda. In October 1993 Tokyo hosted an International Conference on African Development attended by representatives of donor states, African states, and appropriate international organizations to stimulate action to reverse the previous decline in economic prosperity in many African states.

AFRICAN FAMINE. Since the drought and famine in 1972–74 in the Sahel region of Africa, various African countries have been periodically plagued with problems of hunger and mass starvation. United Nations agencies including the **World Food Programme (WFP),** established in 1963, the **United Nations Development Program (UNDP),** and the **United Nations Children's Fund (UNICEF)** in cooperation with governmental and private relief agencies have shipped hundreds of millions of tons of food and established distribution systems in order to alleviate famine in these emergencies. Since 1980 countries heavily affected, often as a result of civil wars, have included Somalia, Ethiopia, Angola, Mozambique, Sudan, and Lesotho.

AGING (WORLD ASSEMBLY ON AGING). At the initiative of the Commission for Social Development of the **Economic and Social Council,** the World Assembly, in recognition of the problems arising from the rapidly growing proportion of older people in the world's population, convened for two weeks in **Vienna** in 1982. Although most implementation of resulting programs would be carried out by national governments, several United Nations agencies were requested to perform review and coordination activities and in 1987–88 an International Institute on Aging was established in Malta.

ALBANIA *see* CORFU CHANNEL CASE

AMENDMENT OF THE UN CHARTER. **Charter of the United Nations** amendments may be proposed by a vote of two-thirds of the total membership of the **General Assembly** or by a two-thirds vote of a general-review conference convened by the joint action of the General Assembly and the **Security Council.** Such proposed amendments come into force if ratified by the governments of two-thirds of the members including all the permanent members of the Security Council. This latter requirement has made the process very difficult and any change in the status or powers of the permanent members almost impossible. The only amendments that have been made came in response to the expanding number of new member states in the organization and the need to accommodate them in the membership of the Security Council and the **Economic and Social Council.** In 1965 the membership of the Security Council was expanded from 11 to 15 and that of the Economic and Social Council from 18 to 27. In 1973 the size of the Economic and Social Council was doubled to 54 members. Another adjustment in 1968 raised the voting requirement in the Security Council from seven to nine affirmative votes for calling a general-review conference, to conform to the change in voting requirements from seven to nine affirmative votes for adoption of any resolutions as a part of the 1965 increase in the size of the Security Council.

AMNESTY INTERNATIONAL. Although Amnesty International is a private organization it is relied on by the United Nations Commission on **Human Rights** to investigate the persecution of political prisoners in many countries. Amnesty International is a perennial consultant to the Commission and furnishes regular written and oral reports to that body.

ANGLO-IRANIAN OIL DISPUTE (1951–52). In 1951 the premier of the Iranian government, Mohammed Mossadegh, nationalized the Anglo-Iranian Oil Company, in which the British government owned a 51 percent interest. The British took their case to both the UN **Security Council** and the **International Court of Justice** but received no satisfactory result. Then, outside the United Nations, they arranged a boycott of Iranian oil and, with the aid of the United States Central Intelligence Agency, fostered a coup which overthrew the Mossadegh regime, and subsequently negotiated a new oil agreement with the Iranian government.

ANGOLA. The situation in Angola, after its independence in 1975, was closely linked to the independence movement in its neighboring state, Namibia (formerly South West Africa). Cuba sent 50,000 troops to Angola to support the governing Popular Movement for the Liberation of Angola. South African military forces aided the rebel forces of the National Union for the Total Independence of Angola. Southern Angola also served as a staging area for the forces of the South West Africa People's Organization which was recognized by the UN **General Assembly** as the only legitimate representative of the Namibian people. As an adjunct of the agreement for Namibian independence in 1988, the UN **Security Council** authorized the creation of the United Nations Angola Verification Mission (UNAVEM) to verify the phased and total withdrawal of Cuban troops from Angola. This was an unarmed observer group of a maximum strength of 70. The withdrawal was accomplished slightly ahead of schedule, but, with the outbreak of hostilities between the armed forces of the two rival Angolan political factions, UNAVEM was recreated in May 1991 as UN-AVEM II and given a new mandate to monitor a cease-fire and the Angolan election process. For this purpose an expanded force of 750 military police and electoral personnel was authorized. As military violence continued after the September 1992 elections the Security Council extended the mandate for UNAVEM II into 1994. (See also PEACEKEEPING; UNITED NATIONS TRANSITION ASSISTANCE GROUP.)

ANTARCTIC TREATY (1959). The nations having territorial claims in Antarctica concluded a treaty providing for cooperation among the parties and prohibiting military activities of all kinds in Antarctica. This treaty was an outgrowth of the declaration by the **General Assembly** establishing 1957–58 as an International Geophysical Year marked by global scientific cooperation relating to the weather, the oceans, space, and the frigid zones.

APARTHEID. Racial segregation and discrimination policies of the government of South Africa have been on the agenda of the **General Assembly** since 1946 and of the **Security Council** since 1960. Although the General Assembly accused South Africa of gross violations of **human rights** obligations specified in the **Charter of the United Nations,** South Africa denied United Nations jurisdiction on the basis of Article 2 of the Charter, which prohibits United Nations intervention in "matters which are essentially within the domestic jurisdiction of any state." The General Assembly devoted more time and effort to the apartheid issue than to any other human rights question and created extensive administrative machinery for studying the problem and directing the pressures on South Africa. (See also SOUTH AFRICAN RACIAL QUESTIONS.)

ARBITRATION *see* PEACEFUL SETTLEMENT OF DISPUTES

ARMS CONTROL. Although the most important negotiations for arms control, especially with regard to strategic weapons, have been conducted among groups of powerful states, the United Nations has made numerous contributions to the process and has exerted constant pressure on governments to both control and reduce armaments. The **Charter of the United Nations** assigns to the **General Assembly** the consideration of "principles governing disarmament and the regulation of armaments," and to the **Security Council** responsibility "for formulating . . . plans . . . for the establishment of a system for the regulation of armaments." The General Assembly has established a series of special bodies in the field of arms control, from the **Atomic Energy Commission** in 1946, and the Commission for Conventional Armaments the following year, to the **Conference on Disarmament,** which is today the most important negotiating arms control agency within the United Nations. The General Assembly has also tried to emphasize the need for disarmament by holding three special sessions devoted exclusively to the subject. The United Nations has instigated a series of treaties in specific areas of control including the **Partial Test-Ban Treaty** (1963), the **Outer Space Treaty** (1966), the **Nuclear Non-Proliferation Treaty** (1968), the **Sea Bed Treaty** (1971), the Biological Weapons Treaty (1972), and the Chemical Weapons Treaty (1993). (See also ACHESON-LILIENTHAL PLAN; ANTARCTIC TREATY; ATOMIC ENERGY COMMISSION; CONFERENCE ON DISARMAMENT; INTERNATIONAL ATOMIC ENERGY AGENCY; NUCLEAR NON-PROLIFERATION TREATY; OUTER SPACE TREATY; PARTIAL TEST-BAN TREATY; SEA BED DEMILITARIZATION TREATY.)

ATLANTIC CHARTER. A document promulgated in 1941 as a result of a meeting between Prime Minister **Winston Churchill** and President **Franklin D. Roosevelt** aboard ship near Newfoundland, declaring certain war and peace aims including the establishment of a "permanent system of general security." Subsequently all the powers allied against the Axis states subscribed to a broader **Declaration by United Nations** which included an endorsement of the principles of the Atlantic Charter. (See also DECLARA-TION BY UNITED NATIONS; MOSCOW DECLARA-TION.)

ATOMIC ENERGY COMMISSION. Established by the first resolution adopted by the **General Assembly** in 1946, it was composed of all members of the **Security Council** plus Canada. In 1952 it was merged with the Commission for Conventional Armaments into a single **Disarmament Commission** with the same membership.

ATOMIC ENERGY (PEACEFUL USES) *see* INTERNA-TIONAL ATOMIC ENERGY AGENCY (IAEA)

- B -

BACTERIOLOGICAL (BIOLOGICAL) WEAPONS TREATY (1972) *see* CHEMICAL, BACTERIOLOGICAL, AND RA-DIOLOGICAL WEAPONS

BARUCH PLAN *see* ACHESON-LILIENTHAL PLAN

BERNADOTTE, FOLKE (1895–1948). Swedish statesman, diplomat, and Red Cross official. In early May 1948 the special session of the **General Assembly** on **Palestine** decided to replace the previous Palestine Commission with a United Nations Mediator for Palestine, and on May 20 Count Folke Bernadotte, President of the Swedish Red Cross, was appointed as Mediator. During the ensuing weeks Count Bernadotte issued a series of reports to the **Security Council** and tried to negotiate observance of a military truce between the new state of Israel and its neighbors. On September 17, 1948 Count Bernadotte and the chief French observer, Colonel André Sérot, were shot and killed in the Israeli-held sector of Jerusalem. **Ralph Bunche** was appointed as Count Bernadotte's successor.

BOSNIA-HERZEGOVINA *see* YUGOSLAVIA

BOUTROS-GHALI, BOUTROS (1922–). The sixth **Secre-**

tary-General of the United Nations whose term began January 1, 1992. He was the first Secretary-General from Africa and the Arab world. He is an Egyptian scholar and statesman who authored more than 100 publications and who served as Deputy Prime Minister of Egypt. He inherited the problems of (1) financing the UN and its expanding **peacekeeping** activities, (2) the need for further administrative reform, and (3) the defining of the new roles of peacekeeping missions, especially in civil disorders. During his first two years in office nine new peacekeeping missions were established. In June 1992 he issued a 53-page special report entitled ''An Agenda for Peace.'' Administrative reforms included the establishment of a new Department for Policy Coordination and Sustainable Development in the **Secretariat** and the elimination of one of the previous semi-annual meetings of the **Economic and Social Council,** but the **General Assembly** could not agree on the details of a larger reform package.

BRETTON WOODS CONFERENCE. Conference held at Bretton Woods, New Hampshire, in July 1944 which established the **International Bank for Reconstruction and Development (IBRD)** and the **International Monetary Fund (IMF).** (See also INTERNATIONAL BANK FOR RECONSTRUCTION AND DEVELOPMENT; INTERNATIONAL MONETARY FUND.)

BRUNTLAND, GRO HARLEM (1939–   ). Prime Minister of Norway for three intermittent terms of office. She chaired the World Commission on Environment and Development whose report served as background for the **United Nations Conference on Environment and Development.** (See also BRUNTLAND REPORT.)

BRUNTLAND REPORT (1987). The result of a three-year study by the World Commission on Environment and Development chaired by **Gro Harlem Bruntland,** Prime Minister of Norway. This report, calling for ''sustainable development,'' served as an initial major basis for the efforts culminating in the **United Nations Conference on Environment and Development,** often referred to as the ''Earth Summit,'' held

in Rio de Janeiro in June 1992. (See also UNITED NA-
TIONS CONFERENCE ON ENVIRONMENT AND DE-
VELOPMENT.)

BUDGET OF THE UNITED NATIONS. In reality there are
several United Nations budgets. The regular budget is met by
assessing each member state by a complex process and
formula approximating ability to pay. The total annual
amount of this budget, which is used to meet the payroll and
expenses of the organization, has varied from less than $20
million in 1946 to more than $1 billion in the 1990s. The
assessments for members vary from 0.01 percent to 25
percent. A failure by governments to pay full assessments
when due is a major problem for the UN.

The members of the United Nations also join most of the
specialized agencies of the United Nations (such as the
**World Health Organization, the International Labour
Organisation,** and the **Food and Agriculture Organization**)
which are loosely affiliated with the United Nations, and the
assessment formula is similar to that of the United Nations.
The budgets of all the specialized agencies total somewhat
more than that of the United Nations.

From time to time the **General Assembly** has authorized
the creation of special programs with separate budgets raised
by voluntary contributions. For these purposes governments
pledge whatever amounts they wish. The first such program
established the **United Nations Children's Fund
(UNICEF)** in 1946. The largest special fund in this category
is the **United Nations Development Program (UNDP),**
with an annual budget of more than $1 billion.

The fourth category of budgets has become the most
expensive of all. This is the necessary financial support for
sending United Nations **peacekeeping** forces into trouble
spots in many parts of the world. More than 35 such actions
have been authorized, some of the largest and most expensive operations having been initiated since 1988. Various
methods of financing these operations have been tried and
most recent forces have been supported by a modified
assessment formula in which the affluent states pay a larger
share than their assessments for the regular UN budget. The

former Soviet Union and a few other states refused to contribute for earlier peacekeeping projects of which they disapproved. In 1992 the annual budgets of existing peacekeeping operations totalled $2.7 billion.

Unpaid assessments for all member states, for both the regular and peacekeeping budgets, totalled $1.9 billion in May 1992. Of this total the United States owed more than $860 million, the Russian Federation owed more than $340 million, Japan owed more than $150 million, and Germany owed more than $100 million. South Africa was also $45 million in arrears for the regular UN budget.

BUNCHE, RALPH J. (1904–1971). U.S. scholar, Department of State official, and United Nations official. As a scholar he was a faculty member of Howard University and Harvard University. As a government official he specialized in colonial affairs. In 1946 he was appointed by Secretary-General **Trygve Lie** to head the Trusteeship Division of the United Nations **Secretariat.** In 1947 he was assigned to the UN Palestine Commission and became its chief mediator after the assassination of Count **Folke Bernadotte.** In 1950, in recognition of his accomplishments as mediator, he was awarded the Nobel Peace Prize, the first Black to be so recognized. He was later promoted to the United Nations Secretariat rank of Undersecretary and served as special representative of the **Secretary-General** as civilian advisor to the military commanders of UN **peacekeeping** forces in the areas of the Middle East, the Congo, and Cyprus.

BUNKER, ELLSWORTH (1894–1984). U.S. corporate executive and ambassador. In 1962 he served as UN mediator in the Dutch-Indonesian dispute over West New Guinea.

- C -

CAMBODIA-THAILAND BORDER DISPUTES. The disputing states requested the aid of the **Secretary-General** of the UN in 1958–59 and again in 1962–64 in resolving border disputes and alleged acts of aggression. The second mission consisting of the personal representative of the Secretary-

General and a small staff was invited to remain in the area for two years at the expense of the disputing states. Satisfactory resolution of the problems was reported by the Secretary-General to the **Security Council** but the dispute was never debated by the Security Council as an official agenda item.

CAMBODIAN SITUATION. The country officially known as Cambodia until January 1976 and again since February 1990 was renamed Democratic Kampuchea during the 1976–90 interval. During the period 1975–79, when the country was ruled by the Khmer Rouge regime under the leadership of Pol Pot, an estimated two million people, out of a total population of seven million, died as a result of acts of genocide. The Kampuchean question was considered by the UN **Security Council** in January 1979 after the invasion of Kampuchea by Vietnamese military forces. The **General Assembly** later that year took up the issue after the Soviet Union used its veto power to block action by the Security Council. Over the next several years the General Assembly called for the withdrawal of all foreign forces from Kampuchea and for a comprehensive, democratic, political solution to the problem. The General Assembly was assisted in its efforts by an International Conference on Kampuchea (1981), a ten-nation Ad Hoc Committee of the Conference, and the efforts of the UN **Secretary-General** and his special representatives. Humanitarian aid was also provided by several United Nations and private agencies.

During the period 1979–89 Vietnam effectively controlled the central government in Kampuchea. In July–August 1989 a Conference on Peace in Cambodia held in Paris laid the groundwork for a peaceful transition to a new government in Cambodia. In September the Vietnamese government announced the withdrawal of all its troops from Cambodia. In 1990 the representatives of the five permanent members of the Security Council agreed upon the general terms for the transition to a democratic government in Cambodia. These included the creation of a UN Transitional Authority in Cambodia (UNTAC) to provide for organizing free and fair elections, and a Supreme National Council representing the four major political factions within Cambodia as a temporary agent of national sovereignty. The UN Security Council approved these terms and the Cambodian factions set up a 13-member Supreme National Council under the chairmanship of Prince Norodom Sihanouk, the former king and head of state (1941–70).

In 1991 the Security Council authorized the dispatch to Cambodia of an advance mission of 380 military liaison officers in preparation for the more than 20,000-member UNTAC peacekeeping force required to demobilize the armed forces of the Cambodian factions and to supervise all steps leading to a freely elected national government. By July 1992 more than 18,0000 UNTAC forces were in Cambodia, but lack of cooperation by faction leaders impeded rapid progress toward the previously accepted goals and processes. Elections were held in May 1993 and a phased withdrawal of UNTAC occurred during the remainder of the year.

CAPACITY STUDY OF THE UNITED NATIONS DEVELOPMENT SYSTEM. A report issued in 1970 under the leadership of Sir Robert Jackson which examined the need for reform in the UN **development** system. The main criticisms included the proliferation of projects and agencies without relationship to broad global planning, a lack of coordination, and the failure to establish and adhere to clear priorities. The goal was progress toward more rational and coordinated UN development efforts.

CENTRAL AMERICAN PEACE EFFORTS. The 1980s were marked by civil wars in Nicaragua, Honduras, and El Salvador. Thousands of lives were lost in each of these countries, and the cessation of hostilities, the disarming of rebel forces, and the restoration of public order were goals of peace efforts both outside and within the United Nations. The situation in Central America was in 1983 placed on the agendas of the UN **General Assembly** and **Security Council.**

The first efforts toward reconciliation between rebel and government leaders were made by the so-called "Contadora group" of countries—Colombia, Mexico, Panama, and Venezuela. Shortly afterward the Presidents of the five Central American countries—Costa Rica, Nicaragua, Honduras, El Salvador, and Guatemala—held a series of meetings seeking peace in the region. The President of Costa Rica, Oscar Arias Sánchez, drafted a plan for which he was awarded the 1987 Nobel Peace Prize. This plan was incorporated into the Esquipulas II Agreement among the five Central American Presidents in August 1987. These plans were endorsed by the UN General Assembly in October.

The UN has sent three major observer groups to Central America since 1989. The first to be established was the United Nations Observation Mission for the Verification of Elections in Nicaragua (ONUVEN). Nicaragua also accepted other surveillance groups to monitor its electoral process. ONUVEN had more than 100 observers, operated for six months, and was disbanded after the February 1990 elections. In response to a request from the Central American governments, the UN Security Council approved the formation in November 1989 of the United Nations Observer Group in Central America (ONUCA). ONUCA's mission was gradually enlarged to include surveillance over the cessation of aid to insurrectionist forces, the non-use of the territory of one state for attacks on others, and the demobilization and disarmament of insurgent forces. ONUCA had a maximum strength of 1,098 military personnel and ceased operations in January 1992.

Meanwhile, another UN **peacekeeping** group, the UN Observer Mission in El Salvador (ONUSAL) had begun in July 1991 to monitor **human rights** in that country. When, after 20 months of negotiation, a final agreement was reached on December 31 for a cease-fire to end the 12-year civil war in El Salvador, ONUSAL was enlarged to 625 members and its mandate was expanded to include verifying compliance with the cease-fire arrangements and monitoring the maintenance of public order. A UN Commission on Truth, composed of three distinguished persons, was also appointed by the UN **Secretary-General** in July 1992 and charged with investigating serious acts of violence in El Salvador.

CHARTER AMENDMENT *see* AMENDMENT OF THE UN CHARTER

CHARTER OF THE UNITED NATIONS. The basic document establishing the United Nations. It is a multilateral treaty specifying the obligations of member states and the purposes, organizational structure, powers, and procedures of the organization. After much preliminary planning, it was signed by the representatives of 50 states at the **San Francisco Conference** on June 26, 1945. On October 24 of that year it came into force upon receipt of the required number of ratifications. Each year October 24 is observed as United Nations Day. Newly admitted members must in their membership applications specify that they accept the obligations contained in the Charter.

The United Nations Charter consists of 111 articles divided into 18 chapters and is nearly three times the length of the **League of Nations** Covenant. It is much more detailed than the Covenant on economic, social and humanitarian agencies, commitments, and programs. It also includes lengthy provisions for a **trusteeship system** and a declaration of the rights of all non-self-governing peoples. Since the League Covenant concentrated more on peace and security matters than on any other subject, the UN Charter does not expand greatly on these provisions, but the Charter delineates clearly between **peaceful settlement** procedures and procedures for dealing with the more serious threats to peace by referring to the former in Chapter VI and the latter in Chapter VII. Altogether the Charter provides an elaborate framework for the wide-ranging activities of the United Nations.

CHARTER RATIFICATION *see* RATIFICATION OF THE UN CHARTER

CHARTER REVIEW *see* REVIEW OF THE UN CHARTER

CHEMICAL, BACTERIOLOGICAL, AND RADIOLOGICAL WEAPONS (CBR). Since the 1960s a series of UN committees has recommended the complete elimination of all CBR weapons from the arsenals of all countries. Such arsenals still exist and were used in the **Iran-Iraq war** in the 1980s. In 1972 a Convention on the Prohibition of the Development, Production and Stockpiling of Bacteriological (Biological) and Toxin Weapons and on Their Destruction was opened for signature. After ten years of effort the UN **Conference on Disarmament** in 1992 completed and submitted to the **General Assembly** a Convention on the Prohibition of the Development, Production, Stockpiling and Use of Chemical Weapons and on Their Destruction. This treaty was opened for signature in Paris in January 1993. The earliest date for its coming into force is 1995 and nations have ten years to complete the destruction of stockpiles. Uniquely, the convention also provides methods and machinery for verification and enforcement with an Organization for the Prohibition of Chemical Weapons at The Hague.

CHEMICAL WEAPONS TREATY (1993) *see* CHEMICAL, BACTERIOLOGICAL, AND RADIOLOGICAL WEAPONS (CBR)

CHILD WELFARE *see* UNITED NATIONS CHILDREN'S FUND

CHINESE REPRESENTATION IN THE UNITED NATIONS. As a major ally in the war in the Pacific in World War II and as a participant in the planning sessions for the United Nations, China was an original member of the United Nations and a permanent member, with **veto** power, in the **Security Council.** After the political and military victory by the Communist regime on the mainland and the flight of Chiang Kai-shek and his followers to Taiwan in 1949, the Soviet Union, opposed most strongly by the United States, pushed for the replacement of the representatives of the Republic of China by those of the People's Republic of China. The United States was able to prevent this change until 1971 in spite of growing reluctance on the part of other member states, including several close U.S. allies. In that year the **General Assembly** voted overwhelmingly to accord sole representation to the Peking representatives. In spite of some sentiment for separate membership for Taiwan, it remains unrepresented in the United Nations.

CHURCHILL, WINSTON (1874–1965). As British Prime Minister (1940–45) Churchill played a major role in planning for the United Nations. He participated in a series of meetings with President **Franklin D. Roosevelt** and Premier Stalin from 1941 to 1945 which committed the three nations to the establishment of a postwar international organization to keep the peace. Churchill at first favored a regional approach to peace maintenance but shifted gradually to a global emphasis.

COLLECTIVE MEASURES COMMITTEE. A special committee set up by the **General Assembly** as a part of its **Uniting for Peace Resolution** adopted in November 1950. This committee was intended to assist the General Assembly in carrying out its anticipated enhanced activities in the peace and security field when the **Security Council** was deadlocked over a security matter. After brief activity the Collective Measures Committee ceased to function. (See also UNITING FOR PEACE RESOLUTION.)

COLLECTIVE SECURITY. A basic principle and goal on which both the **League of Nations** and the United Nations were founded. The theory of collective security is that it is the obligation of all members of the organization to join in supporting collective action against any state judged to have committed a breach of the peace, a threat to the peace, or an act of aggression. The sanctions authorized may be political, economic, or military in nature. Article 43 of the **Charter of the United Nations** anticipates the working out of further agreements detailing the assignment of armed forces and support facilities for military enforcement under the direction of the **Security Council,** aided by a **Military Staff Committee.**

Hopes of applying collective security measures against aggressor states have been thwarted by the inability to reach any supplementary agreements under Article 43 (partially because of the Cold War climate), the impossibility of taking action against the big powers (due to their **veto** power in the

Security Council), the difficulty of identifying an aggressor state, and the unwillingness of states to make sacrifices in situations which do not directly affect their national interests. Therefore, with a few exceptions involving limited successes in applying economic **sanctions** (e.g., against Southern Rhodesia and South Africa), the application of the principle of collective security has fallen short of fulfilling the goals of the theory. The United States received Security Council legitimization for military action against North Korea in 1950 and against Iraq in 1990, but the subsequent military action did not follow the *collective* intent of the Charter provisions under Security Council direction. (See also KOREAN QUESTION; KUWAIT INVASION BY IRAQ; SANCTIONS.)

COLLECTIVE SELF-DEFENSE. Article 51 of the **Charter of the United Nations** provides that, in case of an armed attack against a member state, nothing in the Charter impairs that state's right of individual or **collective self-defense** until the **Security Council** has acted to restore international peace and security. Any actions taken in self-defense shall be immediately reported to the Security Council, whose authority shall not be affected by these circumstances. In practice the failure of states to comply with their responsibility to report fully to the Security Council, sometimes coupled with the use of the **veto** in the Security Council, has allowed states to substitute action through regional organizations for the intended priority of the Security Council. Article 53 of the Charter additionally forbids the taking of "enforcement action" by regional organizations without Security Council authorization. Several cases of action through the Organization of American States have been based on a narrowing of the meaning of "enforcement action" to allow the United States to substitute regional handling of these disputes for Security Council authority.

COLONIALISM *see* NON-SELF-GOVERNING TERRITORIES

COMMISSION ON HUMAN RIGHTS. One of the functional

commissions set up to assist the **Economic and Social Council (ECOSOC).** This commission has been very active and has produced the Declaration of Human Rights (1948) and the two covenants or treaties on **human rights,** one on civil and political rights and the other on economic, social and cultural rights (1966). The Commission also authorizes investigations and each year hears testimony, from both its own investigators and private groups such as **Amnesty International** and the International Commission of Jurists, on charges of gross violations of human rights in various countries around the globe. (See also HUMAN RIGHTS.)

COMMISSION ON NARCOTIC DRUGS. A functional commission of the **Economic and Social Council (ECOSOC)** established in 1946 to assist the Council in formulating policy on narcotic drugs. A series of treaties on narcotic drugs has been produced, the latest comprehensive treaty being signed in **Vienna** in 1988. A number of additional agencies in the field include the International Narcotics Control Board, a United Nations Fund for Drug Abuse Control and a UN Division of Narcotic Drugs in Vienna.

COMMISSION ON THE STATUS OF WOMEN. Originally established in 1946 as a subcommission of the Commission on **Human Rights** but raised to full commission status in 1947. It operates as a functional and advisory agency to the **Economic and Social Council (ECOSOC).** (See also WOMEN.)

COMMISSION TO STUDY THE ORGANIZATION OF PEACE. An association of leading United States scholars established in 1939 to study and recommend the purposes, principles, and organization of the postwar international agency. This group was one of the most influential **non-governmental organizations** in shaping U.S. official planning for the emerging United Nations organization, and continued to study and issue reports on United Nations issues during the decades after the organization began to function.

COMMITTEE FOR DEVELOPMENT PLANNING. A consultative committee of experts established in the 1960s by the **Economic and Social Council** to assist in formulating and carrying out UN **development** plans for each of the **Development Decades.** (The 1990s is the fourth of these designated decades.)

COMMON FUND FOR COMMODITIES. The idea of a common fund has been discussed since the 1970s but has never been fully implemented or financed. The idea is to finance buffer stocks to bolster and stabilize prices for 18 primary commodities upon which the developing countries depend as a source of foreign exchange. This integrated program for commodities has been promoted primarily through the **United Nations Conference on Trade and Development (UNCTAD).** In lieu of full funding for the integrated program, individual international commodity agreements have been adopted for about one-third of the products included in the proposed more comprehensive package.

CONFERENCE ON DISARMAMENT. This is the most important negotiating agency within the UN on the general subject of **disarmament.** It is the successor agency since 1984 to a series of similar major agencies within the United Nations structure under various titles and varying widely in membership. It has 40 members including all the permanent members of the **Security Council** and a wide representation of middle powers and developing states. The work of the Conference on Disarmament has been supplemented by the establishment of a UN Center for Disarmament in the Secretariat, a United Nations Institute for Disarmament Research (UNIDR), and the convening of three special sessions on disarmament of the **General Assembly** in 1978, 1982, and 1988. (See also DISARMAMENT.)

CONFERENCE TO REVIEW THE ACHIEVEMENTS OF THE UNITED NATIONS DECADE FOR WOMEN (1985). A conference in Nairobi, Kenya to assess the progress on the global status of **women** at the end of the Decade for Women proclaimed at the World Conference of the International Women's Year held in Mexico City in 1975. The conference was attended by 2,000 delegates from 157 countries. The conference adopted a document of Forward-Looking Strategies to Improve the Status of Women for the period until the year 2000. In support of this document the **General Assembly** suggested strengthening the **Commission on the Status of Women** and the **International Research and Training Institute for the Advancement of Women (INSTRAW)**. (See also COMMISSION ON THE STATUS OF WOMEN; INTERNATIONAL RESEARCH AND TRAINING INSTITUTE FOR THE ADVANCEMENT OF WOMEN; WOMEN.)

CONGO OPERATION (1960–64). The former Congo (now Zaire) became independent on June 30, 1960. Immediately, civil and political disorder occurred and within two weeks President Kasavubu and Premier **Patrice Lumumba** appealed to the United Nations for assistance in restoring order. The **Security Council** called for Belgium to withdraw its troops from the Congo and authorized the **Secretary-General** to provide both military and technical assistance to the official government of the country.

Within a month, more than 14,000 UN **peacekeeping** personnel were in the Congo and during the next four years the number reached a maximum of 20,000. Thirty countries contributed military personnel, and several others, including the major powers, furnished transport or other aid. This was the largest and most expensive UN peacekeeping operation in the first 45 years of UN history. This United Nations Operation in the Congo (ONUC, according to the French word order) had to deal not only with restoring order, but with political rivalries within the country, disagreements among the major powers and intervention by Belgium concerning these rivalries, and the attempted secession of the richest province, Katanga.

Special difficulties for ONUC and the UN included: (1) the necessity to become involved in military action to prevent the secession of Katanga (contrary to the ideal peacekeeping role); (2) a charge of partiality and a demand for his replacement brought by the Soviet Union against Secretary-General **Dag Hammarskjöld;** (3) the death of

Dag Hammarskjöld in a plane crash when he was on his way to negotiate with the political leader of Katanga, Moise Tshombe; and (4) the beginning of the long-range financial crisis of the United Nations, with the **budget** for ONUC amounting to $400 million in addition to costs absorbed by countries furnishing troops, and the refusal of some states (including the Soviet Union) to pay their assessments.

Although disorders in the Congo continued afterward, all of the ONUC forces were withdrawn by June 30, 1964. The UN continued to furnish **development** aid after the withdrawal of the peacekeeping personnel.

CONNALLY RESERVATION. Article 36, section 2 of the Statute of the **International Court of Justice** provides that any party to the Statute may declare that it recognizes as compulsory, in relation to any other state accepting the same obligation, the jurisdiction of the Court in all legal disputes concerning a broad range of issues of **international law.** Most members of the United Nations do not subscribe to this "optional clause" and others have subscribed subject to reservations. The most sweeping of these reservations was the Connally Amendment attached to the United States subscription to the clause. This reservation specified that the jurisdiction of the Court would not apply to "disputes with regard to matters which are essentially within the **domestic jurisdiction** of the United States as determined by the United States of America." This self-judging reservation almost nullified the effectiveness of adherence to Article 36(2) of the Statute. In 1986 this became a dead issue when the United States withdrew its adherence to the "optional clause." (See also INTERNATIONAL COURT OF JUSTICE.)

CONVENTION ON THE PRIVILEGES AND IMMUNITIES OF THE UNITED NATIONS. This treaty was drafted under the jurisdiction of the United Nations Preparatory Committee so that it was ready for **General Assembly** approval in February 1946. The Convention provides details concerning the privileges and immunities of various categories of UN personnel, but accords full diplomatic privilege and immunities under international law only to the **Secretary-General** and his chief assistants and their families. Most member states have adhered to the treaty.

CORDIER, ANDREW (1901–1975). One of the chief advisers in the U.S. Department of State in drafting the **Charter of the United Nations.** He served as the executive assistant to UN Secretaries-General **Trygve Lie** and **Dag Hammarskjöld** and was UN Under-Secretary for General Assembly Affairs 1961–62. After retiring from UN service he was Dean of the School of International Affairs of Columbia University 1962–72 and President of the University 1969–70.

CORFU CHANNEL CASE (1947–49). The first case heard by the **International Court of Justice,** brought by the United Kingdom against Albania. The United Kingdom first submitted the dispute to the UN **Security Council,** which recommended that the parties refer the dispute to the Court. The charge was the laying of mines in the Corfu Channel by Albania, resulting in the loss of 44 lives aboard British destroyers. The Court held Albania responsible for the laying of the mines, upheld the right of innocent passage by the British ships through international waters, and assessed damages to be paid by Albania at 843,947 pounds sterling. The Court also declared that the British had violated Albanian **sovereignty** in sweeping the mines from the channel, part of which was within Albanian territorial waters. Albania challenged the jurisdiction of the Court on technical grounds and never paid the monetary judgment. (See also INTERNATIONAL COURT OF JUSTICE.)

CYPRUS QUESTION (1954–   ). One of the long-standing, unsettled disputes before the **Security Council** and the **General Assembly.** Successive **Secretaries-General** have also tried both personally and through appointed representatives to mediate a settlement, but to no avail. In 1960 the British worked out, with the concurrence of Greece and Turkey, a plan for Cypriot independence, with a native Greek president, a native Turkish vice-president, and a complex system of representation including a degree of autonomy in the predominantly Greek majority and Turkish minority sectors. Local violence was prevalent and in 1964 the UN Security Council set up a UN **peacekeeping** force which has varied in size from 2,000 to 7,000. A serious crisis occurred in 1974 with intervention by both Greece and Turkey. Turkish troops took over an expanded area of the island beyond that previously claimed by the Turkish minority. The country remains divided but hostilities have diminished and the UN force remains as a deterrent to excessive violence.

- D -

DECLARATION BY UNITED NATIONS. A document signed by 26 nations in January 1942 in Washington, D.C. and subsequently subscribed to by a score of other wartime opponents of the Axis powers. It represents the first use of the term ''United Nations'' and is an early stepping stone in the development of the **Charter of the United Nations** in 1945. The signatory states were the bulk of those who became original members of the United Nations. (See also ATLANTIC CHARTER; MOSCOW DECLARATION.)

DECLARATION ON THE GRANTING OF INDEPENDENCE TO COLONIAL COUNTRIES AND PEOPLES (1960). A landmark document adopted by the **General Assembly** in the implementation of **Charter of the United Nations** principles pertaining to the rights of all peoples to political independence and self-rule. It was adopted immediately after the admission of 17 previous colonies to UN membership in 1960. The following year a special committee was created by the General Assembly to act as a watchdog over the process of decolonization and to study and urge rapid elimination of the remnants of political colonialism.

DESERTIFICATION see ENVIRONMENT PROGRAMS OF THE UNITED NATIONS

DEVELOPMENT. The **Charter of the United Nations** states as one of its purposes the achievement of ''international cooperation in solving international problems of an economic, social, cultural, or humanitarian character." More specifically, in the Charter's preamble the goals include "to promote social progress and better standards of life in larger freedom," and "to employ international machinery for the promotion of the economic and social advancement of all peoples." The major organ to carry out these purposes is the **Economic and Social Council (ECOSOC),** but a huge complex of additional agencies has been created to assist in this work, and a major part of the **budget** of the United Nations is allocated to these programs.

The original modest development efforts of the United Nations were enlarged in 1949 by U.S. President Harry S Truman's proposal for an **Expanded Program of Technical Assistance (EPTA).** Another expansion occurred in the 1960s after the establishment of the **United Nations Development Program (UNDP),** whose separate annual budget, raised by voluntary contributions, eventually reached $1 billion. (See also BRUNTLAND REPORT; COMMITTEE FOR DEVELOPMENT PLANNING; COMMON FUND FOR COMMODITIES; DEVELOPMENT DECADES; RESIDENT REPRESENTATIVES; UNITED NATIONS CONFERENCE ON ENVIRONMENT AND DEVELOPMENT; UNITED NATIONS CONFERENCE ON TRADE AND DEVELOPMENT; UNITED NATIONS DEVELOPMENT PROGRAM; UNITED NATIONS INDUSTRIAL DEVELOPMENT ORGANIZATION.)

DEVELOPMENT DECADES. By 1960 the number of new state members in the United Nations increased the pressure for attention to issues of **development.** As a result of this pressure the **General Assembly** declared the 1960s as the United Nations **Development Decade** and renewed this declaration each ten years, with the 1970s, 1980s, and 1990s designated as the Second, Third, and Fourth Development Decades. In order to assist in planning for each decade the General Assembly created a **Committee for Development Planning.** The goals set for each decade always exceeded the progress made toward economic development in the less-developed countries of Asia, Africa, and Latin America. The affluent states agreed to targets of annually transferring one percent of their GNP to the developing states, with 0.7 percent as public aid. Only Norway, Sweden, the Netherlands, and Denmark ever reached or exceeded these targets. The overall figure for official or public aid in the period since the early 1970s has remained below 0.4 percent, with the United States, as the largest donor, generally below 0.3 percent. Aid is also unevenly divided, with "client" states receiving the major share. As a result the gap between rich and poor countries has widened since 1960. (See also COMMITTEE FOR DEVELOPMENT PLANNING; UNITED NATIONS DEVELOPMENT PROGRAM.)

DISARMAMENT. The **Charter of the United Nations** stresses regulation of armaments rather than disarmament, and most actions taken during the past 50 years were in the nature of **arms control** rather than any substantial reduction of either nuclear or conventional weapons. However, the **General Assembly** has pressured for real disarmament to throw the spotlight of public opinion on the need to reduce the world's huge burden of armaments. Additionally, after a series of UN committees and commissions since 1946, a 40-member Committee on Disarmament, created in 1978, was renamed in 1984 as the **Conference on Disarmament,** and this Conference is the key UN negotiating agency on the subject. Outside the UN, the first treaty to substantially reduce the nuclear arsenal was agreed to in 1991 between the U.S. and Russia, but the level of the global arms trade in conventional weapons has not significantly declined. (See also ACHESON-LILIENTHAL PLAN; ANTARCTIC TREATY; ARMS CONTROL; ATOMIC ENERGY COMMISSION; CHEMICAL, BACTERIOLOGICAL, AND RADIOLOGICAL WEAPONS; CONFERENCE ON DISARMAMENT; DISARMAMENT COMMISSION; DISARMAMENT DECADES; ECONOMIC CONSEQUENCES OF DISARMAMENT; GENERAL AND COMPLETE DISARMAMENT; GENERAL ASSEMBLY SPECIAL SESSIONS ON DISARMAMENT.)

DISARMAMENT COMMISSION. This UN body was first formed in 1952 by the merging of the **Atomic Energy**

Commission and the Commission for Conventional Armaments. It was enlarged from its original 12 members to 26 members in 1957 and to the full membership of the United Nations in 1958. However, since that time the significant UN negotiating activities have been conducted in sub-groups, and since 1984 the preeminent UN negotiating agency has been the 40-member **Conference on Disarmament.**

DISARMAMENT DECADES. As an indication of the dissatisfaction of many middle and smaller powers with the rate of progress toward reduction of the world's armament arsenals, the **General Assembly** declared the 1970s as the Disarmament Decade, the 1980s as the Second Disarmament Decade, and the 1990s as the Third Disarmament Decade. This is just one of several devices of the General Assembly for focusing global attention on the need for reducing the burden of armaments and the dangers of their use in wars.

DISASTER RELIEF. After two major natural disasters in 1970, an earthquake in Peru and a tidal wave in Bangladesh, the **General Assembly** took steps to establish the Office of United Nations Disaster Relief Coordinator (UNDRO), which began operations in 1972. UNDRO is not a field operating agency but acts principally as a coordinating agency for multilateral, governmental, and private relief operations and for pre-disaster prevention and preparedness planning.

DISPUTES CONSIDERED BY UNITED NATIONS BODIES. *see* PEACEFUL SETTLEMENT OF DISPUTES; Individual Disputes

DOMESTIC JURISDICTION. One of the basic principles included in the **Charter of the United Nations** forbids the UN "to intervene in matters which are essentially within the domestic jurisdiction of any state." States including South Africa and the Soviet Union have invoked the domestic jurisdiction clause against United Nations interference, but, since no hard and fast line can be drawn between domestic affairs and threats to international peace and security, the applicability of the clause is subject to conflicting interpretations. (See also SOUTH AFRICAN RACIAL QUESTIONS.)

DOMINICAN REPUBLIC SITUATION (1965–66). From 1961 until 1965 the situation in the Dominican Republic was marked by political unrest with a series of political coups and short-lived political regimes. In April 1965 the United States intervened by dispatching 24,000 U.S. marines to the capital of Santo Domingo. The United States government notified the UN **Security Council** that the matter was being handled by the Organization of American States (OAS), and used its influence in the OAS to convert the marine force into an ostensibly Inter-American Peace Force by replacing a few U.S. marines by small military contingents from five Latin American countries.

At the request of the Soviet Union the Security Council considered the issue in 28 meetings during May–July 1965. Charges were made that the United States had used the OAS in order to bypass the United Nations. The Security Council called for a cease-fire and authorized the **Secretary-General** to send a personal representative and a small group of military observers to keep the Security Council fully informed. However, most of the efforts toward actual settlement were performed by agents of the OAS. The Security Council could not take effective action because of major power disagreement. Critics of United States policy in the matter held that the United States had violated the mandate of Article 53 of the **Charter of the United Nations** which states that "no enforcement action shall be taken under **regional arrangements** or by regional agencies without the authorization of the Security Council."

DRUGS *see* COMMISSION ON NARCOTIC DRUGS

DULLES, JOHN FOSTER (1888–1959). An expert in **international law** and U.S. government official. Dulles became active in the Federal Council of Churches of America and during the 1940s chaired its Commission on a Just and Durable Peace. This commission was influential as a **nongovernmental organization** in contributing support and ideas to the planning group within the U.S. Department of State in shaping the emerging **Charter of the United Nations.** Dulles was a U.S. delegate to the **San Francisco Conference** which produced the Charter of the United Nations, a delegate to the UN **General Assembly** (1946–48, 1950), and U.S. Secretary of State under President **Dwight D. Eisenhower** (1953–59).

DUMBARTON OAKS CONFERENCE (1944). This major planning conference for the emerging United Nations organization was held at the Dumbarton Oaks estate in Washington, D.C. It involved only the four major allies in World War II and was held in two sessions. The representatives of the allies in the war in Europe—the United States, the Soviet Union, and the United Kingdom—met for nearly five weeks beginning in August 1944, followed by a briefer meeting of the Pacific allies in which Chinese representatives replaced the Soviet delegation. The resulting document served as a working basis for the **Charter of the United Nations,** but concentrated heavily on the role of the **Security Council** in the postwar peace-maintenance system. The principles of permanent membership with **veto** power for the Big Five in the Security Council were established in the agreement and firmly defended against any subsequent modification. The proposals also provided for a **General Assembly,** a Court, and a **Secretariat,** but left most details of a **trusteeship system,** an economic and social system, and an enlarged role of the General Assembly to be determined at the **San Francisco Conference** on the UN Charter in 1945.

- E -

EARTHWATCH. An important aspect of the action program established by the Stockholm Conference on the Global Environment (1972) was the creation of an earthwatch network to monitor land, water, and atmospheric conditions, and changes that might affect the human environment. More than 100 monitoring stations were planned, forming a Global Environmental Monitoring Service (GEMS) linked to a central data bank in **Geneva.** (See also ENVIRONMENT PROGRAMS OF THE UNITED NATIONS.)

ECONOMIC AND SOCIAL COMMISSION FOR ASIA AND THE PACIFIC (ESCAP), formerly ECONOMIC COMMISSION FOR ASIA AND THE FAR EAST (ECAFE). One of the five UN **Regional Commissions** established as subsidiary agencies of the **Economic and Social Council.** ECAFE and the **Economic Commission for Europe (ECE)** were first created in 1947 to aid in reconstruction and rehabilitation work, but ESCAP and the other regional agencies now serve much broader purposes. They act as agents of decentralization of the United Nations economic and social activities, of coordination among regional member governments, and of cooperation with such other UN agencies as the **United Nations Development Program** and the **United Nations Conference on Trade and Development.** They also seek to cooperate with non-UN regional programs such as the Colombo Plan. ESCAP has fostered such projects as the Asian Development Bank, the Mekong River Project, the Asian Highway, and the Asian Institute for Economic Development and Planning.

ECONOMIC AND SOCIAL COMMISSION FOR WESTERN ASIA (ESCWA), formerly ECONOMIC COMMISSION FOR WESTERN ASIA (ECWA). The ECWA was the last of the five regional commissions established in 1974 by the United Nations as subsidiary organs to the **Economic and Social Council.** The delay in its creation was due to the hostility between the Arab states and Israel, and Israel is excluded from membership. All of the **regional commissions** serve mainly as agents of decentralization and coordination within their respective areas for the broad range of United Nations economic and social development programs. (See also ECONOMIC AND SOCIAL COMMISSION FOR ASIA AND THE PACIFIC.)

ECONOMIC AND SOCIAL COOPERATION. The promotion of international economic and social cooperation is one of the major goals of the **Charter of the United Nations.** In order to achieve this goal the **Economic and Social Council** was created as one of the six major organs of the UN. Other agencies of support would be the **General Assembly,** a number of **specialized agencies** brought into relationship with the UN, subsidiary bodies of the Economic and Social Council, and **nongovernmental organizations** brought into consultative status with the UN.

ECONOMIC AND SOCIAL COUNCIL (ECOSOC). One of the six major organs of the United Nations as specified in the **Charter of the United Nations.** At the insistence of the lesser powers it was raised to major organ status during the **San Francisco Conference** which produced the Charter. It originally had 18 members, but, as the UN membership grew, it was increased in size to 27 in 1965 and to 54 in 1973. During most of its history ECOSOC held two sessions a year but in 1992 it shifted to a single session of about five weeks.

The purpose of ECOSOC is to further economic and social welfare throughout the world, especially in the developing nations. Its agenda runs the gamut of economic, social, and humanitarian issues of international concern. It directs research, issues reports on economic and social concerns, and coordinates research conducted by the **specialized agencies** affiliated with the UN. Its most intricate and difficult problems relate to its task of coordinating the work of dozens of international agencies involved in promoting economic and social welfare. These include functional commissions, **regional commissions,** specialized agencies, standing committees, ad hoc committees, and other special bodies and programs such as the **United Nations Development Program (UNDP),** the **United Nations Conference on Trade and Development (UNCTAD),** and the **United Nations Environment Program (UNEP).** ECOSOC also has granted consultative status to more than 800 **nongovernmental organizations.**

ECONOMIC COMMISSION FOR AFRICA (ECA). One of the five regional agencies under the **Economic and Social Council** to further decentralization of UN economic and social development efforts. The ECA was created in 1958 after the admission to UN membership of six African states in the previous three years. Lack of cooperation and harmony among the members has hampered the ECA's effectiveness, but among its achievements is the establishment of the

African Development Bank as a source of loans for African development projects. (See also ECONOMIC AND SOCIAL COMMISSION FOR ASIA AND THE PACIFIC.)

ECONOMIC COMMISSION FOR EUROPE (ECE). One of the first established of the five regional agencies under the **Economic and Social Council.** Beginning in 1947, its early efforts were directed to reconstruction and rehabilitation programs. As the emphasis shifted to development projects the ECE became less important than the similar commissions for Asia, Africa, and Latin America. (See also ECONOMIC AND SOCIAL COMMISSION FOR ASIA AND THE PACIFIC.)

ECONOMIC COMMISSION FOR LATIN AMERICA AND THE CARIBBEAN (ECLAC), formerly ECONOMIC COMMISSION FOR LATIN AMERICA (ECLA). Created in 1948 as the third in the eventual group of five **regional commissions** serving to aid in decentralizing the work of the UN **Economic and Social Council.** ECLAC is probably the most effective of the regional commissions, having served as the catalyst for the formation of the Inter-American Development Bank, the Latin American Free Trade Association, the Central American Common Market, and the **United Nations Conference on Trade and Development (UNCTAD). Raul Prebisch,** the executive secretary of ECLA for its first 15 years, was then appointed as the first Secretary-General of UNCTAD. (See also ECONOMIC AND SOCIAL COMMISSION FOR ASIA AND THE PACIFIC; PREBISCH, RAUL; UNITED NATIONS CONFERENCE ON TRADE AND DEVELOPMENT.)

ECONOMIC CONSEQUENCES OF DISARMAMENT. One concern of countries with heavy investment in arms production and military forces is the displacement of personnel resulting from **disarmament.** Counter arguments declare that, with retraining of workers, these military-related expenditures and skills could be channeled toward the solution of economic, social, and humanitarian problems in both developed and developing countries. The United Nations has since

1962 sponsored four studies by expert committees, all of which concluded that all countries, with proper adjustment measures, would reap economic benefits from substantial disarmament measures. (See also DISARMAMENT.)

ECONOMIC DEVELOPMENT *see* ECONOMIC AND SOCIAL COOPERATION

EDUCATIONAL COOPERATION *see* UNITED NATIONS EDUCATIONAL, SCIENTIFIC AND CULTURAL ORGANIZATION

EISENHOWER, DWIGHT D. (1890–1969). World War II general and 34th President of the United States. In 1953 he presented to the United Nations his "Atoms for Peace" proposal which led to the creation of the **International Atomic Energy Agency.**

ENERGY PROGRAMS OF THE UNITED NATIONS. The first major development in the UN energy activities was the convening of the United Nations Conference on the Peaceful Uses of Atomic Energy in 1955. This conference produced a draft statute for the **International Atomic Energy Agency (IAEA),** which was created to promote the safe and peaceful use of atomic energy and began operations in 1957.

The world's dependence on petroleum as the major energy source led to additional activities. Besides the economic burden in developing countries of purchasing petroleum-based products, these countries are fast depleting their sources of fuel wood. In 1980 the **United Nations Industrial Development Organization (UNIDO)** created a Special Advisory Group on Energy. The following year a United Nations Conference on New and Renewable Sources of Energy met in Nairobi. Resulting from the conference was the establishment of a United Nations Energy Unit in the UN **Secretariat** and a Committee on the Development and Utilization of New and Renewable Sources of Energy to monitor progress in the transition to the use of more desirable energy sources. The UN Secretariat's Department of Technical Cooperation for Development annually supports dozens of national projects on energy matters. After long planning and delays, in 1987 a United Nations Conference for the Promotion of International Cooperation in the Peaceful Uses of Nuclear Energy met in Geneva. In 1992 the **United Nations Conference on Environment and Development (UNCED),** held in Rio de Janeiro, encompassed within its broad theme of sustainable development many aspects of energy problems. (See also INTERNATIONAL ATOMIC ENERGY AGENCY.)

ENVIRONMENT PROGRAMS OF THE UNITED NATIONS. Prior to 1972 the only UN agencies that gave limited attention to environmental matters were several of the **specialized agencies.** For example, the **International Labour Organisation (ILO)** was concerned with workers' exposure to toxic materials; the **World Meteorological Organization (WMO)** with air pollution; the **Food and Agriculture Organization (FAO)** with harmful effects of pesticides; and the **World Health Organization (WHO)** with environmental health.

By 1972 the need for an overall examination of environmental issues prompted the convening in Stockholm of the World Conference on the Human Environment. **Maurice F. Strong** of Canada was selected by Secretary-General **U Thant** as secretary-general of the conference. In addition to adopting a Declaration on the Human Environment and an Action Plan for implementing a broad environmental program, the Conference recommended the establishment of a permanent **United Nations Environment Program (UNEP).** This new agency was approved by the **General Assembly** and opened in Nairobi, Kenya, with Maurice Strong as its first executive director. Because of limited staff and a small budget UNEP has been able to carry on only a modest program.

In 1976–77 UNEP promoted three world conferences related to the environment. These were a United Nations Conference on Human Settlements (HABITAT) held in Vancouver, Canada; a United Nations Water Conference held in Mar del Plata, Argentina; and a United Nations Conference on Desertification which met in Nairobi, Kenya.

The need to check the spread of deserts was also emphasized in the General Assembly's 1986 Programme of Action for African Economic Recovery.

Two problems that have received heavy emphasis since 1980 by UNEP and in other forums are global warming and the destruction of the ozone layer in the atmosphere. A world conference in Toronto in 1988 prescribed a 20 percent reduction of carbon emissions (the chief cause of global warming) into the atmosphere by 2005. Chlorofluorocarbons (CFCs), widely used in refrigeration, have been determined as the chief source of ozone depletion, as well as a contributor to global warming. UNEP initiated the signing in Vienna in 1985 of the Convention for the Protection of the Ozone Layer. As scientists discovered that ozone depletion was occurring much faster than previously assumed, the Convention was supplemented in 1987 by a Montreal Protocol providing for a 50 percent reduction in CFC production by 1988. Subsequent alarm about the problem led to a London agreement in 1990 for a complete phaseout of CFC production by 2000 and announcements by all major producers to end production by 1995.

By the mid-1980s various forums of the UN had linked the global environment with development needs. In 1987 the World Commission on Environment and Development issued a report stressing "sustainable development" as the formula for human well-being in an interdependent world. The Commission report, often referred to as the **Bruntland Report,** served as a major impetus to the calling of the 1992 **United Nations Conference on Environment and Development** in Rio de Janeiro. (See also BRUNTLAND, GRO HARLEM; BRUNTLAND REPORT; EARTHWATCH; STRONG, MAURICE F.; UNITED NATIONS CONFERENCE ON ENVIRONMENT AND DEVELOPMENT.)

ERITREA *see* ITALIAN COLONIES

EVATT, HERBERT V. (1894–1965). From 1941 until 1949 Evatt was both Attorney General and Minister for External Affairs of the Australian government. He was the leading spokesperson at the **San Francisco Conference** in 1945 on behalf of the interests of the small and middle powers in the drafting of the **Charter of the United Nations.** Although he was disappointed in his attempts to limit the **veto** by major powers in the **Security Council,** he achieved greater success in leading the fight for expanded powers of the **General Assembly** and the **Economic and Social Council.** In 1948 he was chairman of the committee which developed the Palestine Partition Plan providing for the new state of Israel. In 1948–49 he was President of the General Assembly.

EXPANDED PROGRAM OF TECHNICAL ASSISTANCE (EPTA). This was the first enlargement of the previous **technical assistance** activities of the UN and its affiliated **specialized agencies.** President **Harry S Truman** in 1949 proposed an expansion of both United States bilateral aid and multilateral aid through the United Nations for the benefit of developing nations. Additional funds were furnished and new UN administrative agencies created to supervise and coordinate the activities. In 1950 the initial 18-month budget was $20 million, with the United States pledging 60 percent of the amount. By 1965 the annual budget was $54 million, with the United States furnishing 40 percent of the total. The program was absorbed into the **United Nations Development Program** in 1965. (See also TECHNICAL ASSISTANCE; UNITED NATIONS DEVELOPMENT PROGRAM.)

- F -

FALKLANDS/MALVINAS DISPUTE. The conflicting territorial claims and eventual war between the United Kingdom and Argentina over the Falkland/Malvinas Islands were discussed in the UN **Security Council** and **General Assembly** in 1982 and subsequently, but no action was possible. The UN **Secretary-General** also failed in his attempts to mediate between the parties. The U.S. eventually tilted toward the British in the situation, thus alienating most Latin American interests.

FINANCIAL PROBLEMS *see* BUDGET OF UNITED NATIONS

FISHERIES CASE. This is a case that was before the **International Court of Justice** during 1949–51. The United Kingdom challenged the method by which Norway had determined the limits of a four-mile zone along its coast reserving exclusive fishing rights for its nationals. The Court decided that the use of straight baselines in the manner used by Norway was in conformity with practice established under **international law.** The case was a landmark one for coastal states in determining certain issues concerning territorial waters. (See also INTERNATIONAL COURT OF JUSTICE.)

FOOD AND AGRICULTURE ORGANIZATION (FAO). One of the 17 **specialized agencies** affiliated with the United Nations. Its headquarters are in Rome and it has its own membership, organization and budget, but coordinates its activities with the United Nations through the **Economic and Social Council** on the basis of a working agreement between the two organizations. Founded in 1945, the FAO's general goal is world food security for all people.

The FAO engages in a wide variety of relatively low-cost activities. It carries on hundreds of **technical assistance** field projects in most of the developing countries of the world. These projects strengthen local institutions, provide for research and training, and develop new agricultural techniques. The FAO assists in **disaster relief.** It organizes seminars and conferences on various issues. It regularly monitors world food needs and problems and publishes these surveys as well as many other publications and reports. It assists countries in preparing investment requests to the **International Bank for Reconstruction and Development** and other sources of financial aid. It is the joint sponsor with the UN of the **World Food Programme.** (See also INTERNATIONAL FUND FOR AGRICULTURAL DEVELOPMENT; WORLD FOOD CONFERENCE; WORLD FOOD COUNCIL; WORLD FOOD PROGRAMME.)

FULBRIGHT RESOLUTION. A resolution adopted in 1943 by the U.S. House of Representatives favoring the formation of a postwar international peace-maintaining organization with membership by the United States. This and a similar Senate resolution helped encourage U.S. leadership in the establishment of the United Nations.

- G -

GENERAL AGREEMENT ON TARIFFS AND TRADE (GATT). Plans for an International Trade Organization as a **specialized agency** of the UN system were thwarted when many states refused to ratify its proposed charter, drafted in 1948. As a substitute GATT was formed initially as a treaty and then transformed into a permanent organization loosely affiliated with the United Nations. Its headquarters are in **Geneva.** It operates with protracted rounds of negotiations among national trade representatives, a Director-General and staff, a Council of Representatives, and 20 specialized committees and other subsidiary bodies. GATT and the **United Nations Conference on Trade and Development** jointly operate the International Trade Center in Geneva for the purpose of promoting the trade interests of developing countries.

The general purpose of GATT is to establish a code of conduct and to promote and regulate trade among its members, who account for more than 80 percent of world trade. Eight series of negotiations have been held for the purpose of reducing tariffs and other trade barriers. The "Uruguay round" of negotiations started in 1986 and were completed only in December 1993 because of stalemates over such issues as the European Community's agricultural subsidies. During the Uruguay round of negotiations a decision was made to establish in 1995 a new World Trade Organization (WTO), replacing and expanding GATT and implementing all the results of the negotiations.

The approval of GATT by the U.S. Congress during the week of November 29–December 2, 1994 virtually assured its acceptance by the other member states.

GENERAL AND COMPLETE DISARMAMENT. Beginning in 1948 the Soviet Union and the United States periodically made sweeping proposals and counterproposals for comprehensive **disarmament.** Each plan usually involved a three-stage process over a four- to 14-year period. No progress toward agreement resulted from these proposals, except for the issuance in 1961 of a Joint Statement of Principles by the United States and the Soviet Union regarding underlying conditions for comprehensive disarmament. Actual negotiations on this subject have generally been outside the United Nations, but have been the subject of widespread discussion and debate in the **General Assembly** and subsidiary bodies. (See also DISARMAMENT.)

GENERAL ASSEMBLY. One of the six major organs of the United Nations. It is essentially the central organ since its agenda encompasses the whole range of UN issues and all other organs report to it. However, unlike the **Security Council,** it lacks authority to pass resolutions that legally bind its members. All UN member states are seated in the General Assembly with one vote per state. Certain important matters require a two-thirds vote for adoption, but all others require a simple majority of those present and voting. The General Assembly holds regular annual sessions of about three months duration, but may meet in both special sessions and in emergency special sessions, each devoted to a single topic. Through 1992 the General Assembly had held 17 special sessions and nine emergency special sessions.

In its functions of discussion and recommendation the General Assembly represents the only existing global forum. Its additional functions include budgetary control to approve the UN **budget** and set a scale of member assessments, and the elective function of choosing members of the Security Council, the **Economic and Social Council,** and the **Trusteeship Council.** It shares with the Security Council the selection of the **Secretary-General** and judges of the **International Court of Justice.** It also admits states to UN **membership** upon receiving recommendations for membership from the Security Council. The General Assembly has the leading role in proposing **amendment of the UN Charter** or revisions as well. (See also BUDGET OF THE UNITED NATIONS; RATIFICATION OF THE UN CHARTER; REVIEW OF THE UN CHARTER.)

GENERAL ASSEMBLY SPECIAL SESSIONS ON DISARMA-
MENT. Because of discontent with major power progress on
disarmament, the lesser powers used the **General Assembly** as a world forum by convening special sessions of that
body in 1978, 1982, and 1988 devoted exclusively to the
subject of disarmament. These consciousness-raising assem-
blages were never planned as negotiating sessions but as
stimuli to urge faster and meaningful action toward reduction
of armaments. Large numbers of **nongovernmental organizations** participated in the sessions and a huge mass rally was
held in New York on June 12, 1982, with people assembled
from all parts of the world.

GENERAL CONVENTION ON THE PRIVILEGES AND IM-
MUNITIES OF THE UNITED NATIONS. The **Charter of
the United Nations** accords to staff personnel "such privileges and immunities as are necessary for the independent
exercise of their functions in connection with the Organization." In order to specify the precise extent of these privileges and immunities, the **General Assembly** in 1946 approved the General Convention on the Privileges and
Immunities of the United Nations and opened it for ratification. The Convention spells out the types of privileges and
immunities enjoyed by each category of personnel. Since the
United States, as host country, did not ratify the General
Convention until 1970, a separate **Headquarters Agreement** was drawn up in 1947 between the United States and
the United Nations. Other supplemental documents were
worked out between the United Nations and **Switzerland**
and the Netherlands, covering the special groups of UN
personnel working in those countries. (See also HEAD-
QUARTERS AGREEMENT.)

GENEVA. The host city to what is literally the European
headquarters of the United Nations. The United Nations
occupies the building that was previously the headquarters of
the **League of Nations** plus a substantial enlargement of that
building. Although most of the major organs of the UN hold
their sessions in New York, approximately as many meetings
of various United Nations bodies are held in Geneva as in

New York. Geneva is also the headquarters city for several **specialized agencies** of the UN system. These are the **International Labour Organisation (ILO)**, the **World Health Organization (WHO)**, the **World Meteorological Organization (WMO)**, the **International Telecommunication Union (ITU)**, and the **World Intellectual Property Organization (WIPO)**. The headquarters of the **General Agreement on Tariffs and Trade** and its successor, the World Trade Organization, are also in Geneva.

GENOCIDE CONVENTION. This treaty was largely prompted as a reaction to the holocaust of Jews in Nazi Germany. The full title of the treaty is the Convention on the Prevention and Punishment of the Crime of Genocide. The Convention defines genocide as "acts committed with intent to destroy, in whole or in part, a national, ethnic, racial or religious group." It was approved and opened for ratification by the **General Assembly** in 1948. Several charges of acts of genocide have been made since 1948. Among the most recent and most flagrant have been the "ethnic cleansing" policies of the Serbs against the Bosnians and Croatians and the massacres of Tutsis and Hutus in Rwanda and Burundi. These acts of murder, rape, shelling, and starvation have been condemned by the UN **Security Council** and General Assembly.

GHANA. The first territory under the UN **trusteeship system** to gain independence and **self-government.** The new state of Ghana was created in 1957 from the former trust territory of British Togoland and the former British colony, the Gold Coast. Prior to independence a plebiscite was held to determine whether the indigenous inhabitants wished to be joined into the new state. Ghana was promptly admitted to **membership in the UN** in 1957.

GOALS OF THE UNITED NATIONS. Article 1 of the **Charter of the United Nations** outlines the goals or purposes of the organization. The first objective is to maintain international peace and security by **peaceful settlement of disputes** and by the removal of threats to the peace and the suppression of acts of aggression. Another major goal is to achieve international cooperation in solving problems of an economic, social, cultural, or humanitarian character. The promotion of **human rights** for all without distinction as to race, sex, language, or religion is a third goal. Additionally, the vague and general objectives of developing friendly relations among nations and of acting as a center for harmonizing the actions of nations are included in the article.

GOLAN HEIGHTS DISPUTE. After the Middle East war of October 1973, incidents continued to occur on the Golan Heights (located between Israel and Syria), much of which had been occupied by Israeli forces. In May 1974 an agreement on disengagement between the military forces of the two countries was signed in **Geneva,** including arrangements for the establishment of a United Nations Disengagement Observer Force (UNDOF). Within a few days advance units of the force arrived in the area. The force was first authorized at 1,250 members and later raised to 1,450 members. UNDOF's task was to supervise the ceasefire and the withdrawal of contending forces from a buffer zone, and to patrol the area and report any violations of the agreement. In December 1981 Israel announced its annexation of the Golan Heights, but this decision was declared null and void by both the UN **Security Council** and **General Assembly,** and did not significantly affect UNDOF operations. UNDOF remains in the buffer zone pending a general Middle East peace settlement.

GOOD OFFICES. Although not specifically mentioned in the UN **Charter** as one of the methods for peaceful settlement of disputes, the **Security Council** and **General Assembly** have used this device on several occasions. In the exercise of good offices a third neutral party offers only a means of communicating between the disputants but may not offer suggestions on the terms for settlement. (See also PEACEFUL SETTLEMENT OF DISPUTES.)

GORBACHEV, MIKHAIL (1931–   ). The last head of state of the Soviet Union before its breakup in December 1991. He took power in March 1985. In 1987 he published an article in *Pravda* which was the forerunner of other statements stressing a new role for the United Nations in Soviet foreign policy. These new policies or proposals included full support for UN **peacekeeping** activities, an enhanced role for both the **Security Council** and the **Secretary-General,** the revival of the **Military Staff Committee,** and the greater use of the **International Court of Justice.** Although these suggested reforms did not result in any restructuring of the UN, the Soviet Union and its successor regimes participated constructively in diverse UN activities.

GRAHAM, FRANK P. (1886–1972). U.S. educator, U.S. senator, and UN official. He served for 19 years as President of the University of North Carolina. He was for several years the UN mediator in the **Indian-Pakistani dispute** over Jammu and Kashmir, and also was a member of the UN Good Offices Commission in the Dutch-Indonesian dispute in the late 1940s.

GULF WAR *see* KUWAIT INVASION BY IRAQ

- H -

HAMMARSKJÖLD, DAG (1905–1961). Second **Secretary-General** of the United Nations (1953–61). Before his term as Secretary-General he had held a series of important posts in the areas of finance and foreign affairs in the Swedish government and had served as Swedish delegate to the Organization for European Economic Cooperation (OEEC) and to the Commission of Ministers of the Council of Europe.

Hammarskjöld was both an intellectual and an able administrator. In contrast to his predecessor, **Trygve Lie,** who was outspoken and often alienated major member states, Hammarskjöld was an advocate of **quiet** and **preventive diplomacy** in achieving UN goals. While avoiding fanfare he championed and furthered the United Nations **Charter** principles of the independence and integrity of the **Secretariat** and of the Secretary-General.

Actually, Hammarskjöld expanded the leadership role of the Secretary-General more than any other incumbent in that office. He accomplished this both by filling in details of directives from the **Security Council** and **General Assembly** and by acting on his own initiative to fill vacuums when the only bases of authority were Charter principles and a broad interpretation of the Secretary-General's powers. In response to a 1954 General Assembly request that he use "the means most appropriate in his judgment" to seek the release of 15 American flyers downed on UN missions and imprisoned in China, he was successful through quiet diplomacy and a visit to China in securing their release within seven months. In the Lebanese crisis of 1958, he acted independently to resolve the crisis when Security Council action was stalemated by a series of Soviet **vetoes.** In disputes in Laos (1959–61) and between Cambodia and Thailand (1958–60) he sent personal representatives to mediate the disputes without first requesting authority and guidance from the political organs of the United Nations. In the **Congo** crisis (1960–61) he carried on the activities of the UN **peacekeeping** force and personal negotiations for conflict resolution after deadlocks in the Security Council failed to provide directives on which to base his actions. He resisted the Soviets' personal attacks on him, which included demands for his resignation and his replacement by a **troika** of three administrative heads of the Secretariat, by appealing to the General Assembly. There, the overwhelming majority of states rejected the Soviet proposal.

Hammarskjöld's most innovative contributions to the development of the United Nations came in the area of the creation and management of two large peacekeeping forces in the Middle East and the Congo. In the Suez crisis of 1956 Hammarskjöld, under a General Assembly directive, developed a plan for the **United Nations Emergency Force (UNEF)** of 6,000 lightly-armed military personnel from ten countries to be stationed in a buffer zone in the Sinai on Egyptian territory, to patrol and report on any cease-fire violations by Egypt or Israel. Hammarskjöld was given responsibility for raising the force, developing its guidelines (which served as principles for all subsequent peacekeeping forces), and directing the operations. Within 11 days after the General Assembly resolution the first forces arrived in the Sinai.

In 1960 the Security Council requested Hammarskjöld to raise a peacekeeping force to restore internal order in the Congo (now Zaire). This was one of the largest such UN forces ever deployed and at its peak numbered 20,000 troops from 34 countries. The guidelines established for UNEF were followed for the Congo force (ONUC). No units were accepted from the major powers, or from any state that, in the Secretary-General's judgment, might have a direct interest in the situation. The forces were to remain neutral with regard to internal factional differences, and were to use force only in self-defense.

The chaos in the Congo eventually contributed to Hammarskjöld's death. In attempting to personally negotiate between opposing factions he was on his way to Northern Rhodesia (now Zambia) to meet with the secessionist leader of the Katanga province when all on board his plane were killed in a crash near Ndola airport on September 17, 1961. The cause of the crash was never determined.

HEADQUARTERS *see* UNITED NATIONS HEADQUARTERS

HEADQUARTERS AGREEMENT. This agreement was drawn up in 1947 between the United States and the United Nations. It was necessary because, as host state, the United States did not immediately ratify the **General Convention on the Privileges and Immunities of the United Nations.** Therefore, this substitute agreement covered the working details necessary to clarify the degree to which the **United Nations headquarters** would be treated as international territory and the degree to which UN staff would be immune from United States legal jurisdiction. (See also GENERAL CONVENTION ON THE PRIVILEGES AND IMMUNITIES OF THE UNITED NATIONS.)

HEALTH *see* WORLD HEALTH ORGANIZATION

HOFFMAN, PAUL (1891–1974). Before his assignments in the United Nations he was with the Studebaker Corporation for more than 40 years and served as its President and Chairman of the Board of Directors. He was a U.S. delegate to the UN in 1956–57. From 1959 until 1965 he was the Managing Director of the **United Nations Special Fund** and then served as Administrator of the **United Nations Development Program** 1966–72.

HULL, CORDELL (1871–1955). U.S. Secretary of State during the planning stage of the United Nations. He personally assumed a role in directing these plans and influenced the nature of the security provisions of the **Charter of the United Nations.**

HUMAN RIGHTS. The United Nations **Charter** emphasizes human rights by mentioning them seven times and making the promotion of human rights a goal of the organization. The Charter instructs the **Economic and Social Council** to set up commissions for the promotion of human rights. This led to the creation in 1946 and 1947 of the **Commission on Human Rights,** the **Commission on the Status of Women,** and the Sub-Commission on Prevention of Discrimination and Protection of Minorities. These commissions continue today as the central UN bodies focusing on Human Rights.

The first major project of the Commission on Human Rights was to produce the Universal Declaration of Human Rights which was adopted by the **General Assembly** in December 1948. To transform the Declaration into legally binding form the Commission spent the next 18 years hammering out the terms of two treaties—the International Covenant on Civil and Political Rights and the International Covenant on Economic, Social and Cultural Rights. Both came into force in 1976 when the required 35 ratifications were received; today a majority of UN members have subscribed to the Covenants.

Other highlights of UN efforts to promote and protect human rights are the **Genocide Convention,** which came into force in 1951, and the Convention on the Elimination of All Forms of Racial Discrimination (1969). The latter has been ratified by more than three-fourths of the UN member states, and states are required to submit regular reports for review by a special committee of experts. The **International**

Labour Organisation has developed a large body of conventions and recommendations constituting its International Labour Code for the protection of workers' rights. Another major UN focus has been on the development of women's rights. The Commission on the Status of Women and a series of world conferences on women's rights and role have been the principal agents of this movement. The United Nations has also established an **International Research and Training Institute for the Advancement of Women (INSTRAW)**.

The United Nations has carried on extensive activities prompted by the racial situations in South Africa. These have served as one of the external pressures toward racial equality in that country. (See also AMNESTY INTERNATIONAL; APARTHEID; COMMISSION ON HUMAN RIGHTS; COMMISSION ON THE STATUS OF WOMEN; GENOCIDE CONVENTION; INTERNATIONAL LABOUR ORGANISATION; ROOSEVELT, ELEANOR; SOUTH AFRICAN RACIAL QUESTIONS; WOMEN; WORLD CONFERENCE ON HUMAN RIGHTS.)

HUNGARIAN CRISIS (1956). In 1956 Soviet military forces invaded Hungary to put down a revolt against the Communist regime there. Since no action could be taken in the UN **Security Council** because of the Soviet **veto** power, the **General Assembly** was called into emergency special session to consider the situation. The General Assembly condemned the Soviet occupation and asked the **Secretary-General** to investigate the state of affairs. The Soviets were intransigent concerning any entry of UN investigators into Hungary and the UN was unable to carry out any further measures.

-I-

INDIAN-PAKISTANI DISPUTE (1948–). In 1947, when India and Pakistan became independent, the state of Jammu and Kashmir (generally referred to as Kashmir) was free to accede to either's jurisdiction. Although the majority of Kashmir's population was Muslim, the ruling maharajah opted to become a part of India, subject, however, to a subsequent plebiscite. Pakistan refused to recognize the accession, India accused Pakistan of aiding irregular military forces in Kashmir, and eventually India claimed full rights in the territory without a plebiscite.

Both countries, in January 1948, referred the dispute to the UN **Security Council** and the matter has been a Security Council agenda item ever since. The Security Council has used single mediators and commissions of inquiry and mediation to attempt to get the parties to reach a settlement, but with no results. India and Pakistan did agree to a cease-fire line and in 1949 the United Nations Military Observer Group in India and Pakistan (UNMOGIP) was established to monitor and report on the cease-fire. This **peacekeeping** force usually varied in size between 35 and 45 observers, but was temporarily increased to 102 during the 1965 India-Pakistan war. This force is still maintained in Kashmir.

In September 1965, increased hostilities spilled over into major fighting, including an Indian invasion of Pakistan territory outside of Kashmir. After two weeks the UN Secretary-General, **U Thant,** arranged a cease-fire and the Security Council authorized a new peacekeeping group, the United Nations India-Pakistan Observation Mission (UNIPOM), to patrol the border area where the invasion had occurred. The maximum strength of UNIPOM was 96 observers. In January 1966 the heads of government of India and Pakistan met in Tashkent at the invitation of the Soviet government and agreed to withdraw all troops from the area of the conflict. UNIPOM was disbanded on March 22, 1966.

INDONESIAN QUESTION. After World War II the Dutch tried to reestablish their hegemony over Indonesia, but in 1945 nationalist leaders had declared independence. During 1946 and 1947 military clashes occurred between nationalist and Dutch forces and the UN **Security Council** took up consideration of the situation in July 1947. In October the Security Council dispatched a Committee of Good Offices to Indonesia, which was able to work out a truce and terms for a final settlement. In December 1948 the Dutch again launched major military operations and took into custody the principal nationalist leaders. The following month the Security Council adopted a comprehensive resolution demanding the release of the republican leaders, the setting up of an interim government, and the transfer of **sovereignty** by July 1950. It also converted the Committee of Good Offices into the United Nations Commission for Indonesia (UNCI) with enlarged powers. With the participation of the UNCI the disputing parties held a conference at The Hague and the transfer of sovereignty actually took place in December 1949.

INTERNATIONAL ATOMIC ENERGY AGENCY (IAEA). Following the initiative of U.S. President **Dwight D. Eisenhower** in an address to the UN **General Assembly** in 1953, a statute was drawn up establishing an organization to promote the peaceful uses of nuclear energy. The IAEA began operations in 1957 with headquarters in **Vienna.** In addition to encouraging peaceful applications of nuclear energy, it developed safeguards against the diversion of fissionable materials to military uses. After the adoption in 1970 of the **Nuclear Non-Proliferation Treaty,** which required all states adhering to the treaty to accept these safeguards and inspection by the IAEA, this became the largest and most important function of the IAEA. Difficulties in carrying out and enforcing its inspection functions were experienced by IAEA personnel in Iraq following the Gulf War in 1990–91 and in North Korea in 1992–94. (See also NUCLEAR NON-PROLIFERATION TREATY.)

INTERNATIONAL BANK FOR RECONSTRUCTION AND DEVELOPMENT (IBRD). Commonly referred to as the World Bank. The IBRD is one of the 17 **specialized agencies** affiliated with the United Nations. It was established as a result of the agreements reached at the general monetary conference held at **Bretton Woods,** New Hampshire, in 1944. Its headquarters are in Washington, D.C. It is the largest multilateral source of loans to developing countries and all loans must be guaranteed by recipient governments. In the past decade the IBRD has annually granted loans in the $15–22 billion range. It received its initial capital from member governments but now relies on borrowing on world capital markets in addition to the repayment of previous loans.

In addition to its lending activities the IBRD provides advice to developing countries on financial matters and assistance in designing applications for projects. It conducts surveys in individual countries and carries on research and training projects.

Voting in the controlling bodies of the IBRD is weighted so that the largest contributing states have effective control over policy. (See also BRETTON WOODS CONFERENCE; INTERNATIONAL DEVELOPMENT ASSOCIATION; INTERNATIONAL FINANCE CORPORATION; INTERNATIONAL MONETARY FUND; McNAMARA, ROBERT S.; MULTILATERAL INVESTMENT GUARANTEE AGENCY.)

INTERNATIONAL CIVIL AVIATION ORGANIZATION (ICAO). One of the 17 **specialized agencies** affiliated with the United Nations. Its headquarters are in Montreal, Canada, and it has its own membership, organization and budget, but coordinates its activities with the United Nations through a working agreement between the two organizations. Founded in 1947, ICAO's basic purpose is to facilitate the safety, regularity, and efficiency of commercial air traffic.

ICAO operates through an Assembly composed of all members, a Council of 33 states which carries on the activities of the organization on a continuous basis, a secretariat of about 1,300 employees, and numerous commissions and committees. Most states of the world are members. ICAO promotes safety standards, issues regulations, and settles disputes relating to civil aviation.

INTERNATIONAL COURT OF JUSTICE (ICJ). Often referred to as the World Court. The ICJ is designated by the **Charter of the United Nations** as one of the six major organs of the United Nations. All members of the United Nations are automatically members of the Court, and other states, by special arrangements, may become parties to the Court Statute. The ICJ is a court of general jurisdiction and its headquarters are in The Hague. It is composed of 15 judges, elected by the **General Assembly** and the **Security Council** for nine-year terms. No two judges may be from the same state. The Statute of the Court is nearly identical to that of the Permanent Court of International Justice established by the **League of Nations.**

Article 36 of the ICJ Statute provides that states may accept the compulsory jurisdiction of the Court over a broad range of legal disputes. However, fewer than 50 states have accepted this provision and many have attached reservations to their acceptance. Because of this factor and the general reluctance of states to submit their disputes to judicial settlement, the Court has often had a light agenda. In 45 years, 59 cases have been submitted to the Court. Of these the ICJ handed down decisions in 34 cases, 11 cases are pending, and 14 were withdrawn by the parties before a judgment was rendered. During this period the Court also issued 20 **advisory opinions,** of which 12 were requested by the General Assembly. (See also ADVISORY OPINIONS; CONNALLY RESERVATION; CORFU CHANNEL CASE; FISHERIES CASE; NICARAGUAN SITUATION; SOUTH-WEST AFRICA CASES.)

INTERNATIONAL DEVELOPMENT ASSOCIATION (IDA). The IDA was created in 1960 as an affiliate of the **International Bank for Reconstruction and Development** in order to serve the special financial needs of the world's least developed countries. Although the IDA is financially and legally a separate entity from the Bank, it is administered by the same staff as the Bank. Until 1987 loans were made for 50 years and were interest free (except for a small administrative fee), with no repayment for the first ten years. In 1987 the loan period was changed to 40 years. Only countries with less than $800 annual per capita gross national product are eligible for IDA assistance, with most loans going to countries with less than $450 per capita. Fund replenishments are mainly pledged by the affluent countries and annual available funds are in the $3–4 billion range. The purposes of most loans have been to meet the basic needs of education, agriculture, health, and family planning. (See also INTER-

NATIONAL BANK FOR RECONSTRUCTION AND DE-
VELOPMENT; INTERNATIONAL FINANCE CORPO-
RATION; INTERNATIONAL MONETARY FUND;
McNAMARA, ROBERT S.; MULTILATERAL INVEST-
MENT GUARANTEE AGENCY.)

INTERNATIONAL FINANCE CORPORATION (IFC). The IFC
was established in 1956 as an affiliate of the **International
Bank for Reconstruction and Development.** Its purpose is
to promote private investment in developing countries by
seeking and providing capital for development projects in
cooperation with private investors. The IFC limits its own
contributions to no more than 25 percent of each project and
acts principally as a catalyst rather than as a primary source
of funds. (See also INTERNATIONAL BANK FOR RE-
CONSTRUCTION AND DEVELOPMENT; INTERNA-
TIONAL DEVELOPMENT ASSOCIATION; INTERNA-
TIONAL MONETARY FUND; MULTILATERAL
INVESTMENT GUARANTEE AGENCY.)

INTERNATIONAL FUND FOR AGRICULTURAL DEVELOP-
MENT (IFAD). One of the 17 **specialized agencies** affiliated
with the United Nations. Its headquarters are in Rome and it
has its own membership, organization and budget, but coordinates its activities with the United Nations through the **Economic and Social Council** on the basis of a working agreement between the two organizations. It also has very close
relations with the **Food and Agriculture Organization.**
    The initiative for formation of the IFAD came from the
1974 **World Food Conference.** The IFAD came into operation in 1977. It is unique in having equal voting rights for
each of three groups of countries: the developed, the oil-
exporting developing countries (OPEC), and the other developing state members. The OPEC countries pledged 40
percent of the initial funds and of the first replenishment, but,
due to falling oil revenues, their share in later replenishments
fell below 25 percent, and total pledges fell to less than half
of the original figure of more than $1 billion dollars.
    The IFAD concentrates on projects benefiting the rural
poor and most of its loans are long-term at nominal rates. It is

intended to provide additional funds for agricultural and rural development in the poorest rural areas, especially in the least developed countries. (See also WORLD FOOD CONFERENCE.)

INTERNATIONAL LABOUR ORGANISATION (ILO). One of the 17 **specialized agencies** affiliated with the United Nations. Its headquarters are in **Geneva,** Switzerland, and it has its own membership, organization and budget, but coordinates its activities with the United Nations through the **Economic and Social Council** on the basis of a working agreement between the two organizations.

The ILO was established in 1919 as an institution affiliated with the **League of Nations** and in 1946 it became the first of the specialized agencies associated with the United Nations. Its major purpose is to promote improved labor conditions and living standards throughout the world. Its system of representation in both its International Labour Conference and its Governing Body features one employers' delegate and one workers' delegate for each two government delegates.

The ILO has promoted improved labor conditions and workers' rights through the adoption of the International Labour Code, composed of more than 350 conventions and recommendations with more than 5,500 ratifications by governments. Government compliance with the Code is monitored and implemented by a vigorous and generally effective review process. Thus, the ILO is credited with major contributions to workers' **human rights** and received the Nobel Peace Prize in 1969.

INTERNATIONAL LAW. One of the purposes of the United Nations is the progressive development of international law, with the **General Assembly** as the agent responsible for this development. The **Charter of the United Nations** itself is a basic instrument of international law since **treaties** are a major source of such law and since, because of its scope and fundamental nature in establishing the only general purpose international organization, the Charter lays the groundwork for the further development of law.

The General Assembly has carried out its responsibilities for the development of international law with the aid of the **International Law Commission** and its own Sixth (Legal) Committee. It has also called for international conferences to formulate treaties. Some broad declarations and rulings of the General Assembly establish new legal principles. The **International Court of Justice,** in deciding cases, primarily applies international law but also, through interpretations, expands legal principles. National and regional courts also apply and interpret international law. (See also INTERNATIONAL COURT OF JUSTICE; INTERNATIONAL LAW COMMISSION; TREATIES.)

INTERNATIONAL LAW COMMISSION (ILC). This commission was established by the **General Assembly** as its major instrument in carrying out the **Charter of the United Nations** mandate that ''the General Assembly shall initiate studies and make recommendations for the purpose of . . . encouraging the progressive development of international law and its codification.'' The commission began its work in 1949 with 15 members, a number which was expanded in 1961 to 25 and in 1982 to 34. The members are legal experts and no two may be of the same nationality.

The work of developing **treaties** and studies in international law is necessarily a slow and painstaking process. However, among its accomplishments, the International Law Commission has done seminal work leading to the series of treaties on the law of the seas, the law of treaties, and conventions on diplomatic relations and on consular relations. It has also submitted several basic legal studies to the General Assembly including a declaration on the rights and duties of states, model rules of arbitral procedure, and the question of defining aggression. (See also INTERNATIONAL LAW.)

INTERNATIONAL MARITIME ORGANIZATION (IMO). The IMO was originally called the Inter-Governmental Maritime Consultative Organization and began functioning as a **specialized agency** of the United Nations system in 1958. It is concerned with promoting maritime safety and navigational efficiency, and with preventing maritime pollution from ships. For these purposes it has produced a series of **treaties** and recommendations. Its headquarters are in London.

INTERNATIONAL MONETARY FUND (IMF). The IMF is one of the 17 **specialized agencies** affiliated with the United Nations. It was established as a result of the agreements reached at the general monetary conference held at **Bretton Woods,** New Hampshire, in 1944. Its headquarters are in Washington, D.C. Control of the use of funds is dominated by the Fund's largest contributors.

The original purpose of the IMF was to promote international monetary cooperation to prevent international currency fluctuations through maintaining fixed currency exchange rates. The United States dollar was the basic standard but was displaced in 1969 by special drawing rights (SDRs) based on a basket of five leading currencies. Increasingly, as a result of worldwide economic distress, the IMF role has expanded and it has become the source of increased funds for extended periods, especially for the developing countries which cannot meet debt and balance of payments obligations. In exchange for IMF aid these countries have been required to meet stringent conditions affecting their economic policies. (See also BRETTON WOODS CONFERENCE; INTERNATIONAL BANK FOR RECONSTRUCTION AND DEVELOPMENT.)

INTERNATIONAL REFUGEE ORGANIZATION (IRO). A temporary **specialized agency** of the United Nations system which operated only from 1947 to 1951. During that period it found new national homes for more than a million wartime refugees and repatriated several tens of thousands to their countries of origin. In 1951 it turned over all remaining international refugee problems to the newly created Office of the United Nations High Commissioner for Refugees (UNHCR). (See also REFUGEE WORK OF THE UNITED NATIONS.)

INTERNATIONAL RESEARCH AND TRAINING INSTITUTE FOR THE ADVANCEMENT OF WOMEN (INSTRAW).

This modest program, with an annual budget of less than $500,000, was established by the **General Assembly** in 1976 and has headquarters in Santo Domingo. It is funded by voluntary contributions from governments, private organizations, and individuals. It focuses primarily on the role of **women** in developing countries. It produces some publications but also tries to act as a catalyst among other agencies promoting women's rights and welfare. (See also WOMEN.)

INTERNATIONAL TELECOMMUNICATION UNION (ITU). One of the 17 **specialized agencies** affiliated with the United Nations. Its headquarters are in **Geneva,** Switzerland. It was originally founded in Paris in 1865 as the International Telegraph Union. Its present title was adopted in 1934 and in 1947 it became a specialized agency of the United Nations.

The ITU allocates radio-frequency assignments and maintains a Master International Frequency Register. It also fosters the development of telecommunications in developing countries, provides technical training for telecommunications personnel, undertakes studies, organizes conferences, and publishes information within its field of competence.

IRAN-IRAQ WAR (1980–88). As soon as war began in 1980 between Iran and Iraq, the UN **Security Council** called upon the parties to cease hostilities and to seek a **peaceful settlement** of their dispute. Beginning in 1984 both countries agreed to accept a small group of representatives of the UN **Secretary-General** in their respective capitals to monitor reports of military attacks on civilian centers of population. In January 1987 the Secretary-General suggested to the members of the Security Council the elements for ending hostilities, and in July the Security Council adopted a sweeping resolution calling for an immediate cease-fire, the return of all forces to internationally recognized boundaries, and a prompt exchange of prisoners of war. One year later both Iran and Iraq notified the Secretary-General of their acceptance of the Security Council resolution's terms. In order to monitor compliance with the cease-fire terms the Security Council authorized the deployment of 400 military observers to the area. This United Nations Iran-Iraq Military

Observer Group (UNIIMOG) remained along the Iran-Iraq border as a peacekeeping operation from August 1988 to February 1991.

IRANIAN QUESTION (1946). This was the first dispute considered by the UN **Security Council.** Iran claimed that Soviet troops had not withdrawn from northern Iranian territory as previously agreed and were using their influence to interfere in Iranian internal affairs. The Soviets denied the charges. The Security Council asked the disputants to continue negotiations and keep the Security Council informed. After four months the issue was dropped from the Security Council agenda upon notification by Iran of the withdrawal of the Soviet troops.

IRANIAN SEIZURE OF UNITED STATES DIPLOMATIC HOSTAGES (1979–81). In the same year that the Ayatollah Khomeini was installed as head of the new Islamic government in Iran, a group of militant supporters of the Ayatollah seized the U.S. embassy in Teheran and held the embassy personnel as hostages for the next 444 days. The action was condemned by the UN **Security Council** and **General Assembly,** and the **International Court of Justice** issued a special order declaring the action a breach of established **international law.** Even other Muslim states joined in the overwhelming condemnation of Iran because the action threatened the basic concepts of diplomatic immunity essential to the legal relationships and practices of national states.

ISRAEL *see* GOLAN HEIGHTS DISPUTE; ISRAELI ATTACK ON IRAQI NUCLEAR REACTOR; ISRAELI INVASIONS OF LEBANON; PALESTINE QUESTION; UNITED NATIONS EMERGENCY FORCES IN THE MIDDLE EAST

ISRAELI ATTACK ON IRAQI NUCLEAR REACTOR. On June 7, 1981 Israeli aircraft attacked and destroyed an Iraqi nuclear facility. Iraq protested and five days later the UN **Security Council** met to consider the matter. Israel claimed that the facility was designed to produce atomic weapons to be used against Israel. Iraq held that the facility was devoted to peaceful uses of nuclear energy and that inspectors from the **International Atomic Energy Agency (IAEA)** had confirmed Iraq's adherence to the safeguards obligations under the **Nuclear Non-Proliferation Treaty** to which Iraq was a party. On June 19 the Council strongly condemned the attack, called upon Israel to become a party to the Non-Proliferation Treaty, and decided that Iraq was entitled to redress for the damages inflicted. Later, the UN **General Assembly** repeatedly condemned the action and Israel's refusal to comply with the Security Council resolution of June 19. The IAEA also denounced the incident as an attack against the Agency and its system of safeguards. No further developments have occurred.

ISRAELI INVASIONS OF LEBANON. In March 1978, in retaliation for a commando raid into Israel from Lebanese territory, Israeli armed forces invaded and occupied a substantial segment of southern Lebanon. Lebanon, in the UN **Security Council,** charged Israel with a violation of its territory. On March 19 the Security Council called for the withdrawal of Israeli forces from Lebanon and established a United Nations Interim Force in Lebanon (UNIFIL) to assist in restoring peace to southern Lebanon. On June 13 the Israelis completed the withdrawal of their forces. However, forces backed by the Palestine Liberation Organization and others supported by Israel remained in southern Lebanon and could not be controlled by either UNIFIL or the Lebanese government.

In early June 1982, after the Israeli Ambassador in London was seriously wounded in a terrorist attack, fighting broke out along the Israeli-Lebanese border. On June 5 the Security Council called for an immediate cease-fire. In June Israeli forces made a massive invasion into Lebanon and overran or bypassed UNIFIL positions. By August 1 Israeli forces reached Beirut, the Lebanese capital. During the ensuing months much of Beirut was destroyed in heavy fighting. In 1982–84 security forces from the United States, France, and Italy intervened at the invitation of the Lebanese government. In spite of numerous resolutions of the Security Council the Israeli withdrawal was delayed until June 1985.

Israel, however, maintained a ''security zone'' in southern Lebanon where the Southern Lebanon Army would continue to function, backed by Israeli forces. UNIFIL remained in southern Lebanon as a deterrent to excessive armed conflict.

ITALIAN COLONIES (1948–52). The peace treaty with Italy after World War II provided that the major powers would determine the future status of each of Italy's African colonies, and, if they failed to reach agreement within one year, the UN **General Assembly** would act as the determining agency. The matter was thus passed to the General Assembly for solution. In November 1949 the General Assembly decided that Libya would become an independent state no later than January 1, 1952, and that Somaliland would be placed under trusteeship for ten years, with Italy as the trustee, and then be independent. The General Assembly studied the future of Eritrea for an additional year before deciding that Eritrea would be federated with Ethiopia as an autonomous region within Ethiopia. All three transitions were completed by September 1952 and Somaliland became independent, as planned, in 1960. After a long period of discontent and warfare, Eritrea gained its independence from Ethiopia in April 1993.

-J-

JARRING, GUNNAR (1907–). Swedish diplomat and Special Representative of the **Secretary-General** of the United Nations on the Middle East situation (1967–91).

-K-

KAMPUCHEAN SITUATION *see* CAMBODIAN SITUATION

KASHMIR DISPUTE *see* INDIAN-PAKISTANI DISPUTE

KOREAN QUESTION. At the close of World War II, the Soviet Union and the United States agreed to divide Korea into a zone north of the 38th parallel under Soviet military occupation, and a zone south of that line under United States occupation, subject to negotiations for restoration of a unified Korea. The two sides could reach no agreement and in 1947 the UN **General Assembly** set up a UN Temporary Commission on Korea to supervise elections for a National Assembly. When the commission was denied access to North Korean territory, elections were held in South Korea with UN recognition of the resulting government as the sole governmental authority for all of Korea. In 1948 the General Assembly created a new United Nations Commission on Korea charged with the oversight of the withdrawal of foreign forces from Korea and with facilitating the unification process.

In June 1950 North Korean military forces mounted a major attack across the 38th parallel and overran most of South Korean territory. The UN **Security Council** met in emergency session and, in the absence of a Soviet representative due to a Soviet boycott of that body, adopted a series of resolutions in the interval before the Soviet government ended its boycott. These resolutions legitimized military action by the United States and other countries to assist South Korea in repelling the attack and authorized a unified military command under a U.S. commander. **President Harry S Truman** appointed General **Douglas MacArthur** to that post. Although 15 other states supplied small military contingents, more than 90 percent of the forces were furnished by the United States and South Korea. The unified forces gradually drove the North Korean army back across the 38th parallel, almost to the North Korean border with China, but in November Chinese military forces helped the North Koreans drive MacArthur's troops back into South Korea, occupying the capital, Seoul, for the second time. In January 1951 the battle lines were reestablished roughly along the 38th parallel.

In January 1951 the General Assembly established a cease-fire commission to aid in a settlement. The following month the Assembly branded the Chinese as an aggressor and in May recommended an embargo of all war-related materials to the People's Republic of China and to North Korea. Armistice negotiations began in July, but progress was slow and two years were required before an agreement

established a demilitarized zone along the 38th parallel.
Security Council and General Assembly resolutions on the
Korean situation have proven generally ineffective, and a
perennial stalemate on negotiations has left the Korean
question unresolved. One positive result was that the deadlock in the Security Council prompted the General Assembly
to adopt a procedure for calling the General Assembly into
emergency sessions to deal with threats to the peace when
the Security Council is unable to act because of the use of the
veto power by a permanent member.

KUWAIT INVASION BY IRAQ. On August 2, 1990 Iraqi
military forces invaded and occupied Kuwait, and Iraq
declared it to be a part of Iraqi territory. During the next four
months the UN **Security Council** adopted 15 resolutions
pertaining to the situation, including condemnation of the
invasion, calling for Iraqi troop withdrawal, and imposing
comprehensive economic **sanctions** against Iraq under
Chapter VII of the **Charter of the United Nations,** which
provides for collective measures in cases of aggression. On
November 29 in Resolution 678 the Security Council authorized the use of "all necessary means" to uphold all previous
Council resolutions and to restore international security in
the area if Iraq did not fully implement those resolutions by
January 15, 1991.

On January 16 a United States-led military coalition began
air attacks on Iraq and its military forces, and on February 23
launched ground attacks to push Iraqi forces out of Kuwait.
Although this action was authorized under Council Resolution 678, the military action was in itself not a UN-directed
or -constituted measure, thus falling short of the original
intent of the Charter for UN **collective security** military
forces under UN command. On April 6 Iraq accepted the
terms of Council Resolution 687 which set out stringent
conditions imposed on Iraq for a cease-fire, the destruction of
Iraq's most lethal weapons, the acceptance of inspection
teams to verify this process, and the acceptance by Iraq of
liability for damages resulting from its invasion of Kuwait.
Charges of Iraqi failure to fully meet these terms prolonged
the tensions in the area.

-L-

LABOR *see* INTERNATIONAL LABOUR ORGANISATION

LAW OF THE SEA CONFERENCE (1973–82). Because a comprehensive treaty on the law of the seas was generally accepted as desirable, the United Nations called for a third world conference on the subject. Because of the scope and complexity of the issues and the clash of diverse national interests, the negotiations dragged on for nine years. A comprehensive treaty of 320 articles was finally approved by a vote of 130 yeas, four nays, and 17 abstentions. The United States objected to the provisions on deep-sea mining and cast a negative vote. The Soviet Union was joined by the United Kingdom, Germany, and Italy in abstaining. As a practical matter the treaty would have little effect without the cooperation of these major states. However, a majority of its provisions are observed in state practice.

LAW OF THE SEA CONFERENCES (1958 and 1960). The United Nations instigated conferences on the law of the sea in 1958 and 1960. The 1958 conference produced four conventions on (1) the continental shelf; (2) the territorial sea and contiguous zone; (3) the high sea; and (4) fishing and the conservation of the living resources of the high seas. All of these were ratified by enough states to bring them into force by 1966.

Certain other questions concerning the breadth of the territorial sea and conflicting claims on fishing rights remained unresolved. A second United Nations-sponsored conference in 1960 was unsuccessful in attempting to settle these matters.

LEAGUE OF NATIONS (1919–46). In spite of claims that the United Nations was a totally new organization and different from the League of Nations, the similarities are as great as the differences. In reality the League of Nations pioneered in creating the first general-purpose, almost universal international organization, based on the hope that voluntary cooperation and **collective security** measures could maintain world peace and promote international economic and social well-being. With regard to purposes, principles, and basic structure, the League and the UN were similar. In 1946, when the League was finally dissolved, its property, assets, and some of its functions were transferred to the United Nations. Its buildings in **Geneva** became, in effect, the European headquarters of the United Nations.

Although the League during the 1920s was successful in resolving several conflicts including a Greek-Bulgarian border dispute in 1925, its record during the 1930s was one of weak responses to aggression and resulting ineffectiveness. It failed to stop the Japanese invasion of Manchuria in 1931 and of China in 1937. It invoked limited economic sanctions against Italy in 1935–36 for Italy's invasion of Ethiopia, but these measures were insufficient to prevent Mussolini's victory and annexation of that African territory. No strong measures were taken against Hitler's expansionist moves in the Rhineland and in Eastern Europe.

The League, like the United Nations, was dependent on the voluntary cooperation of its members to force the settlement of disputes or repel aggression. The United States's failure to join the League left Great Britain and France as the leaders of any movement to stop Japan, Italy, and Germany from taking control of additional areas. Great Britain and France lacked the will to use the full potential of the Covenant's provisions for collective action against aggressors.

On the other hand, the economic and social activities of the League developed beyond any initial expectations. Thus, a groundwork was laid for a much more elaborate set of UN programs and agencies.

LEBANESE CRISIS (1958). Lebanon, in 1958, lodged a complaint with the UN **Security Council** charging that its borders with Syria had been penetrated by military forces. The Security Council directed the **Secretary-General** to send an observer group to Lebanon to investigate the charges. At about the same time, United States Marines were dispatched to Lebanon at the request of Lebanese President Chamoun, and subsequently all further action by the Security

Council was blocked by Soviet **vetos**. On his own initiative Secretary-General **Dag Hammarskjöld** increased the size of the observer group and negotiated a pledge of nonintervention by Arab states. The observer group reported minimal infiltration of Lebanese borders and all foreign forces and the observer group were promptly withdrawn from Lebanon.

LEBANON *see* ISRAELI INVASIONS OF LEBANON

LEWIS, STEPHEN H. (1937–). Canadian political leader, columnist, broadcaster, lecturer, and labor arbitrator. He served as Canadian Ambassador to the United Nations (1984–88). In 1986 he chaired the special session of the United Nations **General Assembly** on the Critical Economic Situation in Africa and was then appointed as Special Advisor to the **Secretary-General** on African Economic Recovery. He has also served as a special representative of the **United Nations Children's Fund (UNICEF)**.

LIBYA *see* ITALIAN COLONIES

LIE, TRYGVE (1896–1968). First **Secretary-General** of the United Nations (1946–53). Before his term as UN Secretary-General he had held important posts in the government of Norway, including that of acting foreign minister, and he headed the Norwegian delegation to the **San Francisco conference** which produced the **Charter of the United Nations.**

As UN Secretary-General he disliked administrative detail but tried to establish an independent leadership role for the Secretary-General and often lectured the major powers, accusing them of failure to live up to Charter principles and obligations. He proposed a Twenty-Year Program for Peace which was intended to enhance the role of the United Nations in maintaining world peace and security, but received no support from the major powers, which were suspicious of attempts to strengthen the leadership and prestige of the Secretary-General. Lie used frequent press conferences as a means of publicizing his ideas.

During his tenure as Secretary-General, Lie took stands on disputes which alternately aroused the strong opposition of either the Soviet Union or the United States. In the first dispute considered by the **Security Council,** concerning the Soviet Union's failure to promptly withdraw military forces from northern Iran in 1946, Lie first reluctantly yielded to United States pressure to place the dispute on the Security Council agenda, but later opposed the United States's insistence on retaining the item on the agenda until all Soviet troops had been withdrawn. (See also IRANIAN DISPUTE.) During this dispute Lie established an important precedent for strengthening the leadership role of the Secretary-General: the right of the Secretary-General to take the initiative in presenting oral and written statements to the Security Council at any time.

In other disputes, he alienated the United States in 1950 by advocating the seating of Communist Chinese delegates in the United Nations, and later that year evoked the wrath of the Soviet Union by his support of UN-authorized military action in **Korea.** From that time the Soviets totally ostracized him and opposed the extension of his tenure as Secretary-General. In 1953 he was strongly criticized by delegates of many states for allowing the United States to use the **United Nations headquarters** for carrying on loyalty investigations of United States nationals employed in the United Nations **Secretariat** and for his dismissal of these employees. This was broadly interpreted as a violation of the international character of the headquarters and a threat to Secretariat independence.

At the end of Lie's first term (1946–51) the Security Council was deadlocked over his succession. The Soviet Union vetoed a resolution appointing him to a second five-year term and the United States insisted on his reappointment. Without specific Charter authorization the General Assembly, in the absence of a Security Council recommendation, voted to extend his term for three years. In November 1952 Lie tendered his resignation to the General Assembly, and his successor, **Dag Hammarskjöld,** took office the following April.

LUMUMBA, PATRICE (1925–61). In the elections in the **Congo** (now Zaire) in May 1960, Lumumba emerged as the leader of the strongest political party and became the first prime minister of the newly independent country. In the ensuing months he sought the aid of the United Nations in reestablishing order within the country. The UN response was a large **peacekeeping** force of 20,000 (ONUC) which remained in the Congo until 1964. In September 1960 Lumumba, whose leadership was favored by the Soviet Union, was dismissed by President Kasavubu and, after house arrest, was sent to Katanga province, where his enemies murdered him in early 1961. (See also CONGO OPERATION.)

-M-

MacARTHUR, DOUGLAS (1880–1964). After serving as Commander of U.S. forces in the Far East during World War II, and accepting the Japanese surrender in 1945, General MacArthur was appointed by President **Harry S Truman** as Supreme Commander of the Allied Powers in Japan. In July 1950, after the outbreak of fighting in Korea, he was designated as Commander of United Nations forces (mainly supplied by the U.S. and South Korea) in that country. After China became involved in the Korean conflict, President Truman removed MacArthur from his command in April 1951. (See also KOREAN QUESTION.)

McNAMARA, ROBERT S. (1916–). Prior to his UN service he was with the Ford Motor Company (1946–61) and became its President in 1960. He then was appointed as U.S. Secretary of Defense (1961–68) and served as President of the **International Bank for Reconstruction and Development** (1968–81). As World Bank President he introduced a new policy of funding projects directly beneficial to the poorest 40 percent of the country's inhabitants.

MALVINAS *see* FALKLANDS/MALVINAS DISPUTE

MANDATES SYSTEM OF LEAGUE OF NATIONS. Rather than annex colonies taken from the defeated powers in World War I, the victorious powers sought a more acceptable way of assuming control over them. General Jan Smuts of South

Africa was the author of a plan which was incorporated into the League Covenant which assigned to "advanced nations" the tutelage of these territories "as Mandatories on behalf of the League." The League Council was to be assisted by a Permanent Mandates Commission of nongovernmental experts in exercising this supervision.

Fifteen territories became mandates under the tutelage of Great Britain, France, Belgium, South Africa, Japan, Australia, and New Zealand. The areas of the eastern Mediterranean were considered to be nearly ready for self-government and were classified as A mandates. All of these—Syria, Lebanon, Iraq, Trans-Jordan, and Palestine—were granted independence in 1947. Class B mandates were judged as requiring more time to be ready for self-rule. These included British Cameroons, French Cameroons, British Togoland, French Togoland, Tanganyika under British control, and Ruanda-Urundi assigned to Belgium. Class C mandates, for which self-rule was presumed to be remote, included **South West Africa** under South Africa's administration, the Marianas, Caroline, and Marshall islands with Japan as mandatory, New Guinea and Nauru controlled by Australia, and Western Somoa assigned to New Zealand.

The mandates system relied mainly on annual reports by each mandatory power and questioning of administration officials before the Mandates Commission to provide accountability to the League concerning conditions in each territory. There were no on-site inspections and no assurance that mandatory officials would not screen or withhold petitions of indigenous persons or groups. In spite of these handicaps the cooperation between the administrative officials and the Mandates Commission gradually came to operate at a reasonably satisfactory level.

All B and C mandates except South West Africa became United Nations trust territories. An additional trust territory was the former Italian Somaliland. All except the Pacific Islands group, administered by the United States, had been granted independence by 1975, and even South West Africa became the new state of Namibia in 1990.

MEMBERSHIP IN UN. The **Charter of the United Nations**

provides for two categories of UN membership. Original members were those that participated in the **San Francisco Conference** in 1945 or had previously signed the **Declaration by United Nations** and which ratified the Charter. Other states were to be admitted by a two-thirds vote of the **General Assembly** upon the recommendation of the **Security Council.** Because of Cold War rivalries and the use of the **veto** in the Security Council, 21 applicant states were denied admission between 1946 and 1955. Finally a compromise, admitting 16 states simultaneously, broke the deadlock. New applicants have encountered few obstacles to admission since 1945. The wisdom of according full membership rights to **ministates** has occasionally been questioned, but states judged to be sovereign have been admitted without regard to area or population. UN membership reached 184 in 1993.

No member state has ever been expelled from the organization or has permanently withdrawn from membership. However, states such as South Africa and Yugoslavia have been temporarily suspended from the full exercise of voting rights by the General Assembly. Although it was an active member of the **League of Nations,** and has joined most of the United Nations **specialized agencies, Switzerland** is not a United Nations member because it interprets some of the obligations of the Charter to be in conflict with its traditional policy of neutrality.

MEMBERSHIP IN UN SPECIALIZED AGENCIES. Each of the 17 **specialized agencies** affiliated with the United Nations controls its own process of admission to membership as outlined in its basic constitution or charter. Most of the independent countries of the world belong to both the United Nations and nearly all of the specialized agencies. A few agencies grant associate membership to **non-self-governing territories.**

MILITARY STAFF COMMITTEE. Article 47 of the **Charter of the United Nations** provides for a Military Staff Committee composed of the Chiefs of Staff of the permanent members of the **Security Council** or their representatives. The purpose of the Committee was intended to be to advise and assist the

Security Council on all military matters relating to the Council's duties to maintain international peace and security and to assume strategic direction of any armed forces placed at the direction of the Security Council. Since, due to the Cold War, the major powers were never able to agree on terms for making such armed forces available, the Military Staff Committee was rendered ineffectual. Since 1987 proposals for reviving the Committee's role have surfaced but have received little meaningful support. (See also COLLECTIVE SECURITY.)

MINISTATES. From time to time lip-service has been given to the "problem" of ministates as UN members, but the matter has never been seriously faced to the point of either their exclusion or according them special membership status. The **League of Nations** did exclude such entities as Monaco, San Marino, and Liechtenstein on the grounds that they could not reasonably assume the responsibilities of membership, but all of these, as well as Andorra, have, since 1990, been admitted to UN membership. Other political units such as Saint Kitts and Nevis, Seychelles, Antigua and Barbuda, Dominica, Marshall Islands, and Federated States of Micronesia, each with less than 100,000 population, have been admitted to UN membership with full voting rights in the **General Assembly.** Suggestions for granting associate membership with limited privileges to ministates have never progressed beyond the proposal stage.

MISSIONS TO THE UNITED NATIONS. With few exceptions each member state maintains a permanent mission to the United Nations. The staff is appointed by the home government and is headed by a person of ambassadorial rank who also carries the title "permanent representative to the United Nations." The size of the staff may vary from four or five for a small, underdeveloped country to nearly 200 for major powers. The members of the delegation serve as national representatives in the major organs, committees, and commissions of the UN in which their country has received appointments. They also communicate and negotiate with other delegations, especially within the various voting blocs.

Delegates serve at the pleasure of their home governments and receive their instructions from those governments. Sizable mission staffs serve in **Geneva** as well as New York.

MOBUTU, SESE SEKO (Former name, JOSEPH MOBUTU) (1930–). President of Zaire since 1965. During the UN involvement in the **Congo** (Zaire) in 1960–64 he was the army chief of staff and one of several political figures contending for power. (See also CONGO OPERATION.)

MORSE, BRADFORD (1921–). A U.S. educator, lawyer, congressman, and UN official. He served 12 years in the U.S. House of Representatives. Morse held two important posts in the UN **Secretariat,** as Undersecretary-General for Political and General Assembly Affairs (1972–75) and as Administrator of the **UN Development Program** (1976–86).

MOSCOW DECLARATION (1943). This Declaration, issued at the foreign minister level by representatives of the United States, the Soviet Union, the United Kingdom and China, was the first clear commitment to the early establishment of a general international organization for the maintenance of international peace and security. This is one of a series of key proclamations during World War II leading to the formation of the United Nations. (See also ATLANTIC CHARTER; DECLARATION BY UNITED NATIONS.)

MOZAMBIQUE *see* UNITED NATIONS OPERATION IN MOZAMBIQUE (ONUMOZ)

MULTILATERAL INVESTMENT GUARANTEE AGENCY (MIGA). The MIGA was established in 1988 as an affiliate of the **International Bank for Reconstruction and Development.** Its purpose is to encourage private investment in developing countries by supplying long-term political risk insurance to investors. (See also INTERNATIONAL BANK FOR RECONSTRUCTION AND DEVELOPMENT; INTERNATIONAL DEVELOPMENT ASSOCIATION; INTERNATIONAL FINANCE CORPORATION; INTERNATIONAL MONETARY FUND.)

MULTINATIONAL CORPORATIONS (MNCs) *see* TRANSNATIONAL CORPORATIONS (TNCs)

MYRDAL, GUNNAR (1898–1987). Myrdal was a professor of political economy at the University of Stockholm beginning in 1933. He served as Executive-Secretary of the United Nations **Economic Commission for Europe** from 1947 until 1957. He was widely known for his writings on economic and social development.

-N-

NAMIBIA *see* SOUTH WEST AFRICA CASES; UNITED NATIONS TRANSITION ASSISTANCE GROUP

NARCOTIC DRUGS *see* COMMISSION ON NARCOTIC DRUGS

NAURU. A tiny Pacific island of only eight square miles but rich in phosphate deposits. It was taken from Germany after World War I and placed under the **League of Nations mandates system** with Australia as administrator. In 1947 it became a trust territory under the United Nations **trusteeship system.** Australia again administered it but acted on behalf of New Zealand and the United Kingdom as joint trustees. Nauru was granted independence in 1968.

NEGOTIATION *see* PEACEFUL SETTLEMENT OF DISPUTES

NEW INTERNATIONAL ECONOMIC ORDER (NIEO). This label emerged from a special session of the UN **General Assembly** in 1974 on the subject of raw materials and development. It represented an expanded set of aspirations and demands of the less developed countries for measures that they thought were required to close the rich-poor gap. The proposals included a larger annual transfer of resources from affluent to poor states, a better balance between the prices of imported and exported goods, a reform of the international monetary system, and more favorable trade conditions for developing countries. One principle of the NIEO asserted that each state has an absolute right to control its wealth and natural resources, including the right to nationalize or expropriate foreign property. This principle was strongly opposed by the representatives of the developed market economies. Although the less developed countries have continued to press for the elements of the NIEO, the affluent states, which control a majority of world goods, services, and trade, have made few of the requested concessions, and since 1974 the rich-poor gap in general has widened, not narrowed.

NICARAGUAN SITUATION. Between 1983 and 1988 Nicaragua lodged three complaints with the UN **Security Council** against the United States and another complaint concerning the general situation in Central America. The gist of the charges claimed interference in Nicaraguan internal affairs. In 1984–86 Nicaragua also brought charges against the United States before the **International Count of Justice** concerning intrusions into its territory and waters, including the mining of a harbor, as well as support for antigovernment rebels. The United States refused to recognize the jurisdiction of the Court and the validity of its decision favorable to Nicaragua in spite of U.S. adherence to the optional clause of the Statute of the Court which conferred such jurisdiction. Shortly thereafter the United States gave notice that it was rescinding its adherence to the clause. (See also CENTRAL AMERICAN PEACE EFFORTS.)

NONGOVERNMENTAL ORGANIZATIONS (NGOs). The UN Charter provides that the **Economic and Social Council** may arrange for consultation with appropriate nongovernmental organizations. More than 800 of these private agencies have been granted consultative status in three categories based on the extent of their involvement in ECOSOC's affairs. Twelve of the UN **specialized agencies** also grant consultative status to appropriate NGOs, with **UNESCO** having the longest list. NGOs also consult with such UN agencies as **UNCTAD** and **UNICEF.** The advantages of this consultative relationship occur both for the UN and the private agencies. In the exchange of information and expertise, a division of labor and cooperation are possible which strengthen and unify the joint interests and programs of all involved agencies.

NON-SELF-GOVERNING TERRITORIES. Chapter XI of the **Charter of the United Nations** is entitled "Declaration Regarding Non-Self-Governing Territories" and provides, in effect, a charter of political, economic, social, and educational rights for all people who, in 1945, were still living under colonial rule. Although most of these territories were not placed within the UN **trusteeship system,** the colonial powers were required to furnish regular reports to the UN on their progressive development. The self-government movement started slowly, but after the admission to UN **membership** of 17 newly independent states in 1960, the anticolonial pressure gathered momentum. In December 1960 the **General Assembly** adopted a new, strident **Declaration on the Granting of Independence to Colonial Countries and Peoples.** In this declaration it was asserted that colonial rule constituted a denial of fundamental **human rights** and that all peoples have the rights of self-determination and self-rule without delay. Whether UN pressure was a primary factor in the demise of the colonial system or not, only a few minor remnants of colonialism remain and more than 100 former colonies are UN members today. (See also TRUSTEESHIP SYSTEM.)

NUCLEAR NON-PROLIFERATION TREATY. After nearly ten years of pressure from the **General Assembly** and its Eighteen-Nation Disarmament Committee, the Treaty on the Non-Proliferation of Nuclear Weapons was completed in 1968 and opened for ratification. More than 150 states have adhered to the treaty. The treaty obligates the nuclear nations not to transfer, and the non-nuclear states not to acquire, nuclear weapons, but encourages the use, under safeguards, of nuclear materials for peaceful purposes. In return for the self-denial of non-nuclear states, the nuclear powers were committed to work for nuclear and general disarmament. In review conferences at five-year intervals non-nuclear nations have expressed strong disappointment with the failure of nuclear powers to carry out their part of the treaty obligations. (See also ARMS CONTROL.)

-O-

OCEANS *see* LAW OF THE SEAS CONFERENCES

OPERATIONAL EXECUTIVE AND ADMINISTRATIVE PERSONNEL SERVICES (OPEX). A United Nations service which recruits senior administrators for government positions in developing countries. These administrators serve only until they can train their native replacements.

OUTER SPACE TREATY (1966). Although the **Partial Test-Ban Treaty** (1963) had prohibited nuclear testing in the atmosphere or in space, it did not prohibit the stationing of nuclear weapons in that environment. Through the efforts of its special committee on disarmament, the **General Assembly** in 1966 presented for ratification a general Treaty on Principles Governing the Activities of States in the Exploration and Use of Outer Space. Among the treaty provisions was the prohibition of the orbiting, installing, or stationing of nuclear or other weapons of mass destruction in space. Also prohibited was any military activity on the moon and other extraterrestrial bodies.

-P-

PALESTINE QUESTION (1947–50). Following a request by the United Kingdom, a special session of the UN **General Assembly** to discuss the future of Palestine was held in April–May 1947. The General Assembly established the United Nations Special Committee on Palestine which was authorized to investigate and make recommendations concerning the status of the territory. The Committee in August 1947 submitted a majority and a minority report to the General Assembly. The majority report recommended the partition of Palestine into a Jewish state and an Arab state, with the city of Jerusalem under United Nations trusteeship. The minority plan favored a federation consisting of two subdivisions—one Jewish and one Arab—with Jerusalem as the federal capital. In September the General Assembly created an ad hoc Committee on the Palestine Question, which, after a series of hearings, recommended the majority plan. It was adopted by the Assembly in November. In order to carry out the plan, the Assembly established a United Nations Palestine Commission. As the situation in Palestine continued to deteriorate, the **Security Council** called for another special session of the General Assembly. This special session (April–May 1948) replaced the Palestine Commission with a UN Mediator. Simultaneously, the Security Council called for a truce and established a Truce Commission to oversee it.

On May 14, when the United Kingdom's mandate over Palestine expired, a Jewish state of Israel was announced. Except for a month-long truce in June–July ordered by the Security Council, armed hostilities in the area prevailed for most of the next year. Israel signed armistice agreements with each of its neighbors during the period February–July 1949. The Security Council urged the parties to seek a final peace settlement and in 1949 established the United Nations Truce Supervision Organization (UNTSO) to monitor and report on the degree of compliance with the armistice agreements. UNTSO, an observer **peacekeeping** unit, has continued its functions until the present, pending a comprehensive peace agreement in the Middle East.

PARTIAL TEST-BAN TREATY (1963). By the mid-1950s evidence was growing that atmospheric tests of nuclear weapons were producing major threats to human health that were spreading throughout much of the world. At the urging of the **General Assembly,** the United States, the Soviet Union, and the United Kingdom called a series of negotiating conferences which culminated in an agreement reached in Moscow to eliminate all except underground tests with safeguards to prevent escape of radioactive substances beyond the test sites. The treaty was opened to ratification by other states and approximately 120 states have done so. Although France and China did not ratify the treaty, France has ceased atmospheric tests since 1974.

PASVOLSKY, LEO (1893–1953). Economist and U.S. Department of State official. In 1941 Secretary of State **Cordell Hull** appointed Pasvolsky as his special assistant in charge of the Division of Special Research, the agency for planning the postwar international organization. Pasvolsky enlisted the advice of private groups and coordinated the work that produced the **Dumbarton Oaks** Proposals in 1944. He chaired the Coordinating Committee on Wording at the **San Francisco Conference** that produced the **Charter of the United Nations,** and then chaired the London Preparatory Commission on the United Nations. Thus he could be considered the most significant architect of the Charter.

PEACEFUL SETTLEMENT OF DISPUTES. This is a primary goal and function of the United Nations. Chapter VI of the **Charter of the United Nations** outlines the general procedures for pacific settlement. Parties to a dispute are first of all urged to seek a settlement of the dispute by peaceful means of their own choosing. The **Security Council** is given primary but not exclusive responsibility for dispute settlement and the **General Assembly** has played an important secondary role in the process, especially in the period before 1970. The Charter urges that legal disputes should be referred to the **International Court of Justice,** but this practice has been used sparingly.

The whole range of methods of pacific settlement mentioned in the Charter—negotiation, enquiry, meditation, conciliation, arbitration, judicial settlement, and resort to regional agencies—and such additional devices as **good offices** and cease-fires have been utilized by the Security Council and the General Assembly as appropriate to the circumstances of each dispute. More than 200 disputes have been considered by the United Nations and approximately 90 percent have been settled or are no longer active. Disputes involving military aggression or similar threats to peace may be dealt with by the Security Council under the collective action provisions of Chapter VII of the Charter. (See also COLLECTIVE SECURITY.)

PEACEKEEPING. This is a innovative technique, not envisaged

in the **Charter of the United Nations,** for controlling hostilities. The ideal conditions for its application include: (1) the establishment of a cease-fire between contending parties; (2) the creation of a buffer zone from which hostile forces withdraw and into which lightly-armed neutral forces are dispatched; (3) the peacekeeping force is under UN command and is drawn from middle and small powers; (4) peacekeepers are authorized to fire only in self-defense; and (5) the forces perform functions of observing, patrolling, keeping order, and acting as a buffer until such time as a peace settlement can be negotiated. The size of the force may vary from a few observers to military contingents of more than 20,000.

During the five-year period beginning in 1988, the number of UN peacekeeping missions and the number of personnel involved increased dramatically, and the variety of functions to be performed also expanded. The supervision of elections or regime changes were assisted in such places as Namibia, **Central America, Western Sahara,** and **Cambodia.** Involvement in Somalia, **Rwanda,** and **Yugoslavia** demanded the protection of human lives and the delivery of relief supplies in the midst of civil wars. The ideal requirements for peacekeeping had to be modified to the point that the line between peacekeeping and peace-enforcing became indistinct. Paying the costs of peacekeeping, which had always been a problem, became a major concern. (See also AFGHANISTAN SITUATION; ANGOLA; BUDGET OF THE UNITED NATIONS; CAMBODIAN SITUATION; CONGO OPERATION; CENTRAL AMERICAN PEACE EFFORTS; CYPRUS QUESTION; GOLAN HEIGHTS DISPUTE; ISRAELI INVASIONS OF LEBANON; INDIAN-PAKISTANI DISPUTE; IRAN-IRAQ WAR; LEBANESE CRISIS; PALESTINE QUESTION; UNITED NATIONS EMERGENCY FORCES IN THE MIDDLE EAST; UNITED NATIONS OPERATION IN SOMALIA; UNITED NATIONS TRANSITION ASSISTANCE GROUP; WESTERN SAHARA; YUGOSLAVIA.)

PEARSON, LESTER B. (1897–1972). Canadian educator, civil servant, diplomat, and prime minister. He served as President of the UN **General Assembly** in 1952. In 1956 he initiated the idea of a UN **peacekeeping** force in the Sinai, and received the Nobel Peace Prize the next year for his innovation in this area. His last major service to the United Nations family of agencies was as chairman of a World Bank Commission on International **Development** in 1968–69.

PÉREZ DE CUÉLLAR, JAVIER (1920–). Fifth **Secretary-General** of the United Nations (1982–91). Pérez de Cuéllar entered the diplomatic service of his country, Peru, in 1944 and served in a variety of important posts. At the time of his appointment as UN Secretary-General he was well known in United Nations circles, having served as Permanent Representative of Peru to the UN (1971–75), as the Secretary-General's special representative in **Cyprus** (1975–77) and in **Afghanistan** (1981), and as UN Undersecretary-General for Special Political Affairs (1979–81).

Pérez de Cuéllar's two five-year terms as Secretary-General are in sharp contrast to each other with regard to the global prestige of the UN. During his first term the widespread perception of the UN, among both powerful and third-world nations, was that the organization was largely impotent in both the political and economic realms and was on the periphery of significant events and actions in world affairs. Disillusionment with the UN was especially strong in the United States within both the Reagan administrative leadership and the U.S. Congress. In his first annual report to the **General Assembly** Pérez de Cuéllar accused the member states of bypassing the United Nations and called for strengthening the role of the **Security Council.** During his first term the financial crisis of the organization became increasingly crucial when the United States withheld more than half of its assessed budgetary contributions and demanded administrative and budgetary reform of the UN.

Pérez de Cuéllar's second term, in sharp contrast to the first, was marked by a series of successes, especially in the political realm, and a sharp rise in the global prestige of the UN. Extensive administrative and budgetary process reforms also resulted in U.S. plans to pay their past assessed arrearages, although large deficits still remained.

In the political arena the roles of both the Secretary-

General and the Security Council greatly increased. Both were involved in ending the wars between **Iran and Iraq** and between the Soviet Union and **Afghanistan.** Both played major roles in sending new UN **peacekeeping** forces to **Central America, Namibia, Angola, Western Sahara,** and **Kuwait** and in formulating plans for other large UN peacekeeping forces in **Yugoslavia** and **Cambodia.** In response to Iraq's invasion of Kuwait the Security Council adopted 15 resolutions in 1990 authorizing and legitimizing national collective actions against Iraq, although not instigating a UN **collective security** military operation. Pérez de Cuéllar also played a key role in negotiations leading to the release of Western hostages held in Lebanon.

PERMANENT MEMBERS *see* SECURITY COUNCIL

PETROLEUM *see* ENERGY PROGRAMS OF THE UNITED NATIONS

POPULATION PROGRAMS OF THE UNITED NATIONS. During the 1940s and 1950s the population activities of the United Nations were carried out by the **Economic and Social Council** and its Population Commission, with the assistance of the Secretariat's Population Division and Statistical Office. These activities were limited to fact-finding, statistical analysis, training in census methods, and data publication including the annual *Demographic Yearbook.* Since 1960, UN interest in population matters has expanded to include frequent conferences, seminars, and committees of experts. In 1967 Secretary-General U **Thant** established a modest United Nations Fund for Population Activities (UNFPA), which gradually expanded into a major program. The United States was at first the largest donor, but in 1985 withheld $10 million from its $46 million appropriation and in 1986 cut off all contributions on the unsubstantiated claim that UNFPA funds were supporting abortions in China. In spite of this U.S. refusal to contribute, other countries increased their donations to the extent that a budget of $131 million for 1986 grew to $230 million by 1992. The United States resumed its contributions in 1993.

Beginning in 1954, the UN has sponsored world population conferences at ten-year intervals. The 1974 conference in Bucharest adopted a World Population Plan of Action calling on states to reduce fertility, extend life expectancy, reduce infant mortality, and improve the quality of life of their residents. In planning the 1994 world conference the Population Commission linked population concerns to development planning, to aging and international migration matters, and to the status of women. During three years of preparatory work the representatives of the Vatican opposed any language in the proposed Plan of Action which would encourage abortion or artificial contraception as legitimate means of birth control. Some fundamentalist Muslim governments also expressed reservations concerning the status and rights of women as a key element in population control. Saudi Arabia and Sudan did not attend the conference.

The International Conference on Population and Development met in Cairo, September 5–13, 1994. After intense debate, a spirit of compromise in adjusting phraseology objectionable to minority representatives while maintaining the basic integrity of the document resulted in the adoption of the Plan of Action by consensus of all 179 states, albeit with some expressed reservations by the representatives of the Vatican and 20 Muslim and Latin American states.

By expanding previous proposals to control population, which primarily encouraged family planning through the use of contraceptives, to additional emphases on economic development, the equality, education, and rights of women, and a tripling of resources spent on population programs, it is hoped that implementation of the Plan of Action will result in a further reduction in global rates of fertility, which have been declining since 1950. In fact, population growth since that date is largely a result of increased life expectancy in both the developed and developing countries. It is further hoped to stabilize world population at a level of no more than 11 million people by the end of the 21st century.

PORTUGUESE COLONIALISM AND THE UN. From 1955 until 1974 Portugal was under heavy UN pressure because of its refusal to report to the UN on its African colonies.

Portugal claimed that its overseas territories were not colonies but integral parts of Portugal. Rebellious forces in those territories required heavy Portuguese military expenditures for control and, after a change of governmental regime in Portugal, the colonies of Guinea-Bissau, **Mozambique,** and **Angola** were granted independence in 1974–75, thus ending UN surveillance.

PREBISCH, RAUL (1901–1986). Argentine economist who challenged the classical world trade theory of comparative advantage and believed that the terms of trade worked to the disadvantage of the primary product-producing countries. While serving as Executive Secretary of the United Nations **Economic Commission for Latin America (ECLA)** (1948–63), he became known as the champion and leading theoretician of the developing countries. He then was appointed as the first Secretary-General of the **United Nations Conference on Trade and Development (UNCTAD),** which became the major UN forum for promoting developing countries' aspirations.

PREVENTIVE DIPLOMACY. This term was used to describe Secretary-General **Dag Hammarskjöld's** approach to the handling of disputes. It involves techniques for preventing or forestalling conflicts or arresting their escalation into higher levels of violence. The development of **peacekeeping** techniques was one tool of this broad approach to conflict containment. (See also HAMMARSKJÖLD, DAG; PEACEKEEPING.)

PRINCIPLES OF THE UNITED NATIONS. Article 2 of the **Charter of the United Nations** deals with the basic principles undergirding the organization, which include the following: (1) the sovereign equality of the members; (2) all members shall refrain from the threat or use of force in any manner inconsistent with UN purposes; (3) all members will settle international disputes by peaceful means; (4) members will support the enforcement actions of the United Nations and refrain from aiding states that are the objects of such actions; (5) members assume collective responsibility to require nonmembers not to interfere with the UN actions for the maintenance of international peace and security; and (6) the United Nations shall not intervene in matters that are essentially within the **domestic jurisdiction** of any state. Other principles scattered throughout the Charter include: (1) respect for **human rights;** (2) the right of self-determination of peoples; (3) the right of individual or **collective self-defense** against armed attack; (4) all **treaties** are to be registered with the United Nations; and (5) obligations under the Charter take precedence over those in other international agreements.

PRIVILEGES AND IMMUNITIES OF UNITED NATIONS PERSONNEL *see* GENERAL CONVENTION ON THE PRIVILEGES AND IMMUNITIES OF THE UNITED NATIONS

-Q-

QUIET DIPLOMACY. A term frequently applied to Secretary-General **Dag Hammarskjöld's** techniques in negotiation, which he pursued with impartiality, tactfulness, and persistence, but with minimal publicity. (See also HAMMARSKJÖLD, DAG.)

-R-

RATIFICATION OF THE UN CHARTER. Article 110 of the **Charter of the United Nations** provided that it would come into force upon the deposit with the United States government of ratifications by the five permanent members of the **Security Council** and by a majority of the other signatories. The United States was the first government to ratify and by October 24, 1945 the required number of ratifications had been deposited to bring it into force. October 24 is celebrated each year as United Nations Day. By the end of 1945 all 51 of the original members had joined the organization by depositing instruments of ratification.

REFUGEE WORK OF THE UNITED NATIONS. Several million refugees were displaced as a result of World War II. As one part of its mandate the **United Nations Relief and Rehabilitation Administration (UNRRA),** assisted by the military occupation authorities, repatriated or resettled the bulk of these refugees. In 1947 UNRRA turned over to a temporary UN specialized agency, the **International Refugee Organization (IRO),** the task of finding homes for the remainder. In 1951 the newly created Office of the United Nations High Commissioner for Refugees (UNHCR) assumed the responsibility for resolving refugee problems worldwide. With limited resources UNHCR mainly acts as coordinating agency for the efforts of governments and private agencies. It also promotes legal protection and the general welfare of refugees.

In recent years the refugee population has burgeoned to at least 19 million, with an additional 25 million of internally displaced persons. Africa accounts for the largest number, with others from **Afghanistan,** the former **Yugoslavia,** and the Philippines. A separate UN agency to administer to the needs of Palestine refugees displaced by the Arab-Israeli conflicts was created in 1950. This agency is the **United Nations Relief and Works Agency for Palestine Refugees in the Near East (UNRWA).** (See also INTERNATIONAL REFUGEE ORGANIZATION; UNITED NATIONS RELIEF AND REHABILITATION ADMINISTRATION; UNITED NATIONS RELIEF AND WORKS AGENCY FOR PALESTINE REFUGEES IN THE NEAR EAST.)

REGIONAL ARRANGEMENTS. In the **Charter of the United Nations,** Chapter VIII, containing only Articles 52–54, specifies the relationships between regional organizations and the United Nations. On the one hand, regional organizations are encouraged to peacefully settle regional disputes or may be called on by the **Security Council** to act as enforcement agencies. However, regional organizations are forbidden to take enforcement action without Security Council authorization, and the Security Council is to be kept fully informed of actions taken or contemplated by regional agencies for maintaining international peace and security. These requirements have been reinterpreted and violated in several situations, to the point of weakening the Security Council's supremacy of control over regional disputes.

Article 51 of the Charter, without mentioning regional arrangements, specifies the right of states for individual or **collective self-defense.** This article served as the justification for the formation of such military alliance-type organizations as the North Atlantic Treaty Organization (NATO) and the Soviet-led Warsaw Pact.

REGIONAL COMMISSIONS OF THE UNITED NATIONS. These agencies are subsidiary bodies of the United Nations **Economic and Social Council** for the purpose of decentralizing and coordinating the UN economic and social programs and activities on a regional basis. Their goals include the improvement of the economic well-being and the strengthening of economic ties within and among the countries of the region. There are five such agencies in the areas of Asia and the Far East, Western Asia, Africa, Europe, and Latin America and the Caribbean. (See also ECONOMIC AND SOCIAL COMMISSION FOR ASIA AND THE PACIFIC (ESCAP); ECONOMIC AND SOCIAL COMMISSION FOR WESTERN ASIA (ESCWA); ECONOMIC COMMISSION FOR AFRICA (ECA); ECONOMIC COMMISSION FOR EUROPE (ECE); ECONOMIC COMMISSION FOR LATIN AMERICA AND THE CARIBBEAN (ECLAC).)

REPRESENTATION IN THE SPECIALIZED AGENCIES OF THE UNITED NATIONS. Each state member of the various **specialized agencies** of the United Nations is free to choose appropriate delegates to the representation bodies of each such agency. Expertise in the appropriate subject matter of the particular agency (health, science, meteorology, etc.) will be a major criterion in the selection of delegates, but each foreign office will instruct delegates concerning broad policy and budgetary restraints.

REPRESENTATION IN THE UNITED NATIONS. Although the **Charter of the United Nations** specifies only the number of official national delegates in each major representative organ, and that each member of the **Security Council** "shall . . . be represented at all times at the seat of the Organization," the member states, with few exceptions, maintain permanent **missions** in New York and in **Geneva.** Each government determines its own representatives' qualifications, tenure, and compensation. The head of each delegation normally has ambassadorial rank. Because of the diversity of the UN program, and the need for public relations and support staff, the larger delegations may comprise as many as 200 persons, including a variety of expert advisers.

In 1988 Yasir Arafat, as head of the Palestine Liberation Organization (PLO), which had been granted observer status at the UN, was invited to address the **General Assembly.** When the United States government refused to grant him a visa, the General Assembly temporarily moved its session to Geneva to hear his address. In 1987 the U.S. Congress also attempted to force the closing of the PLO mission in New York, but this action was declared illegal by the courts, including an **advisory opinion** of the **International Court of Justice.** (See also CHINESE REPRESENTATION IN THE UNITED NATIONS; MISSIONS TO THE UNITED NATIONS; REPRESENTATION IN THE SPECIALIZED AGENCIES OF THE UNITED NATIONS.)

RESIDENT REPRESENTATIVES. In order to coordinate the UN economic and social projects within each recipient state, the United Nations appoints a field agent to reside in each country. This agent should assist the host government in planning request proposals, and, as overall coordinator of diverse programs within the country, should serve as chief United Nations representative. The lack of real authority, and the degree of cooperation of the host government and the diverse donor agencies, often act as limitations upon his/her potential effectiveness.

REVIEW OF THE UN CHARTER. Many of the smaller states attending the **San Francisco Conference** for drafting the **Charter of the United Nations** were dissatisfied with the elements of the Charter, especially the **veto** power of the permanent members of the **Security Council.** They managed to include in the Charter a provision that a general-review Conference could be called at any time by a two-thirds vote of all members of the **General Assembly** and a vote of any seven (later changed to nine) members of the Security Council. Also, the question of calling such a conference was to be automatically included in the agenda of the 10th General Assembly in 1955. Such a review conference has never been called since the time and circumstances have not seemed appropriate. The General Assembly has created two special committees, one in 1955 and the other in 1974, to study the matter, but the major powers have resisted ideas for broad reform.

RHODESIAN DISPUTE *see* ZIMBABWE

RIKHYE, INDAR JIT. Major-General Rikhye of India served as chief of staff of the **United Nations Emergency Force (UNEF)** in the Sinai from 1958 to 1960 and then as military advisor to the **Secretary-General** for the next eight years. During this period he also was engaged in direction of UN **peacekeeping** forces in the **Congo, West Irian,** Yemen, and **Cyprus.**

ROCKEFELLER, JOHN D., Jr. (1874–1960). Business executive and philanthropist. In 1946 Rockefeller donated land then worth more than $8 million along the East River in New York City for the permanent headquarters of the United Nations.

ROMULO, CARLOS P. (1899–1985). Romulo was the best-known Filipino diplomat and also won the Pulitzer Prize in 1941 for a series of articles on Southeast Asia. He was a delegate to the **San Francisco Conference** to draft the **Charter of the United Nations,** became Philippine Ambassador to the United Nations (1946–54), was elected President of the UN **General Assembly** in 1949, and served as Philippine Ambassador to the United States for a longer period than any other person. Romulo was widely known and respected as a strong advocate of the United Nations and as a statesperson and writer.

ROOSEVELT, ELEANOR (1884–1962). Wife of U.S. President **Franklin D. Roosevelt,** as well as an independent columnist, diplomat, and supporter of various peace movements. She served as a U.S. delegate to the UN **General Assembly** (1946, 1949–52, and 1961). She was a strong advocate of **human rights** and chaired the UN Commission on Human Rights (1947–51) which in 1948 produced the Universal Declaration on Human Rights. In her later years she was active in the United Nations Association, a private support group, and chaired its Board of Directors.

ROOSEVELT, FRANKLIN D. (1882–1945). The 32nd President of the United States (1933–45). During the war years Roosevelt met with the leaders of the United Kingdom and the USSR and initiated a series of meetings of high-level representatives of the four powers, including China, that agreed upon the broad principles of a general international organization. The culmination of this series of meetings was the **Dumbarton Oaks** conversations among representatives of the four powers in August–October 1944 which thrashed out the security provisions of the subsequent **Charter of the United Nations.** Although Roosevelt died a few days before the opening of the **San Francisco Conference** which produced the Charter, his administration had originated a major part of the elements of the final document. Also during his tenure, meetings hosted by the United States resulted in the establishment of the **Food and Agriculture Organization,** the **International Bank for Reconstruction and Development,** and the **International Monetary Fund** which became **specialized agencies** of the United Nations.

RWANDA *see* UNITED NATIONS PEACEKEEPING MISSIONS TO RWANDA

-S-

SAN FRANCISCO CONFERENCE (1945). San Francisco served as the site of the conference which produced the draft of the **Charter of the United Nations.** The Conference met from April 25 to June 26, 1945 with 282 delegates participating from 50 states. Although the basic peace and security principles and arrangements had been determined by the major powers at **Dumbarton Oaks** the previous year, the task of agreeing upon the elaborate details of the document were handled effectively and efficiently at the conference. (See also CHARTER OF THE UNITED NATIONS; DUMBARTON OAKS CONFERENCE.)

SANCTIONS. These are defined as coercive measures adopted by a group of nations against a nation violating **international law.** In the United Nations these are enforcement measures of a political, economic, or military nature applied in **collective security** actions provided for in Chapter VII of the **Charter of the United Nations.** Military sanctions against North Korea in 1950 and Iraq in 1990 were authorized by the **Security Council** to be carried out under United States's direction, rather than under United Nations's command and control. Examples of the adoption of economic sanctions by the Security Council occurred against Southern Rhodesia in 1966 and 1968, and against South Africa in 1977. (See also COLLECTIVE SECURITY; KOREAN QUESTION; KUWAIT INVASION BY IRAQ; SOUTH AFRICAN DISPUTE; ZIMBABWE.)

SCIENTIFIC COOPERATION *see* UNITED NATIONS EDUCATIONAL, SCIENTIFIC AND CULTURAL ORGANIZATION

SEA BED DEMILITARIZATION TREATY (1971). In 1968 the **General Assembly** established a Committee on the Peaceful Uses of the Seabed and the Ocean Floor and encouraged the **Disarmament Commission** to develop a treaty for demilitarization of this environment. By 1971 a limited treaty was produced and opened for signature; it prohibits the placing of weapons of mass destruction, or structures for storing, testing, or launching such weapons on or under the seabed and ocean floor, but does not prohibit military devices within territorial waters or detection devices beyond those limits.

SEAS *see* LAW OF THE SEAS CONFERENCE; SEA BED DEMILITARIZATION TREATY

SECRETARIAT. One of the six major organs of the United Nations. These international civil servants serve under the direction of the **Secretary-General.** They are recruited internationally on the basis of **Charter of the United Nations** provisions that cite "the necessity of securing the highest standards of efficiency, competence, and integrity" with due regard to geographical distribution. The Charter principles also safeguard these individuals' neutrality in serving the entire membership free from national or other external influence. They are charged with performing the wide range of duties necessary to servicing all the programs and functions of the United Nations. Each of the 17 **specialized agencies** affiliated with the United Nations also has a secretariat whose role is similar to that of the UN but with a more limited program field.

The total staff of the Secretariat is more than 30,000, more than half of whom are assigned to such field agencies as the **United Nations Development Program (UNDP),** the **United Nations Children's Fund (UNICEF),** and the Office of the United Nations High Commissioner for Refugees (UNHCR). In the 1980s and 1990s many attempts have been made to improve the efficiency of the administration, including the weeding out of "dead wood." In 1986 a Group of High-level Intergovernmental Experts issued a set of 71 recommendations to streamline the UN structure, which they described as "too complex, fragmented, and top-heavy." Other charges have been made that there have been waste, abuse, and fraud in the system. In partial response to these many criticisms the Secretary-General, in 1993, announced the reduction in Secretariat high-level posts from 48 to 35. A hiring freeze was also instituted to reduce the size of the Secretariat by 15 percent. Another reform is the introduction of competitive examinations for posts at the lower professional staff levels. The United States Congress in 1994 threatened to withhold 20 percent of its current assessments and 50 percent of funds owed for previous years unless the United Nations established a powerful and independent post of Inspector-General for the UN system in order to assure greater fiscal accountability. The post was created later that year.

SECRETARY-GENERAL. The administrative head of the United Nations. He is appointed by the **General Assembly** upon receipt of a recommendation of the **Security Council,** which recommendation requires unanimity of its permanent members. He is the official secretary to the four major delegate organs of the UN, is responsible for carrying out the functions assigned by these bodies, and is required to submit an annual report to the General Assembly on the work of the organization. He is granted authority by the **Charter of the United Nations** to call to the attention of the Security Council any matter which he believes to be a threat to international peace and security. Six Secretaries-General have occupied that office. (See also BOUTROS-GHALI, BOUTROS; HAMMARSKJÖLD, DAG; LIE, TRYGVE; PÉREZ DE CUÉLLAR, JAVIER; THANT, U; WALDHEIM, KURT.)

SECURITY COUNCIL. One of the six major organs of the United Nations. Originally there were five permanent members and six elective members, but a **Charter amendment** in 1965 added four elective members for a total of 15. The permanent members, the United States, the Russian Federation, China, the United Kingdom, and France have the power of **veto** over any substantive proposal, thus creating a "majority of one" possibility in any situation deemed threatening to their national interests. All resolutions require nine affirmative votes for adoption. The 1965 amendment was adopted in order to accommodate a broader geographical representation after the admission of many newly independent countries.

With the passage of time, the wisdom of maintaining the present size of the Council and the position of the five permanent members has been called into question. Because the permanent members can veto any proposal to change their status or voting privilege, the status quo established in 1945 has been maintained into the 1990s, in spite of changes in power and influence among the world's states. The **General Assembly** has considered the question of equitable representation on and membership of the Council since 1979. Reaching agreement on another Charter amendment to change the composition of the Security Council will be difficult, but the pressure to do so is mounting. Germany and Japan would like to be permanent members, but should they be granted veto powers? The total size of the Council will, no doubt, be eventually increased, but any increase of more than five or six members may make the Council unwieldy and less efficient. India and Brazil also aspire to permanent membership, but would they accept a Charter change to allow them to be reelected after a two-year term, without acquiring the veto power that goes with permanent membership? Such questions, and the prestige of additional states seeking greater participation in the Council, compound the problems of finding an acceptable formula.

The Security Council is a continuous body subject to convening on a few hours' notice. The chairmanship is rotated monthly according to the English alphabetical order of the member states. The Charter confers on the Security Council "primary responsibility for the maintenance of international peace and security." Also, the Charter prescribes that the decisions of the Security Council are binding on all UN member states, but this provision is impractical to enforce with regularity.

SELF-GOVERNMENT *see* NON-SELF-GOVERNING TERRI-TORIES; TRUSTEESHIP SYSTEM

SEYNES, PHILIPPE DE. United Nations Under Secretary-General for Economic and Social Affairs (the largest division of the Secretariat) during the administrations of Secretaries-General **Dag Hammarskjöld, U Thant,** and **Kurt Waldheim.**

SHOTWELL, JAMES T. (1874–1965). University professor and foundation executive. In 1939 Shotwell helped establish and became chairman of the **Commission to Study the Organization of Peace,** an organization of leading U.S. scholars concerned with the formation of a postwar international organization. The Commission's first four reports, issued during 1941–44, represented a comprehensive plan for the proposed organization and influenced Department of State preparations for the forthcoming planning conferences. During the **San Francisco Conference,** which produced the **Charter of the United Nations,** Shotwell served as chairman of a consultants' group to the U.S. delegation. As director of the Division of Economics and History of the

Carnegie Endowment for International Peace and later as the Endowment's president, he used his influence in the formation, study, and strengthening of the United Nations.

SMITH, IAN *see* ZIMBABWE

SOCIAL DEVELOPMENT *see* ECONOMIC AND SOCIAL COOPERATION

SOMALIA *see* UNITED NATIONS OPERATION IN SOMALIA

SOMALILAND *see* ITALIAN COLONIES

SOUTH AFRICA *see* SOUTH AFRICAN RACIAL QUESTIONS

SOUTH AFRICAN RACIAL QUESTIONS. The first complaint of ethnic discrimination in South Africa was made by India to the UN **General Assembly** in 1946 concerning treatment of the Indian minority in South Africa. The next year Pakistan joined India in a similar allegation. By 1962 these charges were combined with those of treatment of the black majority in South Africa under the agenda topic of **apartheid** or separation of the races. Since that time the subject has become an issue discussed by the General Assembly every year, with recommendations for drastic political and economic sanctions against South Africa and with the creation of special bodies within the **Secretariat** to pursue and publicize all aspects of the problem. The government of South Africa has always claimed that the issue is one for internal jurisdiction under the provision in the **Charter of the United Nations** prohibiting UN intervention in domestic affairs. UN bodies have claimed that Charter provisions concerning the **human rights** obligations of states and those pertaining to threats to international peace and security provide justification for UN jurisdiction.

The **Security Council** first took up the apartheid issue in 1960 after the Sharpeville massacre by South African troops of scores of black protestors against the "pass laws" which required black workers in white areas to carry passbooks serving as identification as work and travel permits. From time to time the Security Council adopted increasingly stronger measures but, because of the opposition of South Africa's major trading partners (the United States, France, the United Kingdom and Germany), could never agree to impose sweeping economic **sanctions.** In 1963 the Security Council adopted a limited arms embargo against South Africa and in 1977 strengthened the embargo to close some of the loopholes. After violence increased in 1985–86, and the South African government declared a state of emergency and jailed 8,000 political dissidents, the Security Council in 1986 adopted its strongest set of demands. These included (1) release of all political prisoners; (2) lifting of the state of emergency; (3) abolition of apartheid; and (4) free movement of peoples within South Africa.

After 1988 the movement toward dismantling apartheid and sharing political power gained internal momentum among citizen groups and government leaders in South Africa. In February 1990 Nelson Mandela, the leader of the African National Congress, the strongest black political party, was released after 27 years in prison. In December 1991 all major political party leaders agreed to a process for establishing a new democratic and nonracial constitution for South Africa. President de Klerk and Mandela cooperated in planning for a peaceful, democratic election to select a new President and a constituent assembly to write the new permanent constitution. In October 1993 the UN General Assembly lifted all sanctions against South Africa. In the April 1994 election Mandela won the Presidency by nearly two-thirds of the vote and proceeded to form a coalition cabinet including leaders of all major political parties.

SOUTH WEST AFRICA CASES. South West Africa (now Namibia) was a mandate under the **League of Nations mandate system** with South Africa as the supervising power. When the transfer was made to the UN system, South Africa claimed that it had no obligations to the new organization and that it intended to annex the territory. The UN **General Assembly** requested an **advisory opinion** on the legal obligations of South Africa and in July 1950 the **International Court of Justice** advised that: (1) South African obligations under the mandate continued; (2) South Africa was not required to put South West Africa under the UN **trusteeship system;** and (3) South Africa had no right to annex the territory unless the General Assembly agreed.

In 1960 Ethiopia and Liberia filed a suit in the Court against South Africa charging that it was violating its legal obligations under the mandate. In 1962 the Court, by an 8–7 margin, issued a preliminary finding that Ethiopia and Liberia, as former League members, were competent to bring the charges. However, in 1966 the Court reversed this finding and dismissed the case without ruling on the substance of the charges.

Controversy continued over the future status of South West Africa but during the 1980s a compromise was finally worked out and Namibia gained its independence as a self-governing state in 1990. (See also ADVISORY OPINIONS; INTERNATIONAL COURT OF JUSTICE.)

SOVEREIGNTY. Sovereignty is defined as supremacy of authority exercised by a state. State sovereignty is a basic principle on which the United Nations was founded, thus limiting the organization's power, with minor exceptions, to the voluntary cooperation of the member states. Internal state sovereignty is guaranteed in the **Charter of the United Nations** by the provision that the United Nations is forbidden "to intervene in matters which are essentially within the **domestic jurisdiction** of any state," with the possible exception that "this principle shall not prejudice the application of enforcement measures" against a state accused of a breach of the peace or act of aggression. General sovereignty is recognized in the Charter statement that "The Organization is based on the principle of the sovereign equality of all its Members." Even the Charter provision that **Security Council** resolutions are binding on all members has proven, in practice, to be a minor limitation on the state's freedom of action.

SPACE. In 1958 the **General Assembly** established a Committee on the Peaceful Uses of Outer Space. Subsequently, the

Assembly asserted that outer space and celestial bodies are free to exploration by any state, but not subject to national territorial claims. In 1963 the Eighteen Nation Disarmament Committee presented to the General Assembly the draft of a treaty banning weapons from outer space. From this evolved a broad Treaty on Principles Governing the Activities of States in the Exploration and Use of Outer Space, which came into force in 1967. This treaty remains the landmark document governing the uses of outer space.

SPAIN. In 1946 the **General Assembly** declared that the Franco regime was illegally established and requested all United Nations members to break diplomatic relations with Spain. It further recommended that Spain not be granted membership in any of the UN **specialized agencies.** In 1950 the Assembly reversed its 1946 action and Spain became a UN member in 1955.

SPECIALIZED AGENCIES OF THE UNITED NATIONS. These are autonomous intergovernmental agencies that are brought into a working relationship with the United Nations by agreements between the agencies and the UN **Economic and Social Council** subject to **General Assembly** approval. These 17 agencies have their own membership, headquarters, budget, staff, and charter or constitution. They report on their activities to the UN, but the UN can only make recommendations concerning their programs or budgets. Consultation is the means available for coordination and cooperation between the United Nations and the specialized agencies. (See also FOOD AND AGRICULTURE ORGAN-IZATION; INTERNATIONAL BANK FOR RECON-STRUCTION AND DEVELOPMENT; INTERNATIONAL CIVIL AVIATION ORGANIZATION; INTERNATIONAL DEVELOPMENT ASSOCIATION; INTERNATIONAL FI-NANCE CORPORATION; INTERNATIONAL FUND FOR AGRICULTURAL DEVELOPMENT; INTERNA-TIONAL LABOUR ORGANISATION; INTERNA-TIONAL MARITIME ORGANIZATION; INTERNA-TIONAL MONETARY FUND; INTERNATIONAL TELECOMMUNICATION UNION; MULTILATERAL IN-

VESTMENT GUARANTEE AGENCY; UNITED NA-
TIONS EDUCATIONAL, SCIENTIFIC AND CULTURAL
ORGANIZATION; UNITED NATIONS INDUSTRIAL
DEVELOPMENT ORGANIZATION; UNIVERSAL
POSTAL UNION; WORLD HEALTH ORGANIZATION;
WORLD INTELLECTUAL PROPERTY ORGANIZA-
TION; WORLD METEOROLOGICAL ORGANIZA-
TION.)

SPINELLI, PIER. During the administrations of Secretaries-
General **Dag Hammarskjöld** and **U Thant,** Pier Spinelli
served for ten years as director of the European Office of the
United Nations in **Geneva.** Additionally, during his tenure, he
was assigned at various times as special representative of the
Secretary-General in the Middle East, **Yemen,** and **Cyprus.**

STEVENSON, ADLAI E. (1900–65). U.S. lawyer and public
servant. Stevenson was an ardent supporter of the United
Nations and, as special assistant to the Secretary of State,
helped prepare the transition from the writing of the **Charter
of the United Nations** through the first session of the
General Assembly in 1945–46. He served as U.S. Ambassador to the United Nations from 1961 until his death in 1965,
but felt that he often exercised little influence over U.S.
policies in the UN and was disappointed in the lack of
support from Washington for his ideas for more vigorous use
of the organization.

STRONG, MAURICE F. (1929–). Canadian business executive
and public servant. His UN service has been mainly in
environmental programs. He was Secretary-General of the
Global Conference on the Human Environment in 1972 and
was Executive Director of the **UN Environment Program**
(1972–75). Again in 1992 he served as principal architect
and Secretary-General of the **UN Conference on Environment and Development (UNCED)** in Rio de Janeiro.

SUEZ CANAL QUESTION *see* UNITED NATIONS EMER-
GENCY FORCE; UNITED NATIONS TRUCE SUPERVI-
SION ORGANIZATION—SUEZ CANAL

SWITZERLAND. Although Switzerland was a member of the **League of Nations** with **Geneva** as the seat of the League, it has not joined the United Nations because it interprets the **collective security** obligations of the **Charter of the United Nations** to be in conflict with its long-established policy of neutrality. It is an active member of the various UN **specialized agencies** and the **International Court of Justice**. (See also GENEVA.)

-T-

TECHNICAL ASSISTANCE. This involves the transfer of technical knowledge and skills from one country to another. It is the principal mission of the **Economic and Social Council** and most of the UN **specialized agencies** in order to assist developing countries to improve the economic and social status of their peoples. Technical assistance is furnished not only by United Nations agencies, but also by individual governments and private and regional organizations. (See also EXPANDED PROGRAM OF TECHNICAL ASSISTANCE; UNITED NATIONS DEVELOPMENT PROGRAM.)

TERRORISM. The United Nations has been minimally involved in combatting terrorism. However, Libya's refusal to extradite two suspects in the bombing of Pan Am Flight 103 in December 1988 over Lockerbie, Scotland, with the loss of 270 lives, prompted the **Security Council** to impose an arms and air traffic embargo on Libya, effective 15 April 1992. The embargo continued into 1994.

THANT, U (1909–1974). Third **Secretary-General** of the United Nations (1961–71). At the time of his appointment he was the Permanent Representative of Burma (now Myanmar) to the United Nations. His previous career was as a teacher and journalist and he had served as press director for the Burmese government. His appointment reflected the first move toward choosing a third-world top administrator for the United Nations.

Thant was not successful in maintaining the momentum of

his predecessor, **Dag Hammarskjöld,** in assuming a dynamic role in conflict resolution, but he spoke out on a series of crises, while maintaining support of the big powers and fostering the interests of the developing nations. In some circles he was criticized for rapid withdrawal of the **UNEF peacekeeping** force from the Sinai in 1967 in response to Egyptian demands. He frequently tried to mediate an end to the Vietnam War in spite of United States opposition. The **financial crisis** of the United Nations grew critical during his tenure and was one of his major problems. He played a constructive role in political disputes in West Irian, the **Congo** (now Zaire), and the **Indian-Pakistani conflicts** of 1965 and 1971. In 1964, in response to a **Security Council** directive, he established a United Nations Peacekeeping Force in Cyprus (UNFICYP) and vigorously pursued a settlement of the **Cyprus conflict.** He publicly denounced the Soviet invasion of Czechoslovakia in 1968. In the same year he dispatched a personal representative to Nigeria to aid in distribution of food and medicine to victims of the Nigerian civil war. During the last three years of his tenure he vigorously promoted the preparations for the 1972 World Conference on the Human **Environment** held in Stockholm. In general, he was able to preserve and exercise the principles and prerogatives established by his predecessors.

TRADE *see* GENERAL AGREEMENT ON TARIFFS AND TRADE; UNITED NATIONS CONFERENCE ON TRADE AND DEVELOPMENT

TRANSNATIONAL CORPORATIONS (TNCs). The United Nations has generally adopted the term "transnational corporations" in place of the widely used "multinational corporations." The influence of TNCs in matters of development and trade attracted the attention of the **Economic and Social Council** in the early 1970s. In 1974, after a preliminary study, it created a Commission on Transnational Corporations and a United Nations Center on Transnational Corporations. A major task of these agencies was to try to develop a code of conduct to be followed by TNCs. This complex task has been in process for 20 years. In 1992 the Center was merged with the Development Administration Division of the **Secretariat** into the Transnational Corporations and Management Division.

TREATIES. Treaties are fundamental to the development of **international law.** The **Charter of the United Nations** and the basic instruments establishing the UN **specialized agencies** are treaties. The Charter assigns to the **General Assembly** the task of initiating studies and making recommendations for "encouraging the progressive development of international law." The Charter also requires all member states to register all treaties with the United Nations and provides that any treaty not so registered may not be invoked before any UN organ. The publication of the voluminous UN Treaty Series is one of the diverse tasks of the UN **Secretariat.** (See also INTERNATIONAL LAW; INTERNATIONAL LAW COMMISSION.)

TREATY ON THE NON-PROLIFERATION OF NUCLEAR WEAPONS *see* NUCLEAR NON-PROLIFERATION TREATY

TROIKA. A troika is either a Russian carriage drawn by three horses abreast or rule by a group of three persons. In 1960, because of Soviet displeasure over Secretary-General **Dag Hammarskjöld's** policies in the **Congo,** Khrushchev demanded that Hammarskjöld resign and be replaced by a three-member executive group. These would be representative of socialist, Western, and neutralist interests and each would have **veto** power over decisions. This would have destroyed the neutrality of the **Secretariat,** and the proposal was overwhelmingly rejected by the **General Assembly.**

TRUMAN, HARRY S (1854–1972). Judge, U.S. Senator, Vice-President of the United States (1945), and President of the United States (1945–53). As soon as he took office as President, Truman vigorously supported the preparations for the completion of the **Charter of the United Nations** and the launching of the new organization. Under his leadership the United States was the first country to ratify the Charter. In his

1949 inaugural address he emphasized four major points. The first expressed strong support for the United Nations. The fourth proposed increased economic aid to developing countries, which resulted in considerably greater bilateral aid and inspired the United Nations **Expanded Program of Technical Assistance (EPTA).** In 1950 he received UN legitimization for what was primarily a United States and South Korean military action against North Korea. His executive order in 1953 authorizing investigations of U.S. nationals who were employees or applicants for positions in the UN **Secretariat** was widely resented in UN circles.

TRUSTEESHIP COUNCIL. One of the six major organs of the United Nations. Its purpose is to supervise the administration of trust territories placed under the **trusteeship system.** Its composition was specified as an equal number of administering and non-administering states but also included automatic membership for the five permanent members of the **Security Council.** As soon as most trust territories gained independence, the only members of the Trusteeship Council were these five members of the Security Council. The Trusteeship Council performed its functions by reviewing annual reports from the administering authorities, examining petitions from the inhabitants of the territories, and undertaking periodic visiting missions to each trust territory. (see also TRUSTEESHIP SYSTEM.)

TRUSTEESHIP SYSTEM. The **Charter of the United Nations** provides that territories that might be voluntarily placed under trusteeship by an administering state were (1) territories held under **League of Nations mandate,** (2) territories detached from enemy states as a result of World War II, and (3) additional territories voluntarily placed under the system. In fact only 11 former mandates became trust territories. The purpose of the system was to promote the political, economic, social, and educational advancement of the inhabitants of the territories and their development toward self-government and independence. At the insistence of the United States, the Trust Territory of the Pacific Islands was designated as a strategic territory, subject to **Security Coun-**

cil jurisdictional review. All other trust territories were under **General Assembly** jurisdiction with the assistance of the **Trusteeship Council.** By 1975 all trust territories had become independent except the Trust Territory of the Pacific Islands. These island groups were eventually divided into four political units and in the mid-1990s the trusteeship system ended its work. (See also NON-SELF-GOVERNING TERRITORIES; TRUSTEESHIP COUNCIL.)

-U-

UNIFIED TASK FORCE (UNITAF) *see* UNITED NATIONS OPERATION IN SOMALIA

UNITED NATIONS ADMINISTRATIVE TRIBUNAL. This judicial organ was established by the UN **General Assembly** to hear and decide cases involving complaints of **Secretariat** employees concerning the terms of their employment. In 1953–54 the **International Court of Justice,** in an **advisory opinion** requested by the General Assembly, upheld the legitimacy of the Tribunal's creation and jurisdiction, and its ruling granting compensation to 11 dismissed employees.

UNITED NATIONS ANGOLA VERIFICATION MISSION (UNAVEM) AND (UNIVEM II) *see* ANGOLA

UNITED NATIONS ASSISTANCE MISSION TO RWANDA (UNAMIR) *see* UNITED NATIONS PEACEKEEPING MISSIONS TO RWANDA

UNITED NATIONS CENTRE FOR SOCIAL DEVELOPMENT AND HUMANITARIAN AFFAIRS (CSDHA). This Centre, located in **Vienna,** deals with issues related to **women, youth,** the **aging,** children, the disabled, and crime.

UNITED NATIONS CHARTER *see* CHARTER OF THE UNITED NATIONS

UNITED NATIONS CHILDREN'S FUND (UNICEF). The UN **General Assembly** created UNICEF in 1946 as an emergency organization to provide aid to European children in the aftermath of World War II. Its full original title was the United Nations International Children's Emergency Fund. When it became a permanent agency in 1953, its present title was adopted but its acronym, UNICEF, was retained. UNICEF is a program created within the UN structure rather than an autonomous intergovernmental **specialized agency.** It is supported by voluntary governmental and private contributions, with private sources accounting for more than 25 percent of its funds. Its program emphasizes nutrition, education, and health of children and mothers in developing countries, African countries receiving the greatest attention. Its grants for each project must be more than matched by the recipient government. UNICEF relies on the **World Health Organization,** the **Food and Agriculture Organization,** and the **United Nations Educational, Scientific, and Cultural Organization** to furnish the experts required for carrying out its projects. UNICEF was awarded the Nobel Peace Prize in 1965 in recognition of its accomplishments. In 1990 a Convention on the Rights of the Child was submitted to states for ratification and has been adopted by most countries. Also in 1990 a World Summit for Children laid out an ambitious set of targets for improving the health and well-being of children by the year 2000.

UNITED NATIONS COMMISSION FOR INDONESIA (UNCI) *see* INDONESIAN QUESTION

UNITED NATIONS COMMISSION ON INTERNATIONAL TRADE LAW (UNCITRAL). This 36-member commission established by the UN **General Assembly** in 1966 provides coordination of agencies involved in international trade law, preparation of new conventions relating to this field, and training and advice on such matters, especially for developing countries. UNCITRAL works closely with both the General Assembly and the **United Nations Conference on Trade and Development.** Among the treaties it has produced are the United Nations Convention on the Carriage of Goods by Sea (1978), the United Nations Convention on Contracts for the International Sale of Goods (1980), and the

United Nations Convention on International Bills of Exchange and International Promissory Notes (1988). It has also published a set of arbitration rules and another of conciliation rules.

UNITED NATIONS CONFERENCE ON DESERTIFICATION *see* ENVIRONMENT PROGRAMS OF THE UNITED NATIONS

UNITED NATIONS CONFERENCE ON ENVIRONMENT AND DEVELOPMENT (UNCED). This conference, also known as the Earth Summit, was the largest-ever gathering of heads of state or government, numbering more than 100. It met for two weeks in Rio de Janeiro in June 1992. By this time the linkage between environmental and development issues had been generally accepted under the rubric "sustainable development." Two years of intensive preparatory work produced the preliminary drafts of the main documents produced at the conference. These included: (1) Agenda 21, a detailed plan for global action to achieve the goals of the conference; (2) the Rio Declaration on Environment and Development consisting of 27 principles for sustainable development; (3) a set of principles for the sustainable management of the world's forests; (4) a Convention on Climate Change; and (5) a Convention on Biological Diversity. To monitor the results of the conference, the UN created a new high-level Commission on Sustainable Development and the **Secretariat** was reorganized to create a Department for Policy Coordination and Sustainable Development. Public interest in the Rio conference was expressed by the attendance in parallel forums of 30,000 representatives of **nongovernmental organizations.** (See also BRUNTLAND REPORT; ENVIRONMENT PROGRAMS OF THE UNITED NATIONS; STRONG, MAURICE F.)

UNITED NATIONS CONFERENCE ON HUMAN SETTLEMENTS *see* ENVIRONMENT PROGRAMS OF THE UNITED NATIONS

UNITED NATIONS CONFERENCE ON NEW AND RENEW-

ABLE SOURCES OF ENERGY *see* ENERGY PRO-GRAMS OF THE UNITED NATIONS

UNITED NATIONS CONFERENCE ON THE PEACEFUL USES OF NUCLEAR ENERGY *see* ENERGY PRO-GRAMS OF THE UNITED NATIONS

UNITED NATIONS CONFERENCE ON TRADE AND DE-VELOPMENT (UNCTAD). This program is often referred to as "the poor man's lobby." It was authorized by the UN **General Assembly** in 1962 and held its first conference in 1964. The conferences have met at three- to five-year intervals, with the eighth conference at Cartagena in 1992. The developing states have cooperated to dominate each conference and to approve a pattern of demands on the affluent states for concessions which they hope will narrow the rich-poor gap and speed economic and social development. At the 1964 conference permanent machinery to support the program was created with headquarters in **Geneva.** The executive arm is a Trade and Development Board assisted by a number of committees and a special section of the UN **Secretariat.** The UNCTAD organs report directly to the General Assembly, thus bypassing the **Economic and Social Council.** After decades of strident demands and frustration over failure to obtain major concessions, the Cartagena conference sought reconciliation with the affluent states in a new partnership for sustainable development. (See also DEVELOPMENT.)

UNITED NATIONS DAY *see* RATIFICATION OF THE UN CHARTER

UNITED NATIONS DEVELOPMENT FUND FOR WOMEN (UNIFEM) *see* WOMEN

UNITED NATIONS DEVELOPMENT PROGRAM (UNDP). The UNDP was created in 1965 by the merger of two previous programs—the **Expanded Program of Technical Assistance** and the **United Nations Special Fund.** It is the largest multilateral source of grants for **development** projects. Its annual resources have grown from less than $150 million to $1.5 billion furnished by governmental voluntary contributions. Over the years it has supported tens of thousands of development projects in dozens of areas of economic and social development. In its program it works in close cooperation with governments, regional organizations, other multilateral agencies, and **nongovernmental organizations.** (See also DEVELOPMENT; EXPANDED PROGRAM OF TECHNICAL ASSISTANCE; UNITED NATIONS SPECIAL FUND.)

UNITED NATIONS DISASTER RELIEF COORDINATOR (UNDRO) *see* DISASTER RELIEF

UNITED NATIONS DISENGAGEMENT OBSERVER FORCE (UNDOF) *see* GOLAN HEIGHTS DISPUTE

UNITED NATIONS EDUCATIONAL, SCIENTIFIC AND CULTURAL ORGANIZATION (UNESCO). UNESCO was established in 1946 and entered into an agreement with the United Nations as one of the autonomous **specialized agencies** within the United Nations system. Its headquarters are in Paris. Its mandate is especially broad, encompassing the three fields suggested by its title as well as the area of communications. Among its goals in education is the universal achievement of basic education. It has fostered **human rights** and democracy and the combatting of discrimination. Safeguarding the cultural heritage is one dimension of its cultural activities. It has worked closely with scientific organizations throughout the world. In 1984 the United States withdrew from membership and was followed the next year by the United Kingdom and Singapore. Their objections were both to the administration of the Director-General and to some of the recent policy decisions. The loss of 30 percent of its financial support prompted major administrative and programmatic restructuring under a new Director-General to attempt to induce the renewal of membership by the states that withdrew.

UNITED NATIONS EMERGENCY FORCES IN THE MIDDLE

EAST (UNEF AND UNEF II). In 1956 Egypt announced that it was nationalizing the Suez Canal. After brief negotiations Israeli forces advanced toward the canal, followed on October 31 by British and French air attacks against Egypt, and two days later by invasion by their land forces. A **Security Council** session on October 30 was unable to act because of British and French **vetos** of demands for Israeli withdrawal, so the first-ever emergency special session of the **General Assembly** convened on November 1. A series of General Assembly resolutions demanded the withdrawal of all foreign forces from Egyptian territory and authorized the setting up of the first large-scale United Nations **peacekeeping** force operating under rules and principles which served as a model for all such subsequent operations. By November 15 the first peacekeeping contingents arrived in Egypt and by February 1957 more than 6,000 military personnel from ten countries were assigned to UNEF. The functions of UNEF included the supervision of the withdrawal of foreign forces from Egyptian territory, and subsequently acting as a buffer between Egyptian and Israeli forces in the Gaza and Sinai areas. The force remained on the Egyptian side of these borders for more than ten years until the outbreak of a major war between Israel and its Arab neighbors in June 1967.

With the outbreak of warfare between Israel and both Egypt and Syria in October 1973, a second major UN peacekeeping force (UNEF II) was sent to the area. This time the Security Council, through the cooperation of the permanent members, authorized the action. A force of 7,000 from 13 countries was dispatched to the areas of the Suez Canal and the Sinai peninsula. The mandate for the force was to supervise the cease-fire between Egyptian and Israeli forces, to supervise their redeployment and to patrol the buffer zones established under various agreements. The UNEF II operation was terminated in July 1979. (See also PEACEKEEPING.)

UNITED NATIONS ENVIRONMENT PROGRAM (UNEP) *see* ENVIRONMENT PROGRAMS OF THE UNITED NATIONS

UNITED NATIONS FORCE IN CYPRUS (UNFICYP). The UN **peacekeeping** force sent to Cyprus in 1964 which still monitors the cease-fire there. (See also CYPRUS QUESTION.)

UNITED NATIONS FUND FOR POPULATION ACTIVITIES (UNFPA) *see* POPULATION PROGRAMS OF THE UNITED NATIONS

UNITED NATIONS GOALS *see* GOALS OF THE UNITED NATIONS

UNITED NATIONS HEADQUARTERS. After considering sites in several countries, the UN **General Assembly** accepted an invitation to locate the United Nations permanent headquarters in the United States. In December 1946 the General Assembly accepted an offer by **John D. Rockefeller, Jr.** to purchase an area in Manhattan, New York City, for the site of the headquarters. Construction began in 1947. Occupancy of the various buildings began in 1950 and all buildings were in use by October 1952. The four main structures are a 39-story Secretariat Building, the Conference Building, the General Assembly Hall, and the Dag Hammarskjöld Library. (See also GENEVA.)

UNITED NATIONS HIGH COMMISSIONER FOR REFUGEES (UNHCR) *see* REFUGEE WORK OF THE UNITED NATIONS

UNITED NATIONS INDIA-PAKISTAN OBSERVATION MISSION (UNIPOM) *see* INDIAN-PAKISTANI DISPUTE

UNITED NATIONS INDUSTRIAL DEVELOPMENT ORGANIZATION (UNIDO). In 1965 the UN **General Assembly** approved the formation of the UNIDO and it began operations in 1967 with headquarters in **Vienna.** Its central purpose was, as its title suggests, to promote industrialization in developing countries. It was originally directly responsible to the General Assembly and received funds from the UN regular **budget,** from the **United Nations Development Program,** and from voluntary contributions. In 1975 a campaign was begun to convert UNIDO to the status of a UN **specialized agency** with its own membership and a budget raised by assessment of members. This process was finally completed in 1985. UNIDO assists in the industrialization process through training, surveys, research, exchange of information, and **technical assistance.**

UNITED NATIONS INSTITUTE FOR TRAINING AND RESEARCH (UNITAR). UNITAR was established in 1965 to provide support for enhancing the effectiveness of the United Nations. It has produced a large number of research studies and has conducted training seminars for members and staffs of government delegations. It is supported by voluntary contributions of governments, intergovernmental organizations, and **nongovernmental organizations.** In 1987, the UN **General Assembly** directed that UNITAR concentrate primarily on training activities because of uncertain and fluctuating financial support. Recent training programs have included an emphasis on natural resource and environmental management.

UNITED NATIONS INTERIM FORCE IN LEBANON (UNIFIL) *see* ISRAELI INVASIONS OF LEBANON

UNITED NATIONS INTERNATIONAL SCHOOL. First founded in 1947 as a nursery school by parents from the UN **Secretariat,** the school has expanded to include nearly 1,500 students on two campuses in grades kindergarten through twelve. About half the students are children of diplomats or UN staff members and represent more than 100 nationalities. Ten languages are taught and English as a second language is stressed. The rest of the curriculum is also internationally oriented. Although the school is private, six members of the board are appointed by the UN **Secretary-General** and graduation ceremonies are held in the General Assembly Hall. A new building in Manhattan, completed in 1973, was financed by grants from the Ford Foundation and the Rockefeller Brothers Fund.

UNITED NATIONS IRAQ-KUWAIT OBSERVER MISSION (UNIKOM). This **peacekeeping** force was deployed in the demilitarized zone between the two countries at the end of the Gulf War in 1991. In February 1993 the **Security Council** converted the observer group to a military-type operation by authorizing action to prevent violations of the demilitarized zone and increasing the size from 500 to more then 3,500 personnel. (See also KUWAIT INVASION BY IRAQ.)

UNITED NATIONS MILITARY OBSERVER GROUP IN INDIA AND PAKISTAN (UNMOGIP) *see* INDIAN-PAKISTANI DISPUTE

UNITED NATIONS MISSION FOR THE REFERENDUM IN WESTERN SAHARA (MINURSO) *see* WESTERN SAHARA DISPUTE

UNITED NATIONS OBSERVATION MISSION FOR THE VERIFICATION OF ELECTIONS IN NICARAGUA (ONUVEN) *see* CENTRAL AMERICAN PEACE EFFORTS

UNITED NATIONS OBSERVER GROUP IN CENTRAL AMERICA (ONUCA) *see* CENTRAL AMERICAN PEACE EFFORTS

UNITED NATIONS OBSERVER GROUP IN LEBANON (UNOGIL). This was a small UN **peacekeeping** operation of the observer type in Lebanon in 1958. The crisis was of short duration after the UNOGIL forces reported minimal military penetration of the Lebanese-Syrian border. (See also LEBANESE CRISIS [1958].)

UNITED NATIONS OBSERVER MISSION IN EL SALVADOR (ONUSAL) *see* CENTRAL AMERICAN PEACE EFFORTS

UNITED NATIONS OBSERVER MISSION IN GEORGIA (UNOMIG). This observer-type **peacekeeping** operation was the first on the territory of the former Soviet Union. It was established by the **Security Council** in August 1993. With somewhat less than 100 military personnel, its assignment was to verify compliance with a cease-fire agreement between Georgia and the separatist forces of the region of Abkhazia. The **Secretary-General** also dispatched a personal representative to the area to assist in negotiations for a political settlement.

UNITED NATIONS OBSERVER MISSION IN LIBERIA (UNOMIL). This **peacekeeping** operation was established by the **Security Council** in September 1993. Its mandate was to monitor the July cease-fire agreement, observe elections in 1994, and coordinate humanitarian aid. This UN mission worked in cooperation with a previously-established peacekeeping operation of the Economic Community of West African States.

UNITED NATIONS OBSERVER MISSION IN SOUTH AFRICA (UNOMSA). This set of UN observers was sent to South Africa in September 1992 to assist in the peace process and discourage violence during the transition period leading to free general elections in 1994. First authorized at 50 members, it was later expanded to more than 100. The UN mission collaborated with other observers from the European Community, the Commonwealth, and the Organization of African Unity. (See also SOUTH AFRICAN RACIAL QUESTIONS.)

UNITED NATIONS OBSERVER MISSION UGANDA-RWANDA (UNOMUR) *see* UNITED NATIONS PEACEKEEPING MISSIONS TO RWANDA

UNITED NATIONS OPERATION IN MOZAMBIQUE (ONUMOZ). Civil war began in Mozambique in 1978, just three years after independence from Portugal, and continued until the signing of a series of peace agreements in Rome in 1992 between government officials and leaders of the rebel forces, the Resistência Nacional Moçambicana (RENAMO). In December 1992 the **Security Council** authorized the creation of ONUMOZ with more than 7,000 military and civilian personnel. Its multiple tasks included monitoring and verifying the cease-fire, supervising the withdrawal of foreign forces, demobilization of 80,000 government and RENAMO troops, coordinating and monitoring humanitarian assistance operations, and providing **technical assistance** and monitoring the entire electoral process. A part of the process involved the work of the UN High Commissioner for Refugees (UNHCR) in helping to repatriate 1.5 million Mozambican **refugees** from six neighboring countries. The Security Council urged the parties to set a date for electing a new government which occurred on November 19, 1994. (See also REFUGEE WORK OF THE UNITED NATIONS.)

UNITED NATIONS OPERATION IN SOMALIA (UNOSOM). This **peacekeeping** operation was established in April 1992 to monitor a cease-fire and to safeguard the distribution of humanitarian aid in Somalia. Civil strife, clan warfare, and armed attacks on and looting of aid convoys prompted the **Security Council** in December 1992 to authorize a United States-led Unified Task Force (UNITAF) with a mandate to use "all necessary means" to establish order and protect aid-distribution facilities. In March 1993 the Security Council replaced UNITAF with UNOSOM II, the largest UN peacekeeping force in UN history comprised of more than 30,000 personnel. UNOSOM II was also specifically authorized to use force under the provisions of Chapter VII of the **Charter of the United Nations** and to promote a political settlement to replace the anarchy in Somalia.

UNITED NATIONS OPERATION IN THE CONGO (ONUC) *see* CONGO OPERATION

UNITED NATIONS PEACEKEEPING MISSIONS TO RWANDA. In June 1993 the **Security Council** authorized the United Nations Observer Mission Uganda-Rwanda (UNOMUR) to monitor the border between the two countries to prevent military assistance from reaching Rwanda. In October UNOMUR was absorbed into a broader United Nations Assistance Mission to Rwanda (UNAMIR) to monitor a peace agreement between the factions in a three-year civil war. The UNAMIR forces were also to observe the process of establishing a provisional government prior to 1995 elections. Civil war broke out again in April 1994 following the deaths of the Presidents of Rwanda and Burundi in a plane crash.

Government soldiers and mobs of machete-wielding Hutus, the majority ethnic group, slaughtered hundreds of thousands of Tutsis, the minority ethnic group. However, the armed forces of the Rwandan Patriotic Front (RPF), the rebel Tutsi-dominated faction, by mid-summer had captured Kigali, the capital, and gained control of most of Rwandan territory. More than a million Hutus, including most of the government soldiers, fearing reprisals by the RPF, fled to Zaire. On the march to the Zairian border and in the **refugee** camps in Zaire hundreds of thousands of expatriates died of hunger, cholera, and dysentery, in spite of one of the world's largest relief efforts by governments and private agencies. The Tutsis agreed to set up a coalition government in Rwanda and not to take revenge against any except those proven to have engaged in atrocities, but most refugees, in spite of urging by many authorities, including UN agencies, refused to go home. (See also REFUGEE WORK OF THE UNITED NATIONS.)

UNITED NATIONS PRINCIPLES *see* PRINCIPLES OF THE UNITED NATIONS

UNITED NATIONS PROTECTION FORCE (UNPROFOR) *see* YUGOSLAVIA

UNITED NATIONS RELIEF AND REHABILITATION ADMINISTRATION (UNRRA). This was a temporary agency created by the Allied Powers in 1943 to carry out relief programs and economic and social rebuilding in the war-torn countries of Europe and Asia at the end of hostilities. Food, clothing, and medical supplies were vitally needed. The United States furnished more than two-thirds of the supplies and funding, but each assisted country was responsible for the administration of the programs. In late 1946 UNRRA was terminated, with the **United Nations**

Children's Fund receiving some remaining assets and the **International Refugee Organization** assuming responsibility for the unrepatriated or unrelocated wartime refugees. (See also INTERNATIONAL REFUGEE ORGANIZATION; UNITED NATIONS CHILDREN'S FUND.)

UNITED NATIONS RELIEF AND WORKS AGENCY FOR PALESTINE REFUGEES IN THE NEAR EAST (UNRWA). UNRWA began operations in 1950 with a mandate to provide relief and social services to Palestinian **refugees** displaced as a result of the Middle East conflicts. In the 1990s there are 2.6 million refugees registered with UNRWA, more than one-third of them living in refugee camps in Jordan, Lebanon, Syria, the West Bank, and the Gaza Strip. UNRWA is primarily supported by voluntary contributions and expends about $300 million annually for regular and emergency operations. Almost half of its regular budget goes for education, approximately one-sixth for health services, and about 11 percent for relief and social services. It employs almost 19,000 local staff, including more than 10,000 teachers, with 99 percent of all staff being Palestine refugees. UNRWA's headquarters are in **Vienna** and there are field offices in the five service areas. (See also REFUGEE WORK OF THE UNITED NATIONS.)

UNITED NATIONS SECURITY FORCE (UNSF) *see* WEST IRIAN (WEST NEW GUINEA) QUESTION

UNITED NATIONS SPECIAL COMMITTEE ON THE BALKANS (UNSCOB). A series of complaints concerning foreign interference in Greece and outside aid to Greek guerrilla forces opposed to the Greek government came before the **Security Council** and the **General Assembly** between 1946 and 1951. In 1947 the General Assembly set up UNSCOB to investigate charges that this interference was coming from Albania, Bulgaria, and Yugoslavia. Poland and the USSR, two of the 11-member committee, refused to participate in its investigations. After a series of on-the-spot inquiries and reports in which cross-border activity was verified, UNSCOB was discontinued in December 1951.

UNITED NATIONS SPECIAL FUND. At the urging of the developing countries, the Special Fund was established in 1959 to carry on pre-investment activities, research, surveys, and pilot projects in addition to the less expensive operations of the **Expanded Program of Technical Assistance (EPTA).** In 1965 the Special Fund and the EPTA were merged into the **United Nations Development Program.** (See also DEVELOPMENT; EXPANDED PROGRAM OF TECHNICAL ASSISTANCE; UNITED NATIONS DEVELOPMENT PROGRAM.)

UNITED NATIONS TEMPORARY EXECUTIVE AUTHORITY (UNTEA) *see* WEST IRIAN (WEST NEW GUINEA) QUESTION

UNITED NATIONS TRANSITION ASSISTANCE GROUP (UNTAG). Although South Africa remained in de facto control of the territory of South West Africa, the UN **General Assembly** and **Security Council,** in a series of resolutions beginning in 1966, declared the territory to be the direct responsibility of the United Nations and adopted the name "Namibia" for the area. From 1978 until 1989 negotiations were carried on for a transition of control, with the United States as principal mediator supported by major Western states and the Soviet Union. In December 1988 South Africa, Angola, and Cuba agreed to a plan for free elections and independence for Namibia. In order to ensure a peaceful and orderly process the Security Council authorized the creation of UNTAG to assist the Special Representative of the **Secretary-General** in monitoring the cease-fire and the conduct of the elections. UNTAG was composed of 4,500 military personnel, 1,500 police forces, and 2,000 civilians assigned to election supervision. The personnel were scattered among 42 political offices throughout Namibia. The operation proceeded smoothly and effectively and was terminated in March 1990 with a duration of just under one year. (See also ANGOLA; PEACEKEEPING; SOUTH WEST AFRICA CASES.)

UNITED NATIONS TRANSITIONAL AUTHORITY IN CAMBODIA (UNTAC) *see* CAMBODIAN SITUATION

UNITED NATIONS TRUCE SUPERVISION ORGANIZATION (UNTSO) *see* PALESTINE QUESTION (1947–50)

UNITED NATIONS TRUCE SUPERVISION ORGANIZATION—SUEZ CANAL. This was a small, temporary UN observer mission sent to the Suez Canal area after the June 1967 war. It was under the direction of the United Nations Truce Supervision Organization which had been operating in the Middle East since 1949. (See also PALESTINE QUESTION (1947–50); UNITED NATIONS EMERGENCY FORCES IN THE MIDDLE EAST.)

UNITED NATIONS UNIVERSITY. In 1969 the UN **General Assembly** requested that the **United Nations Educational, Scientific and Cultural Organization** prepare a feasibility study for the establishment of a United Nations University. After a favorable report the University began operations in 1975 with headquarters in Tokyo. It has no students or faculty, but it coordinates research through a network of research institutions, individual scholars, and its own research and training centers and programs in various parts of the world.

UNITED NATIONS VOLUNTEERS. This program established in 1970 by the UN **General Assembly** involves approximately 2,000 field workers on two-year contracts in more than 100 developing countries. Heavy emphasis is placed on advising the least developed countries. Although the volunteers are highly qualified within their specialties, they receive only modest stipends. The largest project to date, involving 400 volunteers, was election supervision in **Cambodia** in 1992–93.

UNITED NATIONS WATER CONFERENCE (1977) *see* ENVIRONMENT PROGRAMS OF THE UNITED NATIONS

UNITED NATIONS YEMEN OBSERVATION MISSION (UNYOM). During the early 1960s a civil war was fought in Yemen with Saudi Arabia and the United Arab Republic supporting opposing factions. In 1963 all parties involved agreed to a cease-fire, the establishment of a demilitarized zone, the withdrawal of foreign military forces, and the acceptance of United Nations observers to verify compliance with the terms of the agreement. UNYOM operated in Yemen from July 1963 until September 1964, with Saudi Arabia and the United Arab Republic sharing equally all costs of the mission.

UNITING FOR PEACE RESOLUTION. This resolution was adopted by the UN **General Assembly** in November 1950. Its main purpose was to provide for calling emergency special sessions of the General Assembly within 24 hours when the **Security Council** is unable to agree on a course of action in situations involving a threat to or breach of the peace or act of aggression. The resolution was in response to the **Korean** situation in which the Security Council had been able to act during the temporary boycott of its sessions by the Soviet Union but was stalemated on this issue after the boycott ended in August 1950. The resolution also requested members to designate military units for United Nations service and it established a Peace Observation Commission and a **Collective Measures Committee,** both of which were active for a brief time. Nine emergency special sessions of the General Assembly have been called, but none since 1982.

UNIVERSAL POSTAL UNION (UPU). This organization has been in existence since 1875 and was established by the Berne Treaty drawn up the previous year. It became a **specialized agency** of the United Nations system in 1948. Its main purpose is to promote and expedite the international flow of mail in all parts of the world. The UPU establishes rules and regulations concerning the passage of mail and provides technical aid to train personnel in developing countries. Its headquarters are in Berne, **Switzerland.**

URQUHART, Sir BRIAN E. (1919–). British public servant. He

was Executive Secretary of the Preparatory Commission of the United Nations in London 1945–46 and then served longer in the United Nations **Secretariat** than any other person (1946–86). He held a succession of major Secretariat positions including responsibility for overseeing UN **peacekeeping** operations.

-V-

VETO. Although the term "veto" does not appear in the **Charter of the United Nations,** the voting formula accords to each of the five permanent members of the **Security Council**—the United States, the Russian Federation, the United Kingdom, France, and China—the power to block any substantive decision by its negative vote. In spite of the protests of the other states represented at the **San Francisco Conference** in 1945, the permanent members held firm against any limitations on this privilege.

In practice the veto has been used to protect the vital national interests of the permanent members. In the first ten years of United Nations operations, the Soviet Union was deliberately forced by the Western bloc to use large numbers of vetoes to block the admission to UN **membership** of states favorable to the West, while the pro-Communist candidates could not be admitted because, without using the veto, the Western states would not give their candidacy the required majority approval. The United Kingdom and France used their veto power to block Security Council action in the 1956 Suez Crisis. Although the United States was initially able to control the situation without resort to the veto, since it cast its first veto in 1971 it has used the veto more often than the Soviet Union/Russian Federation.

Actually the veto has been used sparingly in the past two decades. Even during the Cold War the United States and the Soviet Union realized that their common interest lay in utilizing the smaller Security Council, which they could more easily control, than to allow many decisions to be shifted to the unwieldy **General Assembly.** The end of the Cold War reenforced this commonality of interests. In fact, in several recent years, as the use of the veto diminished, the

Security Council has announced a majority of all its decisions by consensus, without a roll-call vote. (See also SECURITY COUNCIL.)

VIENNA. Vienna may be termed the third major UN headquarters after New York and **Geneva.** In the 1970s the city built a large complex, generally known as "UNO City," in order to attract and accommodate UN agencies. The principal agencies with headquarters there are the **International Atomic Energy Agency (IAEA),** the **United Nations Relief and Works Agency for Palestine Refugees in the Near East (UNRWA),** and a large Centre for Social Development and Humanitarian Affairs (CSDHA) of the UN Office at Vienna, which is a branch of the **Secretariat** serving diverse social and humanitarian programs.

VOTING IN THE GENERAL ASSEMBLY *see* GENERAL ASSEMBLY

VOTING IN THE SECURITY COUNCIL *see* SECURITY COUNCIL

-W-

WALDHEIM, KURT (1918–). Fourth **Secretary-General** of the United Nations (1972–81). At the time of his appointment he was the Permanent Representative of Austria to the United Nations, having served in various posts in the diplomatic service of Austria since 1945, including that of Minister of Foreign Affairs (1968–70).

Waldheim's tenure as Secretary-General was marked by the increasing demands from the developing states for a more equitable distribution of global economic resources and benefits, the repercussions on the global economy of huge increases in petroleum prices, and the pressures from the affluent states for UN budgetary and administrative reform as well as their resistance to third-world economic demands. The major powers also successfully withstood most challenges to their leadership role in the UN by the Secretary-General or the **General Assembly.** For the most part, Waldheim practiced even-handed, **quiet diplomacy** and administrative neutrality, thus contributing to his acceptability for reelection to a second five-year term as Secretary-General.

Waldheim's peacemaking efforts included the deployment of three new United Nations **peacekeeping** forces in the Middle East—the second **United Nations Emergency Force (UNEF-II)** between Israeli and Egyptian forces (1973–1979); the United Nations Disengagement Observer Force (UNDOF) in the **Golan Heights** (1974–); and the United Nations Interim Force in Lebanon (UNIFIL) (1978–). Waldheim also carried on extensive personal negotiations in the **Cyprus** dispute and tried, without success, to involve the UN in the Vietnam conflict. He used his powers under article 99 of the Charter to call the **Security Council** into session in 1979 to consider the hostage crisis in **Iran.** He appointed special personal representatives to attempt to mediate settlements of the **Iran-Iraq** and Soviet-**Afghanistan** wars.

In 1974 the demands of the third-world nations for a radical reordering of the global economic system culminated in the calling of a special session of the General Assembly on the subject of Raw Materials and Development. Out of this session came the set of demands known as the **New International Economic Order (NIEO),** followed later that year by a General Assembly document known as the Charter of Economic Rights and Duties of States. The hopes of the developing countries for greater control of the global economy, a redistribution of resources, and the narrowing of the gap between rich and poor states have been largely frustrated, but Waldheim was generally supportive of third-world aspirations.

Evidence of Waldheim's direct or indirect connection with German war crimes in Yugoslavia and Greece during World War II did not surface until 1986, when he was elected President of Austria. He had concealed his wartime service with the German army in those countries. According to one investigation he was apparently aware of war crimes, but the degree of his involvement remained a debatable issue. Had his war record been fully known in 1971 he undoubtedly would not have been chosen as UN Secretary-General.

WEIGHTED VOTING *see* INTERNATIONAL BANK FOR RECONSTRUCTION AND DEVELOPMENT; INTERNATIONAL MONETARY FUND

WEST IRIAN (WEST NEW GUINEA) QUESTION. After the independence of Indonesia in 1949 both the Netherlands and Indonesia continued to claim jurisdiction over West New Guinea. In 1961–62 fighting occurred in the territory between military forces of the claimant states. Through the efforts of UN Secretary-General **U Thant** an agreement for the transfer of authority was signed at **UN headquarters** in August 1962. The agreement provided that for a period of seven months the Dutch would turn over to the United Nations the administration of the territory, after which jurisdiction would be transferred to Indonesia. A United Nations Temporary Executive Authority (UNTEA) was created to assume the necessary administrative role and it was assisted by a 1,500-member United Nations Security Force (UNSF). This is the only situation in which the United Nations assumed administrative control of a territory. All costs were shared by Indonesia and the Netherlands. Indonesia never conducted a promised future plebiscite to ascertain the wishes of the indigenous people but used questionable substitutes to claim legitimacy for annexing West Irian as a part of Indonesia.

WESTERN SAHARA DISPUTE. The status of Western Sahara has been in dispute since 1975 when Spain gave up its claim to the territory previously called Spanish Sahara. The following year Morocco and Mauritania divided the territory, but an indigenous movement, the Polisario Front, simultaneously declared the independence of Western Sahara. The UN **General Assembly,** backed by an **advisory opinion** of the **International Court of Justice,** pressured for a self-determination referendum to determine the wishes of the inhabitants of the territory. Shortly after, Mauritania withdrew its claim in favor of the Polisario, who were also supported by Algeria. The Organization of African Unity (OAU) took up the issue but was badly split. The UN **Secretary-General** and the Chairman of the OAU in 1988 persuaded Morocco and the Polisario to adopt a peace plan, including a cease-fire and a self-determination referendum, with assistance from UN observers and security units. Since 1988 the **Security Council** has urged implementing the terms of the peace plan, but the disputing parties cannot agree on many details. In 1990 the Security Council created a UN **peacekeeping** force, the UN Mission for the Referendum in Western Sahara (MINURSO). The eventual strength was authorized as 2,900, with the task of monitoring the cease-fire, the referendum, and the post-referendum establishment of a government. Because of continued stalemate over voting rules and eligibility, a force of only 500 had been dispatched by 1994 to serve only as cease-fire monitors.

WILSON, WOODROW (1856–1924). U.S. President (1913–21) who led the movement to establish the **League of Nations,** the forerunner of the United Nations. President Wilson chaired the Commission at the Paris Peace Conference in 1919 which produced the final draft of the Covenant of the League. It is ironic that the United States was the only major country that never joined the League. An anti-League Senate minority crafted 14 reservations to the Covenant which were opposed by President Wilson. Wilson made a 22-day tour of the country, appealing for support for an unencumbered Covenant. At the end of his tour Wilson's health broke and he was incapable of presidential leadership for the remainder of his term in office. Although a majority of the Senate and of U.S. public opinion favored U.S. membership in the League, the Senate failed to produce a two-thirds majority to approve the treaty, with the reservations attached. Some of the negative votes were cast by supporters of the Wilson position on the reservations. (See also LEAGUE OF NATIONS.)

WOMEN. There are five references to equal rights of the sexes in the **Charter of the United Nations.** The **Economic and Social Council** early established a **Commission on the Status of Women** as the principal body to promote women's rights. The **International Labour Organisation** has produced several treaties safeguarding the health and safety of women workers. In 1979 a Convention on the Elimination of

All Forms of Discrimination Against Women was approved by the UN **General Assembly** and opened for ratification, and it has been adopted by more than 100 states. The first global intergovernmental conference on women's issues was held in Mexico City in 1975, and the General Assembly declared the period 1976–85 as the United Nations Decade for Women. Subsequent world conferences were held in Copenhagen in 1980 and Nairobi in 1985, with another planned for Beijing in 1995. The Nairobi Conference was attended by 2,000 delegates from 157 countries, and a parallel forum of 13,500 **nongovernmental organization** representatives conducted hundreds of workshops on women's issues. The conference also laid out a 15-year plan called the Forward-Looking Strategies to Improve the Status of Women.

Several conferences on development have stressed the importance of women's contributions to social and economic development activities. Since 1979 the **International Research and Training Institute for the Advancement of Women (INSTRAW),** with headquarters in Santo Domingo, and supported by voluntary contributions, has carried on projects to promote the role of women in development. Another program, also supported by voluntary contributions, the United Nations Development Fund for Women (UNIFEM), supplies modest allocations for projects providing women's access to credit and training in developing countries. In spite of all these emphases and activities, women are far from achieving equal economic and social rights and status in most societies. (See also COMMISSION ON THE STATUS OF WOMEN; CONFERENCE TO REVIEW THE ACHIEVEMENTS OF THE UNITED NATIONS DECADE FOR WOMEN; INTERNATIONAL RESEARCH AND TRAINING INSTITUTE FOR THE ADVANCEMENT OF WOMEN.)

WORLD BANK *see* INTERNATIONAL BANK FOR RECONSTRUCTION AND DEVELOPMENT

WORLD CONFERENCE ON HUMAN RIGHTS. In June 1993 this Conference was convened in **Vienna.** It was attended by representatives of most countries, including 70 Foreign

Ministers and 11 Heads of State or Government. The final document was the Vienna Declaration and Programme of Action for Human Rights. Among the Declaration's recommendations was a proposal to establish a High Commissioner for Human Rights. The Conference also condemned "ethnic cleansing" and other acts of **genocide.** (See also HUMAN RIGHTS.)

WORLD CONFERENCE ON THE HUMAN ENVIRONMENT (1972) *see* ENVIRONMENT PROGRAMS OF THE UNITED NATIONS

WORLD FOOD CONFERENCE (1974). This two-week conference was convened in Rome at the instigation of the UN **General Assembly,** to focus on the multiple problems of the world food supply. Among its accomplishments were recommendations leading to the formation of the **International Fund for Agricultural Development (IFAD)** and the **World Food Council.** It adopted a Universal Declaration on the Eradication of Hunger and Malnutrition affirming the right of all human beings to be free of those evils and calling on the world community to provide aid, technology, and equitable food distribution to achieve these ends. The conference called for the expansion of agricultural production in developing countries by at least four percent annually, and urged that a food reserve be established to provide at least ten million tons of grain annually in food aid. It also recommended that the **Food and Agriculture Organization** set up a Global Information and Early Warning System on Food and Agriculture. (See also FOOD AND AGRICULTURE ORGANIZATION; INTERNATIONAL FUND FOR AGRICULTURAL DEVELOPMENT; WORLD FOOD COUNCIL; WORLD FOOD PROGRAMME.)

WORLD FOOD COUNCIL. This agency was created by the UN **General Assembly** as a result of a recommendation of the 1974 **World Food Conference.** It is a 36-member group at the ministerial level charged with reviewing and coordinating the work of all international agencies involved in global food problems. Thus, it is the highest-level UN policy body in food and agriculture matters. It normally meets annually and for many years has focused major attention on problems in sub-Saharan Africa. (See also FOOD AND AGRICULTURE ORGANIZATION; INTERNATIONAL FUND FOR AGRICULTURAL DEVELOPMENT; WORLD FOOD CONFERENCE; WORLD FOOD PROGRAMME.)

WORLD FOOD PROGRAMME. This program initiated by the UN **General Assembly** was started in 1963 as a joint undertaking of the United Nations and the **Food and Agriculture Organization.** It started with a fund of $100 million pledged by governments and recently has received more then $600 million per year in commodities, cash, and services. One of its unique aspects is its use of a food-for-work concept to improve nutrition among the rural poor. It engages in both **development** and emergency projects. In recent years its heaviest commitments have been in sub-Saharan Africa. (See also FOOD AND AGRICULTURE ORGANIZATION; INTERNATIONAL FUND FOR AGRICULTURAL DEVELOPMENT; WORLD FOOD CONFERENCE; WORLD FOOD COUNCIL.)

WORLD HEALTH ORGANIZATION (WHO). One of the 17 **specialized agencies** of the UN system of organizations. It is autonomous, with its own staff, headquarters, membership, and budget, and coordinates its activities with the **Economic and Social Council** of the United Nations. It started its operations in 1948 and its headquarters are in **Geneva.** In 1977 it adopted as its goal "Health for All by the Year 2000." By that date one of its subgoals is the immunization of 90 percent of the world's children against six major communicable diseases of childhood. It is also the leading agency in combatting malaria, smallpox, yaws, river-blindness (onchocerciasis), HIV, and **Acquired Immune Deficiency Syndrome (AIDS).** (See also Acquired Immune Deficiency Syndrome.)

WORLD INTELLECTUAL PROPERTY ORGANIZATION (WIPO). One of the 17 **specialized agencies** of the UN system. Prior to its formation similar purposes were provided for under the 1883 Paris Convention for the Protection of Industrial

Property and the 1886 Berne Convention for the Protection of Literary and Artistic Works. The Convention providing for WIPO was signed in 1967 and it became a UN specialized agency in December 1974. Its headquarters are in **Geneva.** WIPO's objectives are to maintain and increase respect for intellectual property and to facilitate creative activity, the transfer of technology, and the dissemination of literary and artistic works. It promotes the enforcement of rights established by patents, trademarks, copyrights, and related rights under laws and treaties, and encourages the wider acceptance of such standards.

WORLD METEOROLOGICAL ORGANIZATION (WMO). One of the 17 **specialized agencies** of the UN system of organizations. It is autonomous, with its own staff, headquarters, membership, and budget, and coordinates its activities with the **Economic and Social Council** of the United Nations. It began operating as a UN specialized organization in 1957. Its headquarters are in **Geneva.** WMO is the center for coordinating and developing meteorological information throughout the world. It operates a World Weather Watch and a World Climate Program. It is assisted by six regional associations and eight expert technical commissions organized around every important phase of meteorological research and information.

WORLD POPULATION CONFERENCES *see* POPULATION PROGRAMS OF THE UNITED NATIONS

WORLD TRADE ORGANIZATION *see* GENERAL AGREEMENT ON TARIFFS AND TRADE

-Y-

YALTA CONFERENCE (1945). This conference in February 1945 was the last conference attended by **Franklin D. Roosevelt, Winston Churchill,** and Stalin and their Foreign Ministers. Although there were several other matters pertaining to the war under discussion, three important decisions pertaining to the forthcoming United Nations organization were agreed upon. The first was the voting formula in the **Security Council;** the second was a concession to include membership of the Ukraine and Byelorussia in the new organization; and the third was an agreement to hold the conference for writing the **Charter of the United Nations** in **San Francisco** beginning on April 25. (See also SAN FRANCISCO CONFERENCE; SECURITY COUNCIL.)

YEMEN DISPUTE *see* UNITED NATIONS YEMEN OBSER-VATION MISSION (UNYOM)

YOUTH. A substantial number of UN agencies have given attention to problems of young people. These include the **General Assembly,** the **Economic and Social Council,** the Commission for Social Development, UNICEF, UNESCO, WHO, ILO, and FAO. The General Assembly denoted 1985 as International Youth Year. Special attention has been focused on physical abuse, neglect, unemployment, poverty, drug abuse, juvenile delinquency, and illiteracy among young people.

YUGOSLAVIA. In 1991–92 the former Yugoslavia broke into several new states. Serbia and Montenegro formed the Federal Republic of Yugoslavia, and Croatia, Slovenia, Bosnia-Herzegovina, and the former Yugoslav Republic of Macedonia declared their independence and were admitted to United Nations **membership** in 1992–93. A civil war broke out in which Serbs, Croatians, and Bosnians were involved and a rebel Bosnian Serb army occupied 70 percent of Bosnia-Herzegovina. The **Security Council,** beginning in 1991, held numerous sessions and adopted dozens of resolutions on the situation. The **Secretary-General** dispatched a personal representative to the area and personally visited Sarajevo. The Security Council authorized a United Nations Protection Force in Yugoslavia (UNPROFOR) and gradually expanded its size to 27,000 military and civilian personnel. Several **sanctions** were imposed on the Federal Republic of Yugoslavia, overflights by Serbian planes over Bosnian territory were prohibited, and five Bosnian cities were declared to be safe havens. By mid-1994 more than 200,000 civilians had been killed and there were millions of **refugees.** The UN High Commissioner for Refugees was heavily involved in coordinating humanitarian aid. Because of extensive and severe **human rights** violations the Security Council and the **General Assembly** set up an 11-member International Tribunal to try war criminals for serious violations of humanitarian law. No permanent peace settlement is in immediate prospect.

-Z-

ZAIRE *see* CONGO OPERATION

ZIMBABWE. The British claimed this area as a colony after 1923, first under the title Southern Rhodesia and later simply Rhodesia. Since Britain had granted internal self-rule, it refused to report to the United Nations on its administration of the territory. However, when the white minority government of Ian Smith declared independence in 1965, the British urged the United Nations to impose **sanctions** against the Smith regime. In 1966 the **Security Council** declared partial sanctions and in 1968 enlarged them to comprehensive sanctions. These measures were only partially successful because of the non-cooperation of South Africa and Portugal. After years of internal conflict, the British finally helped negotiate a settlement establishing black majority rule. The territory was recognized as the independent state of Zimbabwe and became a UN member in 1980.

BIBLIOGRAPHY

Any bibliography for a single volume dealing with the United Nations must be selective. The United Nations annually publishes thousands of documents in addition to other reports and publications of a more general nature. All of the 17 specialized agencies also publish voluminous documents, studies, and other publications. Official and privately published indexes and guides may be used for detailed scholarly research into the plethora of subjects relating to the United Nations. The *United Nations Documents Index* covers the official documentation of both the United Nations and its specialized agencies.

Official Publications

"Annual Report of the Secretary-General on the Work of the United Nations."

Everyman's United Nations (8th ed.), 1968. Handbook of activities of the United Nations, 1945–65.

Everyman's United Nations—Supplement, 1971. Summary of activities of the United Nations, 1966–70.

Everyone's United Nations (9th ed.), 1979. Highlighting the UN activities of 1966–77.

Everyone's United Nations (10th ed.), 1986. Covers 40 years of UN activity with special focus on 1978–85.

Repertory of Practice of United Nations Organs.

United Nations Demographic Yearbook.

United Nations Documents Index.

United Nations Statistical Yearbook.

United Nations Treaty Series.

Yearbook of the United Nations.

Documents of the United Nations Conference on International Organization, 22 vols., is the official record of the conference in San Francisco in 1945 which drafted the United Nations Charter. Volumes 1–16 were published in London and New York in 1945–46 by the United Nations Information Organizations. The remaining volumes were published in New York by the United Nations in 1954–55.

The United Nations has published a valuable series of periodicals as follows:

United Nations Bulletin (August 1946–June 1954). First weekly, then twice monthly.

United Nations Review (July 1954–April 1964). Monthly.

United Nations Chronicle (May 1964–present). Monthly through February 1986, then quarterly.

Other Basic General Sources

Annual Review of United Nations Affairs, annual volumes. Dobbs Ferry, New York: Oceana Publications, Inc.

Britain and the United Nations. London: Great Britain, Central Office of Information, 1964.

Commission to Study the Organization of Peace. *Building Peace: Reports of the Commission to Study the Organization of Peace, 1939–72.* Metuchen, NJ: Scarecrow Press, 1973.

Goodrich, Leland M., Edvard Hambro, and Anne P. Simons. *United Nations Charter: Commentary and Documents* (3rd ed.). New York: Columbia University Press, 1969.

Greenfield, Stanley R., ed. *Who's Who in the United Nations and Related Agencies* (2nd ed.). Detroit: Omnigraphics, Inc., 1992.

Issues Before the General Assembly of the United Nations. Annual volumes. New York: United Nations Association of the United States of America.

OsmańczykЕdmund J. *The Encyclopedia of the United Nations and International Relations* (2nd ed.). New York: Taylor and Francis, 1990.

Patil, Anjali V. *The UN Veto in World Affairs, 1946–1990.* Sarasota, FL: UNIFO Publishers, 1992.

Worldmark Encyclopedia of the Nations, 1, The United Nations (7th ed.). New York: John Wiley & Sons, Inc., 1988.

Yearbook of International Organizations, published biennially. Brussels: Union of International Associations.

Reference Works

Baratta, Joseph Preston. *United Nations System.* Oxford: Clio Press, 1994.

Fetzer, Mary K. *United Nations Documents and Publications: A Research Guide.* New Brunswick, NJ: Graduate School of Library Service, Rutgers—The State University of New Jersey, 1978.

Hajnal, Peter I. *Guide to United Nations Organization, Documentation and Publishing for Students, Researchers, Librarians.* Dobbs Ferry, NY: Oceana Publications, 1978.

Marulli, Luciana. *Documentation of the United Nations System: Co-ordination in Its Bibliographic Control.* Metuchen, NJ: Scarecrow Press, 1979.

United Nations. *The Complete Reference Guide to United Nations Sales Publications, 1946–1978.* Pleasantville, NY: UNIFO Publishers, 1982.

United Nations Library (Geneva, Switzerland). *The United Nations Library at Geneva: Collections and Reader's Services.* Geneva, Switzerland: United Nations Library, 1990.

Winton, Harry N. M. *Publications of the United Nations System: A Reference Guide.* New York: R. R. Bowker Co., 1972.

Background

Armstrong, Hamilton Fish. *The Calculated Risk.* New York: Macmillan Co., 1947.

Bonnet, Henri. *The United Nations on the Way: Principles and Policies.* Chicago: World Citizens Association, 1942.

Cecil, Lord Robert. *A Great Experiment.* New York: Oxford University Press, 1939.

Claude, Inis L., Jr. *The Changing United Nations.* New York: Random House, 1967.

Eagleton, Clyde. "The Charter Adopted at San Francisco," *American Political Science Review,* 39 (October 1945), 934–42.

Eichelberger, Clark Mell. *Organizing for Peace: A Personal History of the Founding of the United Nations.* New York: Harper & Row, 1977.

Goodrich, Leland M. "From League of Nations to United Nations," *International Organization,* 1 (February 1947), 3–21.

Hilderbrand, Robert C. *Dumbarton Oaks: The Origins of the*

United Nations and the Search for Postwar Security. Chapel Hill: University of North Carolina Press, 1990.

Hovet, Thomas. *A Chronology and Fact Book of the United Nations, 1941–1985.* Dobbs Ferry, NY: Oceana Publications, 1986.

League of Nations. *The Development of International Cooperation in Economic and Social Affairs.* Geneva: League Secretariat, August 1939.

Luard, Evan. *A History of the United Nations,* Vol. I, *The Years of Western Domination, 1945–1955.* New York: St. Martin's Press, 1982.

Mangone, Gerard J. *A Short History of International Organization.* New York: McGraw-Hill, 1954.

Miller, David Hunter. *The Drafting of the Covenant.* 2 vols. New York: Putnam, 1928.

Nicholas, H. G. *The United Nations as a Political Institution* (4th ed.). New York: Oxford University Press, 1971.

Northledge, F. S. *The League of Nations: Its Life and Times 1920–1946.* New York: Holmes & Meier, 1986.

Preparatory Commission of the United Nations Report. London: 1945.

''Report to the President on the Results of the San Francisco Conference. . . .'' Department of State Publication 2349, Conference Series 71. Washington, DC: Government Printing Office, 1945.

Romulo, Carlos Pena. *Forty Years: A Third World Soldier at the UN.* Westport, CT: Greenwood Press, 1986.

Russell, Ruth B., and Jeanette E. Muther. *A History of the United*

Nations Charter: The Role of the United States, 1940–1945. Washington, DC: Brookings Institution, 1958.

Walters, F. P. *A History of the League of Nations*. 2 vols. New York: Oxford University Press, 1952.

Structure of the UN

Alker, Hayward R., Jr., and Bruce M. Russet. *World Politics in the General Assembly*. New Haven, CT: Yale University Press, 1965.

Bailey, Sydney D. *The General Assembly of the United Nations: A Study of Procedure and Practice*. Westport, CT: Greenwood Press, 1978.

————. *The Procedure of the UN Security Council*. New York: Oxford University Press, 1988.

————. *The United Nations: A Short Political Guide*. Basingstoke, Hampshire, England: Macmillan, 1989.

————. *Voting in the Security Council*. Bloomington: Indiana University Press, 1969.

Beckel, Graham. *Workshops for the World: The Specialized Agencies of the United Nations*. New York: Abelard-Schuman, 1954.

Chiang, Pei-heng. *Non-governmental Organizations at the United Nations: Identity, Role, and Function*. New York: Praeger, 1981.

Dormael, Armand van. *Bretton Woods: Birth of a Monetary System*. New York: Holmes & Meier, 1978.

Hadwen, John G. *How United Nations Decisions Are Made*. New York: Oceana Publications, 1962.

Junn, Robert S. "Voting in the United Nations Security Council," *International Interactions,* 9, no. 4 (1983), 315–52.

Kaufmann, Johan. *United Nations Decision Making.* Alphen aan den Rijn, Netherlands: Sijthoff & Noordhoff, 1980.

Keohane, Robert O. "Political Influence in the General Assembly," *International Conciliation,* no. 557 (March 1966).

Luard, Evan. *The United Nations: How It Works and What It Does.* New York: St. Martin's Press, 1994.

Meron, Theodor. *The United Nations Secretariat: The Rules and the Practice.* Lexington, MA: Lexington Books, 1977.

Newcombe, Hanna, Michael Ross, and Alan G. Newcombe. "United Nations Voting Patterns," *International Organization,* 24 (Winter 1970), 100–21.

Nicholas, H. G. *The United Nations as a Political Institution.* London, New York: Oxford University Press, 1971.

Pitt, David, and Thomas G. Weiss, eds. *The Nature of United Nations Bureaucracies.* London: Croom Helm, 1986.

"The Problem of the Veto in the United Nations Security Council." Staff Study No. 1, Subcommittee on the United Nations Charter, Committee on Foreign Relations, United States Senate, 83rd Congress, 2nd Session. Washington, DC: Government Printing Office, 1954.

"Representation and Voting in the United Nations General Assembly." Staff Study No. 4, Subcommittee on the United Nations Charter, Committee on Foreign Relations, United States Senate, 83rd Congress, 2nd Session. Washington, DC: Government Printing Office, 1954.

Russell, Ruth B. *The General Assembly: Patterns/Problems/*

Prospects. New York: Carnegie Endowment for International Peace, 1970.

Stoessinger, John G. *The United Nations and the Superpowers* (4th ed.). New York: Random House, 1977.

Townley, Ralph. *The United Nations: A View from Within.* New York: Scribner, 1968.

Vincent, Jack Ernest. *Support Patterns at the United Nations.* Lanham, MD: University Press of America, 1991.

Yoder, Amos. *The Evolution of the United Nations System.* Washington, DC: Taylor & Francis, 1993.

Membership Issues

Bachrack, Stanley D. *The Committee of One Million: "China Lobby" Politics, 1953–1971.* New York: Columbia University Press, 1976.

Gunter, Michael M. "What Happened to the United Nations Ministate Problem?" *American Journal of International Law,* 71 (January 1977), 110–24.

Jackson, Richard L. *The Non-aligned, the UN, and the Superpowers.* New York: Praeger, 1983.

Kay, David A. "The Impact of the African States on the United Nations," *International Organization,* 23 (Winter 1969), 20–47.

————. *The New Nations in the United Nations, 1960–1967.* New York: Columbia University Press, 1970.

Nyangoni, Wellington Winter. *Africa in the United Nations System.* Rutherford, NJ: Fairleigh Dickinson University Press, 1985.

"The Problem of Membership in the United Nations." Staff Study No. 3, Subcommittee on the United Nations Charter, Committee on Foreign Relations, United States Senate, 83rd Congress, 2nd Session. Washington, DC: Government Printing Office, 1954.

Rajan, M.S., V. S. Mani, and C. S. R. Marthy, eds. *The Nonaligned and the United Nations*. New Delhi: South Asian Publishers, 1987.

Peace and Security Activities

Abi-Saab, Georges. *The United Nations Operation in the Congo, 1960–1964*. Oxford, New York: Oxford University Press, 1978.

Alker, Hayward R. *World Politics in the General Assembly*. New Haven, CT: Yale University Press, 1965.

Allsebrook, Mary. *Prototypes of Peacemaking: The First Forty Years of the United Nations*. Harlow, Essex, England: Longman, 1986.

Bailey, Sydney D. *How Wars End: The United Nations and the Termination of Armed Conflict, 1946–1964*. Oxford: Clarendon Press; New York: Oxford University Press, 1982.

Baranyi, Stephen. *Stretching the Limits of the Possible: United Nations Peacemaking in Central America*. Ottawa: Canadian Centre for Global Security—Centre canadien pour la sécurité mondiale, 1992.

Boyd, Andrew. *Fifteen Men on a Powder Keg: A History of the United Nations Security Council*. New York: Stein and Day, 1971.

Boyd, James M. *United Nations Peace-Keeping Operations:*

A Military and Political Appraisal. New York: Praeger, 1971.

Burns, Arthur Lee. *Peace-Keeping by UN Forces.* Westport, CT: Greenwood Press, 1975.

Claude, Inis L., Jr. "The OAS, the UN, and the United States," *International Conciliation,* no. 547 (March 1964).

Damrosch, Lori F., ed. *Enforcing Restraint: Collective Intervention in Internal Conflicts.* New York: Council on Foreign Relations Press, 1993.

Diehl, Paul F. *International Peacekeeping.* Baltimore, MD: Johns Hopkins University Press, 1993.

Durch, William J., ed. *The Evolution of UN Peacekeeping: Case Studies and Comparative Analysis.* New York: St. Martin's Press, 1993.

Fabian, Larry L. *Soldiers Without Enemies: Preparing the United Nations for Peacekeeping.* Washington, DC: Brookings Institution, 1971.

Falk, Richard A., and Cyril E. Black, eds. *The Future of the International Legal Order,* Vol. III, *Conflict Management.* Princeton, NJ: Princeton University Press, 1971.

Finger, Seymour M. "The Maintenance of Peace," *Proceedings of the Academy of Political Science.* 32, no. 4 (1977), 195–205.

Finkelstein, Marina S., and Lawrence S. Finkelstein, eds. *Collective Security.* San Francisco: Chandler Publishing, 1966.

Forsythe, David P. *United Nations Peacemaking: The Conciliation Commission for Palestine.* Baltimore, MD: Johns Hopkins University Press, 1972.

Franck, Thomas M. *Nation Against Nation: What Happened to*

the UN Dream and What the U.S. Can Do About It. New York: Oxford University Press, 1985.

Goodrich, Leland M. *Korea: A Study of the U.S. Policy in the United Nations.* New York: Council on Foreign Relations, 1956.

————, and Anne P. Simons. *The United Nations and the Maintenance of International Peace and Security.* Washington, DC: The Brookings Institution, 1955.

Haas, Ernest B. *Collective Security and the Future International System.* Denver, CO: University of Denver Press, 1968.

————. *Why We Still Need the United Nations: The Collective Management of International Conflict, 1945–1984.* Berkeley, CA: Institute of International Studies, University of California, 1986.

Halderman, John W. *The Political Role of the United Nations: Advancing the World Community.* New York: Praeger, 1981.

Harrelson, Max. *Fires All Around the Horizon: The UN's Battle to Preserve the Peace.* New York: Praeger, 1989.

Haviland, Henry Field. *The Political Role of the General Assembly.* Westport, CT: Greenwood Press, 1978.

Higgins, Rosalyn. *United Nations Peacekeeping Documents and Commentary.* London: Oxford University Press, 1981.

Hume, Cameron R. *The United Nations, Iran, and Iraq: How Peacemaking Changed.* Bloomington: Indiana University Press, 1994.

James, Alan. *The Politics of Peace-Keeping.* Published for The Institute for Strategic Studies. New York: Praeger, 1969.

Johnstone, Ian. *Aftermath of the Gulf War: An Assessment of UN Action.* Boulder, CO: Lynne Rienner Publishers, 1994.

Lall, Arthur S. *The UN and the Middle East Crisis, 1967.* New York: Columbia University Press, 1968.

Lefever, Ernest W. *Crisis in the Congo: A United Nations Force in Action.* Washington, DC: Brookings Institution, 1965.

————. *Uncertain Mandate: Politics of the UN Congo Operation.* Baltimore, MD: Johns Hopkins Press, 1967.

Liu, F. T. *United Nations Peacekeeping and the Non-use of Force.* Boulder, CO: Lynne Rienner Publishers, 1992.

Mackinlay, John. *The Peacekeepers: An Assessment of Peacekeeping Operations at the Arab-Israel Interface.* London: Unwin Hyman, 1989.

Malek, Mohammed H., ed. *International Mediation and the Gulf War.* Glasgow, Scotland: Royston House, 1991.

Miller, Linda B. *World Order and Local Disorder: The United Nations and Internal Conflicts.* Princeton, NJ: Published for the Center of International Studies, Princeton University by Princeton University Press, 1967.

Misra, Kashi Prasad. *The Role of the United Nations in the Indo-Pakistani Conflict, 1971.* Delhi: Vikas Publishing House, 1973.

Mitchell, C. R. *Peacemaking and the Consultant's Role.* New York: Nichols Publishing Co., 1981.

Moskos, Charles C. *Peace Soldiers: The Sociology of a United Nations Military Force.* Chicago: University of Chicago Press, 1976.

Murphy, John F. *The United Nations and the Control of International Violence: A Legal and Political Analysis.* Totowa, NJ: Allanheld, Osmun Publishers, 1982.

Nachmani, Amikam. *International Intervention in the Greek Civil*

War: The United Nations Special Committee on the Balkans, 1947–1952. New York: Praeger, 1990.

Naidu, Mumulla V. R. *Collective Security and the United Nations: A Definition of the UN Security System.* New York: St. Martin's Press, 1975.

"Pacific Settlement of Disputes in the United Nations." Staff Study No. 5, Subcommittee on the United Nations Charter, Committee on Foreign Relations, United States Senate, 83rd Congress, 2nd Session. Washington, DC: Government Printing Office, 1954.

Pearson, Lester B. *The Four Faces of Peace and the International Outlook.* Toronto: McClelland and Stewart Ltd., 1964.

Pelcovits, Nathan A. *Peacekeeping on Arab-Israeli Fronts: Lessons from the Sinai and Lebanaon.* Boulder, CO: Westview Press with the Foreign Policy Institute, School of Advanced International Studies, Johns Hopkins University, 1984.

Peterson, M. J. *The General Assembly in World Politics.* Boston: Allen & Unwin, 1986.

Pogany, Istvan. *The Security Council and the Arab-Israeli Conflict.* Aldershot, Hants, England: Gower, 1984.

Rikhye, Indar Jit. *Military Adviser to the Secretary-General: UN Peacekeeping and the Congo Crisis.* New York: St. Martin's Press, 1993.

———. *The Theory and Practice of Peacekeeping.* London: C. Hurst and Co., 1984.

———. *The Thin Blue Line: International Peacekeeping and Its Future.* New Haven, CT: Yale University Press, 1974.

Siekmann, Robert C. R., ed. *Basic Documents on United Nations and Related Peace-Keeping Forces.* Dordrecht: Nijhoff, 1989.

———. *National Contingents in United Nations Peace-Keeping Forces*. Dordrecht: Nijhoff, 1991.

Skogmo, Bjorn. *UNIFIL: International Peacekeeping in Lebanon, 1978–1988*. Boulder, CO: Lynne Rienner Publishers, 1989.

Stegenga, James A. *The United Nations Force in Cyprus*. Columbus: Ohio State University Press, 1968.

Stone, Julius. *Conflict Through Consensus: United Nations Approaches to Aggression*. Baltimore: Johns Hopkins University Press, 1977.

The United Nations and the Iran-Iraq War: A Ford Foundation Conference Report. New York: Ford Foundation, 1987.

United Nations Department of Public Information. *The Blue Helmets: A Review of United Nations Peace-Keeping* (2nd ed.). New York: United Nations, 1990.

United Nations Institute for Training and Research. *The United Nations and the Maintenance of International Peace and Security*. Dordrecht: Nijhoff, 1987.

Verrier, Anthony. *International Peacekeeping: United Nations Forces in a Troubled World*. New York: Penguin, 1981.

Waldheim, Kurt. *Building the Future Order: The Search for Peace in an Interdependent World*. New York: Free Press: 1980.

Weiss, Thomas G., ed. *Collective Security in a Changing World*. Boulder, CO: Lynne Rienner Publishers, 1993.

White, N.D. *Keeping the Peace: The United Nations and the Maintenance of International Peace and Security*. New York: Manchester University Press, 1993.

Zeidan, Abdel-Latif M. *The United Nations Emergency Force,*

1956–1967. Stockholm: Almqvist & Wiksell International, 1976.

Arms Control and Disarmament

Arms Control: Issues for the Public. Published for The American Assembly. Englewood Cliffs, NJ: Prentice-Hall, 1961.

Art, Robert J., and Kenneth N. Waltz, eds. *The Use of Force: International Politics and Foreign Policy.* Boston: Little, Brown, 1971.

Bargman, Abraham. "Nuclear Diplomacy," *Proceedings of the Academy of Political Science,* 32, no. 4 (1977), 159–69.

Beker, Avi. *Disarmament Without Order: The Politics of Disarmament at the United Nations.* Westport, CT: Greenwood Press, 1985.

Bloomfield, Beth. "Strategic Arms Limitation," *Proceedings of the Academy of Political Science,* 32, no. 4 (1977), 184–94.

Bourantonis, Dimitris. *The United Nations and the Quest for Nuclear Disarmament.* Aldershot, Hants, England: Dartmouth Publishing Co.; Brookfield, VT: Gower Publishing Co., 1993.

"Chemical and Bacteriological (Biological) Weapons and the Effects of Their Possible Use." Report of the Secretary-General, United Nations. New York: United Nations, 1969.

"Economic and Social Consequences of the Arms Race and of Military Expenditures." Report of the Secretary-General, UN Document A/8469/Rev. 1. New York: United Nations, 1972.

Falk, Richard A., and Saul H. Mendlovitz, eds. *The Strategy of World Order,* Vol. IV, *Disarmament and Economic Development.* New York: World Law Fund, 1966.

Frei, Daniel. *Perceived Images: U.S. and Soviet Assumptions and Perceptions in Disarmament.* Lanham, MD: Rowman & Allanheld, 1986.

Sivard, Ruth Leger. *World Military and Social Expenditures.* Washington, DC: World Priorities, Inc., 1993.

Slocombe, Walter. "Controlling Strategic Nuclear Weapons." Headline Series, no. 226. New York: Foreign Policy Association, June 1975.

United Nations, Department of Political and Security Council Affairs. *The United Nations and Disarmament, 1945–1970.* New York: United Nations, 1970.

————. *The United Nations and Disarmament, 1970–1975.* New York: United Nations, 1976.

Legal Activities

Boczek, Boleslaw A. *Historical Dictionary of International Tribunals.* Metuchen, NJ: Scarecrow Press, 1994.

Corbett, Percy E. *The Growth of World Law.* Princeton, NJ: Princeton University Press, 1971.

Falk, Richard A., and Cyril E. Black, eds. *The Future of the International Legal Order,* Vol. I, *Trends and Patterns.* Princeton, NJ: Princeton University Press, 1969.

Fischer, Dana D. "Decisions to Use the International Court of Justice," *International Studies Quarterly,* 26, no. 2 (June 1982), 251–77.

Franck, Thomas M. *Judging the World Court.* New York: Priority Press for Twentieth Century Fund, 1986.

Henkin, Louis. *How Nations Behave: Law and Foreign Policy.*

Published for the Council on Foreign Relations. New York: Praeger, 1970.

Higgins, Rosalyn. *The Development of International Law Through the Political Organs of the United Nations.* New York: Oxford University Press, 1963.

International Court of Justice Yearbook. The Hague: International Court of Justice.

International Organizations and Law. New York: Ford Foundation, 1990.

Jenks, C. Wilfred. *A New World of Law?* London: Longmans, Green, 1969.

Jessup, Philip C. *The Price of International Justice.* New York: Columbia University Press, 1971.

Lowe, Vaughn, and Colin Warbrick, eds. *The United Nations and the Principles of International Law: Essays in Memory of Michael Akehurst.* New York: Routledge, 1994.

McWhinney, Edward. *United Nations Law Making: Cultural and Ideological Relativism and International Law Making for an Era of Transition.* New York: Holmes & Meier, 1984.

Ramcharan, B. G. *The International Law Commission: Its Approach to the Codification and Progressive Development of International Law.* The Hague: Nijhoff, 1977.

Sanger, Clyde. *Ordering the Oceans: The Making of the Law of the Sea.* Toronto, Ontario: University of Toronto Press, 1987.

Sebenius, James K. *Negotiating the Law of the Sea.* Cambridge, MA: Harvard University Press, 1984.

Swing, John Temple. ''The Law of the Sea,'' *Proceedings of the Academy of Political Science,* 32, no. 4 (1977), 128–41.

Weiss, Mildred. "The Lawless Depths: The Need for an International Oceans Regime," In *The U.S. and the Developing World: Agenda for Action 1974.* Published for the Overseas Development Council. New York: Praeger, 1974.

Economic and Social Development

Adesishiah, Malcolm S., ed. *Forty Years of Economic Development: UN Agencies and India.* New Delhi: Lancer International in association with India International Centre, 1987.

Ansari, Javed. *The Political Economy of International Economic Organization.* Boulder, CO: Lynne Rienner Publishers, 1986.

Brown, Barbara Jean. *Disaster Preparedness and the United Nations: Advance Planning for Disaster Relief.* Elmsford, NY: Published for UNITAR by Pergamon Press, 1979.

Brown, Lester R. "The Interdependence of Nations." Headline Series, no. 212. New York: Foreign Policy Association, October 1972.

———. "The Social Impact of the Green Revolution," *International Conciliation,* no. 581 (January 1971).

———, and Associates. *State of the World.* Annual volumes. New York: W. W. Norton.

Buehrig, Edward. *The UN and the Palestinian Refugees: A Study in Nonterritorial Administration.* Bloomington: Indiana University Press, 1971.

Feld, Werner J. *Multinational Corporations and UN Politics: The Quest for Codes of Conduct.* New York: Pergamon Press, 1980.

Ferguson, C. Clyde, Jr. "The Politics of the New International

Economic Order," *Proceedings of the Academy of Political Science*, 32, no. 4 (1977), 142–58.

Finlayson, Jock A., and Mark W. Zacher. *Managing International Markets: Developing Countries and the Commodity Trade Regime.* New York: Columbia University Press, 1988.

Forsythe, David P., ed. *The United Nations in the World Political Economy: Essays in Honour of Leon Gordenker.* New York: St. Martin's Press, 1989.

"The Global Partnership for Environment and Development." New York: United Nations, 1992.

The Global 2000 Report to the President: Entering the Twenty-First Century, 3 vols. Washington, DC: U.S. Government Printing Office, 1980.

Gregg, Robert W. "UN Economic, Social, and Technical Activities," In *The United Nations, Past, Present, and Future,* ed. James Barros. New York: Free Press, 1972.

Haas, Peter M. *International Environmental Issues: An ACUNS Teaching Text.* Hanover, NH: Academic Council on the United Nations System, 1991.

Hill, Martin. *The United Nations System: Coordinating Its Economic and Social Work.* Cambridge, England: Cambridge University Press, 1978.

Hollick, Ann L., and Robert E. Osgood. *New Era of Ocean Politics.* Baltimore, MD: Johns Hopkins University Press, 1974.

"The International Development Strategy: First Over-all Review and Appraisal of Issues and Policies." Report of the Secretary-General. New York: United Nations, 1973.

"International Development Strategy: For the Third United Nations Development Decade." New York: United Nations, 1981.

Johnson, Stanley. *World Population and the United Nations: Challenge and Response.* Cambridge, England: Cambridge University Press, 1987.

Leonard, William Ramsdell. *UN Development Aid: Criteria and Methods of Evaluation.* New York: Arno Press, 1971.

Logue, John J., ed. *The Fate of the Oceans.* Villanova, PA: Villanova University Press, 1972.

Mangone, Gerard J. *UN Administration of Economic and Social Programs.* New York: Columbia University Press, 1966.

Menon, B. P. *Bridges Across the South: Technical Cooperation Among Developing Countries.* New York: Pergamon Press, 1980.

North–South: A Programme for Survival. London: Pan Books, Ltd., 1980.

Perspectives on Multilateral Assistance: A Review by the Nordic UN Project. Stockholm, Sweden: Nordic UN Project, 1990.

Pregel, Boris, Harold D. Lasswell, and John McHale, eds. *World Priorities.* New Brunswick, NJ: Transaction Books, 1977.

Rogers, Adam. *The Earth Summit: A Planetary Reckoning.* Los Angeles, CA: Global View Press, 1993.

Schachter, Oscar. *Sharing the World's Resources.* New York: Columbia University Press, 1977.

Sen, Sudhir. *United Nations in Economic Development—Need for a New Strategy.* Dobbs Ferry, NY: Oceana Publications, 1969.

Spero, Joan E. *The Politics of International Economic Relations* (4th ed.). New York: St. Martin's Press, 1990.

Symonds, Richard, ed. *International Targets for Development.* New York: Harper & Row, 1970.

"Towards Accelerated Development: Proposals for the Second United Nations Development Decade." Report of the Committee for Development Planning. New York: United Nations, 1970.

The United Nations in Development. Final Report of the Nordic UN Project. Stockholm: Almqvist & Wiksell International, 1991.

Walls, James. *Land, Man, and Sand: Desertification and Its Solution.* New York: Macmillan Publishing Co., 1980.

Human Rights Activities

Anderson, Mary B. *Focusing on Women: UNIFEM's Experience in Mainstreaming.* New York: UNIFEM, 1993.

Forsythe, David P. *Human Rights and World Politics.* Lincoln: University of Nebraska Press, 1983.

———. "The United Nations and Human Rights: 1945–1985," *Political Science Quarterly,* 100 (Summer 1985), 249–70.

Henkin, Louis. "The Internationalization of Human Rights," *Human Rights: A Symposium.* Columbia University, Proceedings of the General Education Seminar, 6, no. 1 (1977), 5–16.

Kardam, Nuket. *Bringing Women in: Women's Issues in International Development Programs.* Boulder, CO: Lynne Rienner Publishers, 1991.

Kommers, Donald P., and Gilbert D. Loescher, eds. *Human Rights and American Foreign Policy.* Notre Dame, IN: University of Notre Dame Press, 1979.

Korey, William. "The Key to Human Rights—Implementation," *International Conciliation,* no. 570 (November 1968).

Meron, Theodor. *Human Rights Law-Making in the United Nations: A Critique of Instruments and Process.* New York: Oxford University Press, 1986.

Nickel, James W. *Making Sense of Human Rights: Philosophical Reflections on the Universal Declaration of Human Rights.* Berkeley: University of California Press, 1987.

Ozgur, Ozdemir A. *Apartheid, the United Nations & Peaceful Change in South Africa.* Dobbs Ferry, NY: Transnational Publishers, 1982.

Pietila, Hilkka. *Making Women Matter: The Role of the United Nations.* Atlantic Highlands, NJ: Zed Books, 1990.

Tolley, Howard. *The UN Commission on Human Rights.* Boulder, CO: Westview Press, 1987.

United States. Congress. House. Committee on Foreign Affairs. Subcommittee on International Organizations and Movements. "Human Rights in the World Community: A Call for U.S. Leadership; Report." Washington, DC: U.S. Government Printing Office, 1974.

Van Dyke, Vernon. *Human Rights, the United States, and World Community.* New York: Oxford University Press, 1970.

Independence and Self-Government

Allen, Philip M. "Self-Determination in the Western Indian Ocean," *International Conciliation,* no. 560 (November 1966).

Chowdhuri, R. N. *International Mandates and Trusteeship Systems: A Comparative Study.* The Hague: Nijhoff, 1955.

El-Ayouty, Yassin. *The United Nations and Decolonization: The Role of Afro-Asia.* The Hague: Nijhoff, 1971.

Emerson, Rupert. "Colonialism, Political Development, and the UN," *International Organization,* 19 (Summer 1965), 484–503.

————. *From Empire to Nation: The Rise to Self-Assertion of Asian and African Peoples.* Cambridge, MA: Harvard University Press, 1960.

Jessup, Philip C. *The Birth of Nations.* New York: Columbia University Press, 1974.

Kay, David A. "The United Nations and Decolonization," In *The United Nations: Past, Present, and Future,* ed. James Barros. New York: Free Press, 1972.

McHenry, Donald F. *Micronesia: Trust Betrayed.* Washington, DC: Carnegie Endowment for International Peace, 1975.

Murray, James N., Jr. *The United Nations Trusteeship System.* Illinois Studies in the Social Sciences, 40. Urbana: University of Illinois Press, 1957.

Pelt, Adrian. *Libyan Independence and the United Nations: A Case of Planned Decolonization.* New Haven: Published for the Carnegie Endowment for International Peace by Yale University Press, 1970.

Sears, Mason. *Years of High Purpose: From Trusteeship to Nationhood.* Washington, DC: University Press of America, 1980.

Singham, A. W. *Namibian Independence—A Global Responsibility.* Westport, CT: L. Hill, 1986.

Taylor, Alastair MacDonald. *Indonesian Independence and the United Nations.* Ithaca, NY: Cornell University Press, 1960.

UN Leadership and the Secretary-General

Bailey, Sydney D. *The Secretariat of the United Nations.* New York: Carnegie Endowment for International Peace, 1962.

Barros, James. *Trygve Lie and the Cold War: The UN Secretary-General Pursues Peace, 1946–1953.* DeKalb, IL: Northern Illinois University Press, 1989.

Berridge, G. R., and A. Jennings, eds. *Diplomacy at the UN.* New York: St. Martin's Press, 1985.

Boudreau, Tom. *Sheathing the Sword: The UN Secretary-General and the Prevention of International Conflict.* New York: Greenwood Press, 1991.

Claude, Inis L. "Reflections on the Role of the Secretary-General of the United Nations." New York: Ralph Bunche Institute on the United Nations, Occasional Paper Series, 1991.

Cordier, Andrew, comp. *Public Papers of the Secretaries-General of the United Nations.* New York: Columbia University Press, 1969–77.

————, ed. *The Quest for Peace: The Dag Hammarskjöld Memorial Lectures.* New York: Columbia University Press, 1965.

Dayal, Rajeshwar. *Mission for Hammarskjöld: The Congo Crisis.* Princeton, NJ: Princeton University Press, 1976.

Finger, Seymour Maxwell. *American Ambassadors at the UN: People, Politics, and Bureaucracy in Making Foreign Policy.* New York: Holmes & Meier, 1988.

————. *Bending with the Winds: Kurt Waldheim and the United Nations.* New York: Praeger, 1990.

————. *Your Man at the UN: People, Politics, and Bureaucracy in Making Foreign Policy.* New York: New York University Press, 1980.

————, and John Mugno. *The Politics of Staffing the United Nations Secretariat.* New York: Ralph Bunche Institute on the United Nations, Graduate School and University Center of the City University of New York, 1974.

Finkelstein, Lawrence S. "The Coordinative Function of the United Nations Secretary-General: What, If Anything, Should He Coordinate and How Should He Do It?" New York: Ralph Bunche Institute on the United Nations, Occasional Paper Series, 1992.

Foote, Wilder, ed. *Servant of Peace: A Selection of the Speeches and Statements of Dag Hammarskjöld.* New York: Harper & Row, 1963.

Fosdick, Raymond B. *The League and the United Nations After Fifty Years: The Six Secretaries-General.* Newton, CT: Raymond B. Fosdick, 1972.

Gerson, Allan. *The Kirkpatrick Mission: Diplomacy Without Apology: America at the United Nations, 1981–1985.* New York: Maxwell Macmillan International, 1991.

Hammarskjöld, Dag. *Servant of Peace: A Selection of the Speeches and Statements of Dag Hammarskjöld, Secretary-General of the United Nations, 1953–1961.* New York: Harper & Row, 1962.

Hazzard, Shirley. *Countenance of Truth: The United Nations and the Waldheim Case.* New York: Viking, 1990.

Jordan, Robert S., ed. *Dag Hammarskjöld Revisited: The UN Secretary-General as a Force in World Politics.* Durham, NC: Carolina Academic Press, 1983.

"Leadership at the United Nations: The Roles of the Secretary-General and the Member States." First Panel Report, United

Nations Management and Decision-Making Project. New York: United Nations Association of the United States of America, 1986.

Lie, Trygve. *In the Cause of Peace: Seven Years with the United Nations*. New York: Macmillan, 1954.

Miller, Richard I. *Dag Hammarskjöld and Crisis Diplomacy*. New York: Oceana Publications, 1961.

Nassif, Ramses. *U Thant in New York, 1961–1971: A Portrait of the Third UN Secretary-General*. London: Hurst, 1988.

"Report of the Group of High-Level Intergovernmental Experts to Review the Efficiency of the Administrative and Financial Functioning of the United Nations." UN Document A/41/49, 1986.

Rivlin, Benjamin, and Leon Gordenker, eds. *The Challenging Role of the UN Secretary-General: Making "the Most Impossible Job in the World" Possible*. Westport, CT: Praeger, 1993.

Rovine, Arthur W. *The First Fifty Years: The Secretary-General in World Politics, 1920–1970*. Leiden: A. W. Sijthoff, 1970.

Schwebel, Stephen M. *The Secretary-General of the United Nations: His Political Powers and Practice*. Cambridge, MA: Harvard University Press, 1952.

Thant, U. *View from the UN*. Garden City, NY: Doubleday, 1978.

Urquhart, Brian. *Hammarskjöld*. New York: Knopf, 1972.

————. *A Life in Peace and War*. New York: Harper & Row, 1987.

————. *Ralph Bunche: An American Life*. New York: W. W. Norton, 1993.

————, and Erskine Childers. *A World in Need of Leadership: Tomorrow's United Nations.* Uppsala, Sweden: Dag Hammarskjöld Foundation, 1990.

Waldheim, Kurt. *Building the Future Order: The Search for Peace in an Interdependent World.* New York: Free Press, 1980.

————. *The Challenge of Peace.* New York: Rawson, Wade Publishers, 1980.

Winchmore, Charles. "The Secretariat: Retrospect and Prospect," *International Organization,* 19 (Summer 1965), 622–39.

Zacher, Mark W. *Dag Hammarskjöld's United Nations.* New York: Columbia University Press, 1970.

Evaluation and Prospects

Arend, Anthony C. *International Law and the Use of Force: Beyond the UN Charter Paradigm.* New York: Routledge, 1993.

Ashby, Lowell D. *The United Nations' Economic Institutions and the Need for Restructuring.* Washington, DC: Center for UN Reform Education, 1991.

Baehr, Peter R. *The United Nations in the 1990s.* Houndmills, England: Macmillan, 1992.

————. *The United Nations, Reality and Ideal.* New York: Praeger, 1984.

Barnaby, Frank, ed. *Building a More Democratic United Nations.* London: Frank Cass & Co. Ltd., 1991.

Beigbeder, Yves. *Threats to the International Civil Service.* New York: Pinter Publishing, 1988.

Berdal, Mats R. *Whither UN Peacekeeping?: An Analysis of the Changing Military Requirement of UN Peacekeeping with Proposals for its Enhancement.* London: Brassey's Ltd. for the International Institute for Strategic Studies, 1993.

Beres, Louis R. *People, States, and World Order.* Itasca, IL: F. E. Peacock Publishers, Inc., 1981.

Berridge, Geoff. *Return to the UN: UN Diplomacy in Regional Conflicts.* New York: St. Martin's Press, 1991.

Bertrand, Maurice. *The Third Generation World Organization.* Dordrecht, Boston: Nijhoff, 1989.

Camps, Miriam. *Collective Management: The Reform of Global Economic Organizations.* New York: McGraw-Hill, 1981.

Coate, Roger. *Unilateralism, Ideology and U.S. Foreign Policy.* Boulder, CO: Lynne Rienner Publishers, 1988.

Commission to Study the Organization of Peace. *Modernizing the Security Council: Special Report.* New York, 1974.

————. *Restructuring the United Nations System for Economic and Social Cooperation and Development: Twenty-Seventh Report of the Commission to Study the Organization of Peace.* Muscatine, IA: Stanley Foundation, 1980.

Connaughton, R. M. *Military Intervention in the 1990s: A New Logic of War.* New York: Routledge, 1992.

Daley, Ted. *Russia's "Continuation" of the Soviet Security Council Membership and Prospective Russian Policies Toward the United Nations.* Santa Monica, CA: Rand, 1992.

Davis, Lynn E. *Peacekeeping and Peacemaking After the Cold War.* Santa Monica, CA: Rand, 1993.

Dorsey, Gray L. *Beyond the United Nations: A Changing Dis-*

course in International Politics and Law. Lanham, MD: University Press of America, 1986.

Finkelstein, Lawrence S., ed. *Politics in the United Nations System*. Durham, NC: Duke University Press, 1988.

Fromuth, Peter. *The UN at 40: The Problems and Opportunities*. New York: United Nations Association of the United States of America, 1986.

Goodrich, Leland M. *The United Nations in a Changing World*. New York: Columbia University Press, 1974.

Gregg, Robert W. *About Face? The United States and the United Nations*. Boulder, CO: L. Rienner Publishers, 1993.

Harrod, Jeffrey, and Nico Schrijver, eds. *The UN Under Attack*. Aldershot, England: Gower Publishing Co., 1988.

Kaufmann, Johan, and Nico Schrijver. *Changing Global Needs: Expanding Roles for the United Nations System*. Hanover, NH: Academic Council on the United Nations System, 1990.

Kay, David A., ed. *The Changing United Nations: Options for the United States*. Proceedings of the Academy of Political Science, 32, no 4 (1977).

Lee, John M. *To Unite Our Strength: Enhancing the United Nations Peace and Security System*. Lanham, MD: University Press of America, 1992.

McWhinney, Edward. *United Nations Law Making: Cultural and Ideological Relativism and International Law Making for an Era of Transition*. New York: Holmes & Meier, 1984.

Mayer, Martin. *Children of the World: Learning Together at the United Nations International School*. Lanham, MD: Madison Books, 1990.

Moynihan, Daniel P. *A Dangerous Place*. Boston: Little, Brown, 1978.

Muller, Joachim W. *The Reform of the United Nations*. Dobbs Ferry, NY: Oceana Publications, 1992.

Newcombe, Hanna. *Design for a Better World*. Lanham, MD: University Press of America, 1983.

Nordic UN Project. *The United Nations in Development: Reform Issues in the Economic and Social Fields: A Nordic Perspective: Final Report*. Stockholm: The Project; Distributed by Almqvist & Wiksell International, 1991.

Norton, Augustus R. *UN Peacekeepers: Soldiers with a Difference*. New York: Foreign Policy Association, 1990.

Perspectives on Multilateral Assistance: A Review by the Nordic UN Project. Stockholm, Sweden: Nordic UN Project, 1990.

Puchala, Donald J., and Roger A. Coate. *The Challenge of Relevance: The United Nations in a Changing World Environment*. Hanover, NH: Academic Council on the United Nations System, 1989.

"Reform and Restructuring of the UN System." Department of State Pub. 8940, International Organization and Conference Series 135, June 1978.

Rikhye, Indar Jit. *The Theory & Practice of Peacekeeping*. London: Published for the International Peace Academy by C. Hurst & Co., 1984.

———. *The United Nations and the Aftermath of the Gulf Crisis*. Toronto: Editions du Gref, 1992.

———, and Kjell Skjelsbask, eds. *The United Nations and Peacekeeping: Results, Limitations and Prospects: The Lessons of 40 Years of Experience*. Basingstoke, Hampshire,

England: Macmillan in association with the International Peace Academy, 1990.

Rochester, J. Martin. *Waiting for the Millennium: The United Nations and the Future of World Order.* Columbia, SC: University of South Carolina Press, 1993.

Roosevelt, Eleanor. *UN: Today and Tomorrow.* New York: Harper, 1953.

Rosenau, James N. *The United Nations in a Turbulent World.* Boulder, CO: Lynne Rienner Publishers, 1992.

Saksena, K. P. *Reforming the United Nations: The Challenge of Relevance.* New Delhi, Newbury Park: Sage Publications, 1993.

Staley, Robert Stephens. *The Wave of the Future: The United Nations and Naval Peacekeeping.* Boulder, CO: Lynne Rienner Publishers, 1992.

Steele, David. *The Reform of the United Nations.* London; Wolfeboro, NH: Croom Helm, 1987.

Tehranian, Katherine, and Majid Tehranian, eds. *Restructuring for World Peace: On the Threshold of the Twenty-First Century.* Cresskill, NJ: Hampton Press, Inc., 1992.

Urquhart, Brian. *Towards a More Effective United Nations: Two Studies.* Uppsala, Sweden: Dag Hammarskjöld Foundation, 1992.

Yeselson, Abraham. *A Dangerous Place: The United Nations as a Weapon in World Politics.* New York: Grossman Publishers, 1974.

Specialized Agencies and Other Bodies

Abbott, John Cave. *Politics and Poverty: A Critique of the Food and Agriculture Organization of the United Nations.* New York: Routledge, 1992.

Achieving Health for All by the Year 2000: Midway Reports of Country Experiences. Geneva: World Health Organization, 1990.

Alcock, Antony Evelyn. *History of the International Labour Organisation.* London: Macmillan, 1971.

"Annual Report of the Executive Director: United Nations Environment Programme." Nairobi, Kenya: United Nations Environment Programme.

"Annual Review: United Nations Environment Programme." Nairobi, Kenya: United Nations Environment Programme.

Ayres, Robert L. *Banking on the Poor: The World Bank and World Poverty.* Cambridge, MA: MIT Press, 1983.

Besen, Stanley M. *The Role of the ITU in Standardization: Preeminence, Impotence or Rubber Stamp.* Santa Monica, CA: Rand, 1992.

Buergenthal, Thomas. *Law-making in the International Civil Aviation Organization.* Syracuse, NY: Syracuse University Press, 1969.

Coate, Roger A. *Unilateralism, Ideology, and U.S. Foreign Policy: The United States In and Out of UNESCO.* Boulder, CO: Lynne Rienner, 1988.

Codding, George A. *The International Telecommunication Union in a Changing World.* Dedham, MA: Artech House, 1982.

Conable, Barber B. *The Conable Years at the World Bank: Major Policy Addresses of Barber B. Conable, 1986–91.* Washington, DC: World Bank, 1991.

DeLancey, Mark W., and Terry M. Mays. *Historical Dictionary of International Organizations in Sub-Saharan Africa.* Metuchen, NJ: Scarecrow Press, 1994.

DeVries, Barend A. *Remaking the World Bank.* Washington, DC: Seven Locks Press; Lanham, MD: Distributed by National Book Network, 1987.

First Implementation Plan for the World Climate Research Programme. Geneva: World Meteorological Organization, 1985.

Four Decades of Achievement: Highlights of the Work of WHO. Geneva: World Health Organization, 1988.

Ghebali, Victor Yves. *The International Labour Organisation: A Case Study on the Evolution of U.N. Specialized Agencies.* Dordrecht, Boston: Nijhoff, 1989.

Gibbon, Peter. *A Blighted Harvest: The World Bank and African Agriculture in the 1980s.* London: J. Currey, 1993.

Goode, Richard. *Economic Assistance to Developing Nations Through the IMF.* Washington, DC: Brookings Institution, 1985.

Gorman, Robert F. *Historical Dictionary of Refugee and Disaster Relief Organizations.* Metuchen, NJ: Scarecrow Press, 1994.

Hajnal, Peter I. *Guide to UNESCO.* London; New York: Oceana Publications, 1983.

Hinnawi, Essam E. *The State of the Environment.* London, Boston: Butterworths, 1987.

Humphreys, Norman K. *Historical Dictionary of the International Monetary Fund.* Metuchen, NJ: Scarecrow Press, 1994.

Hurni, Bettina S. *The Lending Policy of the World Bank in the 1970s: Analysis and Evaluation.* Boulder, CO: Westview Press, 1980.

Imber, Mark. *The USA, ILO, UNESCO, and IAEA: Politicization and Withdrawal in the Specialized Agencies.* New York: St. Martin's Press, 1989.

Jacobson, Harold Karan. *China's Participation in the IMF, the World Bank, and GATT: Toward a Global Economic Order.* Ann Arbor: University of Michigan Press, 1990.

Jenks, C. Wilfred. *Social Justice in the Law of Nations: The ILO Impact After Fifty Years.* New York: Oxford University Press, 1970.

Johnston, George A. *The International Labour Organisation: Its Work for Social and Economic Progress.* London: Europa Publications, 1970.

Jones, Phillip. W. *International Policies for Third World Education: UNESCO, Literacy and Development.* New York: Routledge, 1988.

Joyce, James Avery. *World Labour Rights and Their Protection.* London: Croom Helm, 1980.

Joyner, Christopher C. "The United States' Withdrawal from the ILO: International Politics in the Labor Arena," *International Lawyer,* 12 (Fall 1978), 721–39.

Labouisse, Henry R. "For the World's Children—UNICEF at 25," *UN Chronicle,* 8 (April 1971), 48–60.

Lambert, Youry. *The United Nations Industrial Development Organization: UNIDO and Problems of International Economic Cooperation.* Westport, CT: Praeger, 1993.

Laves, Walter H. *UNESCO: Purpose, Progress, Prospects.* Bloomington, IN: Indiana University Press, 1957.

Lengyel, Peter. *International Social Science, the UNESCO Experience.* New Brunswick, NJ: Transaction Books, 1986.

Lubin, Carol Riegelman. *Social Justice for Women: The Interna-*

tional Labour Organisation and Women. Durham, NC: Duke University Press, 1990.

M'Bow, Amadou-Mahtar. *Hope for the Future.* Paris: UNESCO, 1984.

McNamara, Robert S. *The McNamara Years at the World Bank: Major Policy Addresses of Robert S. McNamara, 1968–1981.* Baltimore, MD: Published for the World Bank by Johns Hopkins University Press, 1981.

Miller, Morris. *Coping Is Not Enough: The International Debt Crisis and the Roles of the World Bank and International Monetary Fund.* Homewood, IL: Dow Jones-Irwin, 1986.

Morse, David A. *The Origin and Evolution of the ILO and Its Role in the World Community.* Ithaca, NY: New York State School of Industrial and Labor Relations, Cornell University, 1969.

Mosley, Paul. *Aid and Power: The World Bank and Policy-Based Lending in the 1980s.* New York: Routledge, 1991.

Parker, J. Stephen. *UNESCO and Library Development Planning.* London: Library Association, 1985.

Payer, Cheryl. *The World Bank: A Critical Analysis.* New York: Monthly Review Press, 1982.

Price, John. *ILO: 50 Years On.* London: Fabian Society, 1969.

Pritchard, Anthony J. *Lending by the World Bank for Agricultural Research: A Review of the Years 1981 Through 1987.* Washington, DC: World Bank, 1990.

Quimby, Freeman H. *The Politics of Global Health.* Committee Print, Subcommittee on National Security Policy and Scientific Developments, Committee on Foreign Affairs, U.S. House of Representatives, 92nd Congress, 1st Session. Washington, DC: Government Printing Office, 1971.

Rich, Bruce. *Mortgaging the Earth: The World Bank, Environmental Impoverishment, and the Crisis of Development.* Boston, MA: Beacon Press, 1994.

Rothstein, Robert L. *Global Bargaining: UNCTAD and the Quest for a New International Economic Order.* Princeton: Princeton University Press, 1979.

Salda, Anne C.M. *International Monetary Fund.* Oxford, England: Clio Press, 1993.

————. *World Bank.* Oxford, England: Clio Press, 1994.

Savage, James G. *The Politics of International Telecommunications Regulation.* Boulder, CO: Westview Press, 1989.

Talbot, Ross. B. *The Four World Food Agencies in Rome.* Ames, IA: Iowa State University Press, 1990.

————. *Historical Dictionary of the International Food Agencies: FAO, WFP, WFC, IFAD.* Metuchen, NJ: Scarecrow Press, 1994.

The UNESCO Courier (Monthly). Paris: UNESCO.

United Nations Relief and Rehabilitation Administration. *UNRRA: The History of the United Nations Relief and Rehabilitation Administration.* New York: Columbia University Press, 1950.

Wells, Clare. *The UN, UNESCO, and the Politics of Knowledge.* New York: St. Martin's Press, 1987.

Williams, Douglas. *The Specialized Agencies and the United Nations.* New York: St. Martin's Press, 1987.

The Work of WHO: Biennial Report of the Director-General. Geneva: World Health Organization.

The World Bank Annual Report. Washington, DC: World Bank.

World Health Organization. *Global Strategy for Health for All by the Year 2000.* Geneva: World Health Organization, 1981.

Yudelman, Montague. *The World Bank and Agricultural Development: An Insider's View.* Washington, DC: World Resources Institute, 1985.

APPENDIX 1
CHARTER OF THE UNITED NATIONS

WE THE PEOPLES OF THE UNITED NATIONS determined

to save succeeding generations from the scourge of war, which twice in our lifetime has brought untold sorrow to mankind, and

to reaffirm faith in fundamental human rights, in the dignity and worth of the human person, in the equal rights of men and women and of nations large and small, and

to establish conditions under which justice and respect for the obligations arising from treaties and other sources of international law can be maintained, and

to promote social progress and better standards of life in larger freedom and for these ends

to practice tolerance and live together in peace with one another as good neighbors, and

to unite our strength to maintain international peace and security, and

to ensure, by the acceptance of principles and the institution of methods, that armed force shall not be used, save in the common interest, and

to employ international machinery for the promotion of the economic and social advancement of all peoples,

have resolved to combine our efforts to accomplish these aims.

Accordingly, our respective Governments, through representatives assembled in the city of San Francisco, who have exhibited their full powers found to be in good and due form, have agreed to the present Charter of the United Nations and do hereby establish an international organization to be known as the United Nations.

Chapter 1
Purposes and Principles

Article 1

The purposes of the United Nations are:

1. To maintain international peace and security, and to that end: to take effective collective measures for the prevention and removal of threats to the peace, and for the suppression of acts of aggression or other breaches of the peace, and to bring about by peaceful means, and in conformity with the principles of justice and international law, adjustment or settlement of international disputes or situations which might lead to a breach of the peace;
2. To develop friendly relations among nations based on respect for the principle of equal rights and self-determination of peoples, and to take other appropriate measures to strengthen universal peace;
3. To achieve international co-operation in solving international problems of an economic, social, cultural, or humanitarian character, and in promoting and encouraging respect for human rights and for fundamental freedoms for all without distinction as to race, sex, language, or religion; and
4. To be a centre for harmonizing the actions of nations in the attainment of these common ends.

Article 2

The Organization and its Members, in pursuit of the Purposes stated in Article 1, shall act in accordance with the following Principles.

1. The Organization is based on the principle of the sovereign equality of its Members.
2. All Members, in order to ensure to all of them the rights and benefits resulting from membership, shall fulfill in good faith the obligations assumed by them in accordance with the present Charter.

3. All Members shall settle their international disputes by peaceful means in such a manner that international peace and security, and justice, are not endangered.

4. All Members shall refrain in their international relations from the threat or use of force against the territorial integrity or political independence of any state, or in any other manner inconsistent with the Purposes of the United Nations.

5. All Members shall give the United Nations every assistance in any action it takes in accordance with the present Charter, and shall refrain from giving assistance to any state against which the United Nations is taking preventive or enforcement action.

6. The Organization shall ensure that states which are not Members of the United Nations act in accordance with these Principles so far as may be necessary for the maintenance of international peace and security.

7. Nothing contained in the present Charter shall authorize the United Nations to intervene in matters which are essentially within the domestic jurisdiction of any state or shall require the Members to submit such matters to settlement under the present Charter; but this principle shall not prejudice the application of enforcement measures under Chapter VII.

Chapter II
Membership

Article 3

The original Members of the United Nations shall be the states which, having participated in the United Nations Conference on International Organization at San Francisco, or having previously signed the Declaration by United Nations of 1 January 1942, sign the present Charter and ratify it in accordance with Article 110.

Article 4

1. Membership in the United Nations is open to all other peace-loving states which accept the obligations contained

in the present Charter and, in the judgment of the Organization, are able and willing to carry out these obligations.
2. The admission of any such state to membership in the United Nations will be effected by a decision of the General Assembly upon the recommendation of the Security Council.

Article 5

A Member of the United Nations against which preventive or enforcement action has been taken by the Security Council may be suspended from the exercise of the rights and privileges of membership by the General Assembly upon the recommendation of the Security Council. The exercise of these rights and privileges may be restored by the Security Council.

Article 6

A Member of the United Nations which has persistently violated the Principles contained in the present Charter may be expelled from the Organization by the General Assembly upon the recommendation of the Security Council.

Chapter III
Organs

Article 7

1. There are established as the principal organs of the United Nations: a General Assembly, a Security Council, an Economic and Social Council, a Trusteeship Council, an International Court of Justice and a Secretariat.
2. Such subsidiary organs as may be found necessary may be established in accordance with the present Charter.

Article 8

The United Nations shall place no restrictions on the eligibility of men and women to participate in any capacity and under conditions of equality in its principal and subsidiary organs.

Chapter IV
The General Assembly

COMPOSITION

Article 9

1. The General Assembly shall consist of all the Members of the United Nations.
2. Each Member shall have not more than five representatives in the General Assembly.

FUNCTIONS AND POWERS

Article 10

The General Assembly may discuss any questions or any matters within the scope of the present Charter or relating to the powers and functions of any organs provided for in the present Charter, and, except as provided in Article 12, may make recommendations to the Members of the United Nations or to the Security Council or to both on any such questions or matters.

Article 11

1. The General Assembly may consider the general principles of co-operation in the maintenance of international peace and security, including the principles governing disarmament and the regulation of armaments, and may make recommendations with regard to such principles to the Members or to the Security Council or to both.
2. The General Assembly may discuss any questions relating to the maintenance of international peace and security brought before it by any Member of the United Nations, or by the Security Council, or by a state which is not a Member of the United Nations in accordance with Article 35, paragraph 2, and, except as provided in Article 12, may make recommendations with regard to any such questions to

the state or states concerned or to the Security Council or to both. Any such question on which action is necessary shall be referred to the Security Council by the General Assembly either before or after discussion.

3. The General Assembly may call the attention of the Security Council to situations which are likely to endanger international peace and security.

4. The powers of the General Assembly set forth in this Article shall not limit the general scope of Article 10.

Article 12

1. While the Security Council is exercising in respect of any dispute or situation the functions assigned to it in the present Charter, the General Assembly shall not make any recommendations with regard to that dispute or situation unless the Security Council so requests.

2. The Secretary-General, with the consent of the Security Council, shall notify the General Assembly at each session of any matters relative to the maintenance of international peace and security which are being dealt with by the Security Council and shall similarly notify the General Assembly, or the Members of the United Nations if the General Assembly is not in session, immediately the Security Council ceases to deal with such matters.

Article 13

1. The General Assembly shall initiate studies and make recommendations for the purpose of:
   a. promoting international co-operation in the political field and encouraging the progressive development of international law and its codification;
   b. promoting international co-operation in the economic, social, cultural, educational, and health fields, and assisting in the realization of human rights and fundamental freedoms for all without distinction as to race, sex, language, or religion.

2. The further responsibilities, functions and powers of the

General Assembly with respect to matters mentioned in paragraph 1(b) above are set forth in Chapters IX and X.

Article 14

Subject to the provisions of Article 12, the General Assembly may recommend measures for the peaceful adjustment of any situation, regardless of origin, which it deems likely to impair the general welfare or friendly relations among nations, including situations resulting from a violation of the provisions of the present Charter setting forth the Purposes and Principles of the United Nations.

Article 15

1. The General Assembly shall receive and consider annual and special reports from the Security Council; these reports shall include an account of the measures that the Security Council has decided upon or taken to maintain international peace and security.
2. The General Assembly shall receive and consider reports from the other organs of the United Nations.

Article 16

The General Assembly shall perform such functions with respect to the international trusteeship system as are assigned to it under Chapters XII and XIII, including the approval of the trusteeship agreements for areas not designated as strategic.

Article 17

1. The General Assembly shall consider and approve the budget of the Organization.
2. The expenses of the Organization shall be borne by the Members as apportioned by the General Assembly.
3. The General Assembly shall consider and approve any financial and budgetary arrangements with specialized agencies referred to in Article 57 and shall examine the administrative budgets of such specialized agencies with a view to making recommendations to the agencies concerned.

VOTING

Article 18

1. Each member of the General Assembly shall have one vote.
2. Decisions of the General Assembly on important questions shall be made by a two-thirds majority of the members present and voting. These questions shall include: recommendations with respect to the maintenance of international peace and security, the election of the non-permanent members of the Security Council, the election of the members of the Economic and Social Council, the election of members of the Trusteeship Council in accordance with paragraph 1(c) of Article 86, the admission of new Members to the United Nations, the suspension of the rights and privileges of membership, the expulsion of Members, questions relating to the operation of the trusteeship system, and budgetary questions.
3. Decisions on other questions, including the determination of additional categories of questions to be decided by a two-thirds majority, shall be made by a majority of the members present and voting.

Article 19

A Member of the United Nations which is in arrears in the payment of its financial contributions to the Organization shall have no vote in the General Assembly if the amount of its arrears equals or exceeds the amount of the contributions due from it for the preceding two full years. The General Assembly may nevertheless, permit such a member to vote if it is satisfied that the failure to pay is due to conditions beyond the control of the Member.

PROCEDURE

Article 20

The General Assembly shall meet in regular annual sessions and in such special sessions as occasion may require. Special sessions shall be convoked by the Secretary-General at the request of the Security Council or of a majority of the Members of the United Nations.

Article 21

The General Assembly shall adopt its own rules of procedure. It shall elect its President for each session.

Article 22

The General Assembly may establish such subsidiary organs as it deems necessary for the performance of its functions.

Chapter V
The Security Council

COMPOSITION

Article 23

1. The Security Council shall consist of fifteen Members of the United Nations. The Republic of China, France, the Union of Soviet Socialist Republics, the United Kingdom of Great Britain and Northern Ireland, and the United States of America shall be permanent members of the Security Council. The General Assembly shall elect ten other Members of the United Nations to be non-permanent members of the Security Council, due regard being specially paid, in the first instance to the contribution of Members of the United Nations to the maintenance of international peace and security and to the other purposes of the Organization, and also to equitable geographical distribution.
2. The non-permanent members of the Security Council shall be elected for a term of two years. In the first election of the non-permanent members after the increase of the membership of the Security Council from eleven to fifteen, two of the four additional members shall be chosen for a term of

one year. A retiring member shall not be eligible for immediate reelection.

3. Each member of the Security Council shall have one representative.

FUNCTIONS AND POWERS

Article 24

1. In order to ensure prompt and effective action by the United Nations, its Members confer on the Security Council primary responsibility for the maintenance of international peace and security, and agree that in carrying out its duties under this responsibility the Security Council acts on their behalf.
2. In discharging these duties the Security Council shall act in accordance with the Purposes and Principles of the United Nations. The specific powers granted to the Security Council for the discharge of these duties are laid down in Chapters VI, VII, VIII, and XII.
3. The Security Council shall submit annual and, when necessary, special reports to the General Assembly for its consideration.

Article 25

The Members of the United Nations agree to accept and carry out the decisions of the Security Council in accordance with the present Charter.

Article 26

In order to promote the establishment and maintenance of international peace and security with the least diversion for armaments of the world's human and economic resources, the Security Council shall be responsible for formulating, with the assistance of the Military Staff Committee referred to in Article 47, plans to be submitted to the Members of the United Nations for the establishment of a system for the regulation of armaments.

VOTING

Article 27

1. Each member of the Security Council shall have one vote.
2. Decisions of the Security Council on procedural matters shall be made by an affirmative vote of nine members.
3. Decisions of the Security Council on all other matters shall be made by an affirmative vote of nine members including the concurring votes of the permanent members; provided that, in decisions under Chapter VI, and under paragraph 3 of Article 52, a party to a dispute shall abstain from voting.

PROCEDURE

Article 28

1. The Security Council shall be so organized as to be able to function continuously. Each member of the Security Council shall for this purpose be represented at all times at the seat of the organization.
2. The Security Council shall hold periodic meetings at which each of its members may, if it so desires, be represented by a member of the government or by some other specially designated representative.
3. The Security Council may hold meetings at such places other than the seat of the Organization as in its judgment will best facilitate its work.

Article 29

The Security Council may establish such subsidiary organs as it deems necessary for the performance of its functions.

Article 30

The Security Council shall adopt its own rules of procedure, including the method of selecting its President.

Article 31

Any Member of the United Nations which is not a member of the Security Council may participate, without vote, in the discussion of any question brought before the Security Council whenever the latter considers that the interests of that Member are specially affected.

Article 32

Any Member of the United Nations which is not a member of the Security Council or any state which is not a Member of the United Nations, if it is a party to a dispute under consideration by the Security Council, shall be invited to participate, without vote, in the discussion relating to the dispute. The Security Council shall lay down such conditions as it deems just for the participation of a state which is not a member of the United Nations.

Chapter VI
Pacific Settlement of Disputes

Article 33

1. The parties to any dispute, the continuance of which is likely to endanger the maintenance of international peace and security, shall, first of all, seek a solution by negotiation, enquiry, mediation, conciliation, arbitration, judicial settlement, resort to regional agencies or arrangements, or other peaceful means of their own choice.
2. The Security Council shall, when it deems necessary, call upon the parties to settle their dispute by such means.

Article 34

The Security Council may investigate any dispute, or any situation which might lead to international friction or give rise to a dispute, in order to determine whether the continuance of the dispute or situation is likely to endanger the maintenance of international peace and security.

Article 35

1. Any Member of the United Nations may bring any dispute, or
   any situation of the nature referred to in Article 34, to the
   attention of the Security Council or of the General Assembly.
2. A state which is not a Member of the United Nations may
   bring to the attention of the Security Council or of the General
   Assembly any dispute to which it is a party if it accepts in
   advance, for the purposes of the dispute, the obligations of
   pacific settlement provided in the present Charter.
3. The proceedings of the General Assembly in respect of
   matters brought to its attention under this Article will be
   subject to the provisions of Articles 11 and 12.

Article 36

1. The Security Council may, at any stage of a dispute of the
   nature referred to in Article 33 or of a situation of like
   nature, recommend appropriate procedures or methods of
   adjustment.
2. The Security Council should take into consideration any
   procedures for the settlement of the dispute which have
   already been adopted by the parties.
3. In making recommendations under this Article the Security
   Council should also take into consideration that legal disputes should as a general rule be referred by the parties to the
   International Court of Justice in accordance with the provisions of the Statute of the Court.

Article 37

1. Should the parties to a dispute of the nature referred to in
   Article 33 fail to settle it by the means indicated in that
   Article, they shall refer it to the Security Council.
2. If the Security Council deems that the continuance of the
   dispute is in fact likely to endanger the maintenance of
   international peace and security, it shall decide whether to
   take action under Article 36 or to recommend such terms of
   settlement as it may consider appropriate.

Article 38

Without prejudice to the provisions of Articles 33 to 37, the Security Council may, if all the parties to any dispute so request, make recommendations to the parties with a view to a pacific settlement of the dispute.

Chapter VII
Action with Respect to Threats to the Peace, Breaches of the Peace, and Acts of Aggression

Article 39

The Security Council shall determine the existence of any threat to the peace, breach of the peace, or act of aggression and shall make recommendations, or decide what measures shall be taken in accordance with Articles 41 and 42, to maintain or restore international peace and security.

Article 40

In order to prevent an aggravation of the situation, the Security Council may, before making the recommendations or deciding upon the measures provided for in Article 39, call upon the parties concerned to comply with such provisional measures as it deems necessary or desirable. Such provisional measures shall be without prejudice to the rights, claims, or position of the parties concerned. The Security Council shall duly take account of failure to comply with such provisional measures.

Article 41

The Security Council may decide what measures not involving the use of armed force are to be employed to give effect to its decisions, and it may call upon the Members of the United Nations to apply such measures. These may include complete or partial interruption of economic relations and of rail, sea, air, postal, telegraphic, radio, and other means of communication, and the severance of diplomatic relations.

Article 42

Should the Security Council consider that measures provided for in Article 41 would be inadequate or have proved to be inadequate, it may take such action by air, sea, or land forces as may be necessary to maintain or restore international peace and security. Such action may include demonstrations, blockade, and other operations by air, sea, or land forces of Members of the United Nations.

Article 43

1. All Members of the United Nations, in order to contribute to the maintenance of international peace and security, undertake to make available to the Security Council, on its call and in accordance with a special agreement or agreements, armed forces, assistance and facilities, including rights of passage, necessary for the purpose of maintaining international peace and security.
2. Such agreement or agreements shall govern the numbers and types of forces, their degree of readiness and general location, and the nature of the facilities and assistance to be provided.
3. The agreement or agreements shall be negotiated as soon as possible on the initiative of the Security Council. They shall be concluded between the Security Council and Members or between the Security Council and groups of Members and shall be subject to ratification by the signatory states in accordance with their respective constitutional processes.

Article 44

When the Security Council has decided to use force it shall, before calling upon a Member not represented on it to provide armed forces in fulfillment of the obligations assumed under Article 43, invite that Member, if the Member so desires, to participate in the decisions of the Security Council concerning the employment of contingents of that Member's armed forces.

Article 45

In order to enable the United Nations to take urgent military measures, Members shall hold immediately available national air-force contingents for combined international enforcement action. The strength and degree of readiness of these contingents and plans for their combined action shall be determined, within the limits laid down in the special agreement or agreements referred to in Article 43, by the Security Council with the assistance of the Military Staff Committee.

Article 46

Plans for the application of armed force shall be made by the Security Council with the assistance of the Military Staff Committee.

Article 47

1. There shall be established a Military Staff Committee to advise and assist the Security Council on all questions relating to the Security Council's military requirements for the maintenance of international peace and security, the employment and command of forces placed at its disposal, the regulation of armaments, and possible disarmament.
2. The Military Staff Committee shall consist of the Chiefs of Staff of the permanent members of the Security Council or their representatives. Any Member of the United Nations not permanently represented on the Committee shall be invited by the Committee to be associated with it when the efficient discharge of the Committee's responsibilities requires the participation of that Member in its work.
3. The Military Staff Committee shall be responsible under the Security Council for the strategic direction of any armed forces placed at the disposal of the Security Council. Questions relating to the command of such forces shall be worked out subsequently.
4. The Military Staff Committee, with the authorization of the

Security Council and after consultation with appropriate regional agencies, may establish regional sub-committees.

Article 48

1. The action required to carry out the decisions of the Security Council for the maintenance of international peace and security shall be taken by all the members of the United Nations or by some of them, as the Security Council may determine.
2. Such decisions shall be carried out by the Members of the United Nations directly and through their action in the appropriate international agencies of which they are members.

Article 49

The Members of the United Nations shall join in affording mutual assistance in carrying out the measures decided upon by the Security Council.

Article 50

If preventive or enforcement measures against any state are taken by the Security Council, any other state, whether a Member of the United Nations or not, which finds itself confronted with special economic problems arising from the carrying out of those measures shall have the right to consult the Security Council with regard to a solution of those problems.

Article 51

Nothing in the present Charter shall impair the inherent right of individual or collective self-defense if an armed attack occurs against a Member of the United Nations, until the Security Council has taken measures necessary to maintain international peace and security. Measures taken by members in the exercise of this right of self-defense shall be immediately reported to the Security Council and shall not in any way affect the authority and responsibility of the Security Council under the present Charter to take at any time such action as it deems necessary in order to maintain or restore international peace and security.

Chapter VIII
Regional Arrangements

Article 52

1. Nothing in the present Charter precludes the existence of regional arrangements or agencies for dealing with such matters relating to the maintenance of international peace and security as are appropriate for regional action, provided that such arrangements or agencies and their activities are consistent with the Purposes and Principles of the United Nations.
2. The Members of the United Nations entering into such arrangements or constituting such agencies shall make every effort to achieve pacific settlement of local disputes through such regional arrangements or by such regional agencies before referring them to the Security Council.
3. The Security Council shall encourage the development of pacific settlement of local disputes through such regional arrangements or by such regional agencies either on the initiative of the states concerned or by reference from the Security Council.
4. This Article in no way impairs the application of Articles 34 and 35.

Article 53

1. The Security Council shall, where appropriate, utilize such regional arrangements or agencies for enforcement action under its authority. But no enforcement action shall be taken under regional arrangements or by regional agencies without the authorization of the Security Council, with the exception of measures against any enemy state, as defined in paragraph 2 of this Article, provided for pursuant to Article 107 or in regional arrangements directed against renewal of aggressive policy on the part of any such state, until such time as the Organization may, on request of the Governments concerned, be charged with the responsibility for preventing further aggression by such a state.

2. The term enemy state as used in paragraph 1 of this Article applies to any state which during the Second World War has been an enemy of any signatory of the present Charter.

Article 54

The Security Council shall at all times be kept fully informed of activities undertaken or in contemplation under regional arrangements or by regional agencies for the maintenance of international peace and security.

Chapter IX
International Economic and Social Co-operation

Article 55

With a view to the creation of conditions of stability and well-being which are necessary for peaceful and friendly relations among nations based on respect for the principle of equal rights and self-determination of peoples, the United Nations shall promote:
   a. higher standards of living, full employment, and conditions of economic and social progress and development.
   b. solutions of international economic, social, health, and related problems; and international cultural and educational co-operation; and
   c. universal respect for, and observance of, human rights and fundamental freedoms for all without distinction as to race, sex, language, or religion.

Article 56

All Members pledge themselves to take joint and separate action in co-operation with the Organization for the achievement of the purposes set forth in Article 55.

Article 57

1. The various specialized agencies, established by intergovernmental agreement and having wide international

responsibilities, as defined in their basic instruments, in economic, social, cultural, educational, health, and related fields, shall be brought into relationship with the United Nations in accordance with the provisions of Article 63.

2. Such agencies thus brought into relationship with the United Nations are hereinafter referred to as specialized agencies.

Article 58

The Organization shall make recommendations for the coordination of the policies and activities of the specialized agencies.

Article 59

The Organization shall, where appropriate, initiate negotiations among the states concerned for the creation of any new specialized agencies required for the accomplishment of the purposes set forth in Article 55.

Article 60

Responsibility for the discharge of the functions of the Organization set forth in this Chapter shall be vested in the General Assembly and, under the authority of the General Assembly, in the Economic and Social Council, which shall have for this purpose the powers set forth in Chapter X.

Chapter X
The Economic and Social Council

COMPOSITION

Article 61

1. The Economic and Social Council shall consist of fifty-four Members of the United Nations elected by the General Assembly.
2. Subject to the provisions of paragraph 3, eighteen members of the Economic and Social Council shall be elected each

year for a term of three years. A retiring member shall be eligible for immediate re-election.

3. At the first election after the increase in the membership of the Economic and Social Council from twenty-seven to fifty-four members, in addition to the members elected in place of the nine members whose term of office expires at the end of that year, twenty-seven additional members shall be elected. Of these twenty-seven additional members, the term of office of nine members so elected shall expire at the end of one year, and of nine other members at the end of two years, in accordance with arrangements made by the General Assembly.

4. Each member of the Economic and Social Council shall have one representative.

FUNCTIONS AND POWERS

Article 62

1. The Economic and Social Council may make or initiate studies and reports with respect to international economic, social, cultural, educational, health, and related matters and may make recommendations with respect to any such matters to the General Assembly, to the Members of the United Nations and to the specialized agencies concerned.

2. It may make recommendations for the purpose of promoting respect for, and observance of, human rights and fundamental freedoms for all.

3. It may prepare draft conventions for submission to the General Assembly, with respect to matters falling within its competence.

4. It may call, in accordance with the rules prescribed by the United Nations, international conferences on matters falling within its competence.

Article 63

1. The Economic and Social Council may enter into agreements with any of the agencies referred to in Article 57, defining the terms on which the agency concerned shall be

brought into relationship with the United Nations. Such agreements shall be subject to approval by the General Assembly.

2. It may co-ordinate the activities of the specialized agencies through consultation with and recommendations to such agencies and through recommendations to the General Assembly and to the Members of the United Nations.

Article 64

1. The Economic and Social Council may take appropriate steps to obtain regular reports from the specialized agencies. It may make arrangements with the Members of the United Nations and with the specialized agencies to obtain reports on the steps taken to give effect to its own recommendations and to recommendations on matters falling within its competence made by the General Assembly.

2. It may communicate its observations on these reports to the General Assembly.

Article 65

The Economic and Social Council may furnish information to the Security Council and shall assist the Security Council upon its request.

Article 66

1. The Economic and Social Council shall perform such functions as fall within its competence in connection with the carrying out of the recommendations of the General Assembly.

2. It may, with the approval of the General Assembly, perform services at the request of Members of the United Nations and at the request of specialized agencies.

3. It shall perform such other functions as are specified elsewhere in the present Charter or as may be assigned to it by the General Assembly.

VOTING

Article 67

1. Each Member of the Economic and Social Council shall have one vote.
2. Decisions of the Economic and Social Council shall be made by a majority of the members present and voting.

PROCEDURE

Article 68

The Economic and Social Council shall set up commissions in economic and social fields and for the promotion of human rights, and such other commissions as may be required for the performance of its functions.

Article 69

The Economic and Social Council shall invite any Member of the United Nations to participate, without vote, in its deliberations on any matter of particular concern to that Member.

Article 70

The Economic and Social Council may make arrangements for representatives of the specialized agencies to participate, without vote, in its deliberations and in those of the commissions established by it, and for its representatives to participate in the deliberations of the specialized agencies.

Article 71

The Economic and Social Council may make suitable arrangements for consultation with non-governmental organizations which are concerned with matters within its competence. Such arrangements may be made with international organizations and, where appropriate, with national organizations after consultation with the Member of the United Nations concerned.

Article 72

1. The Economic and Social Council shall adopt its own rules of procedure, including the method of selecting its President.
2. The Economic and Social Council shall meet as required in accordance with its rules, which shall include provision for the convening of meetings on the request of a majority of its members.

Chapter XI
Declaration Regarding Non-Self-Governing Territories

Article 73

Members of the United Nations which have or assume responsibilities for the administration of territories whose peoples have not yet attained a full measure of self-government recognize the principle that the interests of the inhabitants of these territories are paramount, and accept as a sacred trust the obligation to promote to the utmost, within the system of international peace and security established by the present Charter, the well-being of the inhabitants of these territories, and, to this end:

a. to ensure, with due respect for the culture of the peoples concerned, their political, economic, social, and educational advancement, their just treatment, and their protection against abuses;
b. to develop self-government, to take due account of the political aspirations of the peoples, and to assist them in the progressive development of their free political institutions, according to the particular circumstances of each territory and its peoples and their varying stages of advancement;
c. to further international peace and security;
d. to promote constructive measures of development, to encourage research, and to co-operate with one another and,

when and where appropriate, with specialized international bodies with a view to the practical achievement of the social, economic, and scientific purposes set forth in this Article; and

e. to transmit regularly to the Secretary-General for information purposes, subject to such limitation as security and constitutional considerations may require, statistical and other information of a technical nature relating to economic, social, and educational conditions in the territories for which they are respectively responsible other than those territories to which Chapters XII and XIII apply.

Article 74

Members of the United Nations also agree that their policy in respect of the territories to which this Chapter applies, no less than in respect of their metropolitan areas, must be based on the general principle of good neighborliness, due account being taken of the interests and well-being of the rest of the world, in social, economic, and commercial matters.

Chapter XII
International Trusteeship System

Article 75

The United Nations shall establish under its authority an international trusteeship system for the administration and supervision of such territories as may be placed thereunder by subsequent individual agreements. These territories are hereinafter referred to as trust territories.

Article 76

The basic objectives of the trusteeship system, in accordance with the Purposes of the United Nations laid down in Article 1 of the present Charter, shall be:

a. to further international peace and security;
b. to promote the political, economic, social, and educational advancement of the inhabitants of the trust territories, and their progressive development towards self-government or independence as may be appropriate to the particular circumstances of each territory and its peoples and the freely expressed wishes of the peoples concerned, and as may be provided by the terms of each trusteeship agreement;
c. to encourage respect for human rights and for fundamental freedoms for all without distinction as to race, sex, language, or religion, and to encourage recognition of the interdependence of the peoples of the world; and
d. to ensure equal treatment in social, economic, and commercial matters for all Members of the United Nations and their nationals, and also equal treatment for the latter in the administration of justice, without prejudice to the attainment of the foregoing objectives and subject to the provisions of Article 80.

Article 77

1. The trusteeship system shall apply to such territories in the following categories as may be placed thereunder by means of trusteeship agreements:
    a. territories now held under mandate;
    b. territories which may be detached from enemy states as a result of the Second World War; and
    c. territories voluntarily placed under the system by states responsible for their administration.
2. It will be a matter for subsequent agreement as to which territories in the foregoing categories will be brought under the trusteeship system and upon what terms.

Article 78

The trusteeship system shall not apply to territories which have become Members of the United Nations, relationship among which shall be based on respect for the principle of sovereign equality.

Article 79

The terms of trusteeship for each territory to be placed under the trusteeship system, including any alteration or amendment, shall be agreed upon by the states directly concerned, including the mandatory power in the case of territories held under mandate by a Member of the United Nations, and shall be approved as provided for in Articles 83 and 85.

Article 80

1. Except as may be agreed upon in individual trusteeship agreements, made under Articles 77, 79, and 81, placing each territory under the trusteeship system, and until such agreements have been concluded, nothing in the Chapter shall be construed in or of itself to alter in any manner the rights whatsoever of any states or any peoples or the terms of existing international instruments to which Members of the United Nations may respectively be parties.
2. Paragraph 1 of the Article shall not be interpreted at giving grounds for delay or postponement of the negotiations and conclusion of agreements for placing mandated and other territories under the trusteeship system as provided for in Article 77.

Article 81

The trusteeship agreement shall in each case include the terms under which the trust territory will be administered and designate the authority which will exercise the administration of the trust territory. Such authority, hereinafter called the administering authority, may be one or more states or the Organization itself.

Article 82

There may be designated, in any trusteeship agreement, a strategic area or areas which may include part or all of the trust territory to which the agreement applies, without prejudice to any special agreement or agreements made under Article 43.

Article 83

1. All functions of the United Nations relating to strategic areas, including the approval of the terms of the trusteeship agreements and of their alteration or amendment, shall be exercised by the Security Council.
2. The basic objectives set forth in Article 76 shall be applicable to the people of each strategic area.
3. The Security Council shall, subject to the provisions of the trusteeship agreements and without prejudice to security considerations, avail itself of the assistance of the Trusteeship Council to perform those functions of the United Nations under the trusteeship system relating to political, economic, social, and educational matters in the strategic areas.

Article 84

It shall be the duty of the administering authority to ensure that the trust territory shall play its part in the maintenance of international peace and security. To this end the administering authority may make use of volunteer forces, facilities, and assistance from the trust territory in carrying out the obligations towards the Security Council undertaken in this regard by the administering authority, as well as for local defense and the maintenance of law and order within the trust territory.

Article 85

1. The functions of the United Nations with regard to trusteeship agreements for all areas not designated as strategic, including the approval of the terms of the trusteeship agreements and of their alteration or amendment, shall be exercised by the General Assembly.
2. The Trusteeship Council, operating under the authority of the General Assembly, shall assist the General Assembly in carrying out these functions.

Chapter XIII
The Trusteeship Council

COMPOSITION

Article 86

1. The Trusteeship Council shall consist of the following Members of the United Nations:
   a. those Members administering trust territories;
   b. such of those Members mentioned by name in Article 23 as are not administering trust territories; and
   c. as many other Members elected for three-year terms by the General Assembly as may be necessary to ensure that the total number of members of the Trusteeship Council is equally divided between those Members of the United Nations which administer trust territories and those which do not.
2. Each member of the Trusteeship Council shall designate one specially qualified person to represent it therein.

FUNCTIONS AND POWERS

Article 87

The General Assembly and, under its authority, the Trusteeship Council, in carrying out their functions, may:

a. consider reports submitted by the administering authority;
b. accept petitions and examine them in consultation with the administering authority;
c. provide for periodic visits to the respective trust territories at times agreed upon with the administering authority; and
d. take these and other actions in conformity with the terms of the trusteeships agreements.

Article 88

The Trusteeship Council shall formulate a questionnaire on the political, economic, social, and educational advancement of the inhabitants of each trust territory, and the administering authority for each trust territory within the competence of the General Assembly shall make an annual report to the General Assembly upon the basis of such questionnaire.

VOTING

Article 89

1. Each member of the Trusteeship Council shall have one vote.
2. Decisions of the Trusteeship Council shall be made by a majority of the members present and voting.

PROCEDURE

Article 90

1. The Trusteeship Council shall adopt its own rules of procedure, including the method of selecting its President.
2. The Trusteeship Council shall meet as required in accordance with its rules, which shall include provisions for the convening of meetings on the request of a majority of its members.

Article 91

The Trusteeship Council shall, when appropriate, avail itself of the assistance of the Economic and Social Council and of the specialized agencies in regard to matters with which they are respectively concerned.

Chapter XIV
The International Court of Justice

Article 92

The International Court of Justice shall be the principal judicial organ of the United Nations. It shall function in accordance with the annexed Statute, which is based upon the Statute of the Permanent Court of International Justice and forms an integral part of the present Charter.

Article 93

1. All Members of the United Nations are *ipso facto* parties to the Statute of the International Court of Justice.
2. A state which is not a Member of the United Nations may become a party to the Statute of the International Court of Justice on conditions to be determined in each case by the General Assembly upon the recommendation of the Security Council.

Article 94

1. Each Member of the United Nations undertakes to comply with the decision of the International Court of Justice in any case to which it is a party.
2. If any party to a case fails to perform the obligations incumbent upon it under a judgment rendered by the Court, the other party may have recourse to the Security Council, which may, if it deems necessary, make recommendations or decide upon measures to be taken to give effect to the judgment.

Article 95

Nothing in the present Charter shall prevent Members of the United Nations from entrusting the solution of their differences to other tribunals by virtue of agreements already in existence or which may be concluded in the future.

Article 96

1. The General Assembly or the Security Council may request the International Court of Justice to give an advisory opinion on any legal question.
2. Other organs of the United Nations and specialized agencies, which may at any time be so authorized by the General Assembly, may also request advisory opinions of the Court on legal questions arising within the scope of their activities.

Chapter XV
The Secretariat

Article 97

The Secretariat shall comprise a Secretary-General and such staff as the organization may require. The Secretary-General shall be appointed by the General Assembly upon the recommendation of the Security Council. He shall be the chief administrative officer of the Organization.

Article 98

The Secretary-General shall act in that capacity in all meetings of the General Assembly, of the Security Council, of the Economic and Social Council, and of the Trusteeship Council, and shall perform such other functions as are entrusted to him by these organs. The Secretary-General shall make an annual report to the General Assembly on the work of the Organization.

Article 99

The Secretary-General may bring to the attention of the Security Council any matter which in his opinion may threaten the maintenance of international peace and security.

Article 100

1. In the performance of their duties the Secretary-General and the staff shall not seek or receive instructions from any

government or from any other authority external to the Organization. They shall refrain from any action which might reflect on their position as international officials responsible only to the Organization.

2. Each Member of the United Nations undertakes to respect the exclusively international character of the responsibilities of the Secretary-General and the staff and not to seek to influence them in the discharge of their responsibilities.

Article 101

1. The staff shall be appointed by the Secretary-General under regulations established by the General Assembly.
2. Appropriate staffs shall be permanently assigned to the Economic and Social Council, the Trusteeship Council, and, as required, to other organs of the United Nations. These staffs shall form a part of the Secretariat.
3. The paramount consideration in the employment of the staff and in the determination of the conditions in the employment of the staff and in the determination of the conditions of service shall be the necessity of securing the highest standards of efficiency, competence, and integrity. Due regard shall be paid to the importance of recruiting the staff on as wide a geographical basis as possible.

Chapter XVI
Miscellaneous Provisions

Article 102

1. Every treaty and every international agreement entered into by any Member of the United Nations after the present Charter comes into force shall as soon as possible be registered with the Secretariat and published by it.
2. No party to any such treaty or international agreement which has not been registered in accordance with the provisions of paragraph 1 of this Article may invoke that treaty or agreement before any organ of the United Nations.

Article 103

In the event of a conflict between the obligations of the Members of the United Nations under the present Charter and their obligations under any other international agreement, their obligations under the present Charter shall prevail.

Article 104

The Organization shall enjoy in the territory of each of its Members such legal capacity as may be necessary for the exercise of its functions and the fulfillment of its purposes.

Article 105

1. The Organization shall enjoy in the territory of each of its Members such privileges and immunities as are necessary for the fulfillment of its purposes.
2. Representatives of the Members of the United Nations and officials of the Organization shall similarly enjoy such privileges and immunities as are necessary for the independent exercise of their functions in connection with the Organization.
3. The General Assembly may make recommendations with a view to determining the details of the application of paragraphs 1 and 2 of this Article or may propose conventions to the Members of the United Nations for this purpose.

Chapter XVII
Transitional Security Arrangements

Article 106

Pending the coming into force of such special agreements referred to in Article 43 as in the opinion of the Security Council enable it to begin the exercise of its responsibilities under Article 42, the parties to the Four-Nations Declaration, signed at

Moscow, 30 October 1943, and France, shall, in accordance with the provisions of paragraph 5 of that Declaration, consult with one another and as occasion requires with other Members of the United Nations with a view to such joint action on behalf of the Organization as may be necessary for the purpose of maintaining international peace and security.

Article 107

Nothing in the present Charter shall invalidate or preclude action, in relation to any state which during the Second World War has been an enemy of any signatory to the present Charter, taken or authorized as a result of that war by the Governments having responsibility for such action.

Chapter XVIII
Amendments

Article 108

Amendments to the present Charter shall come into force for all Members of the United Nations when they have been adopted by a vote of two-thirds of the members of the General Assembly and ratified in accordance with their respective constitutional processes by two-thirds of the Members of the United Nations, including all the permanent members of the Security Council.

Article 109

1. A General Conference of the Members of the United Nations for the purpose of reviewing the present Charter may be held at a date and place to be fixed by a two-thirds vote of the members of the General Assembly and by a vote of any nine members of the Security Council. Each Member of the United Nations shall have one vote in the conference.
2. Any alteration of the present Charter recommended by a two-thirds vote of the conference shall take effect when

ratified in accordance with their respective constitutional processes by two-thirds of the Members of the United Nations including all the permanent members of the Security Council.

3. If such a conference has not been held before the tenth annual session of the General Assembly following the coming into force of the present Charter, the proposal to call such a conference shall be placed on the agenda of that session of the General Assembly, and the conference shall be held if so decided by a majority vote of the members of the General Assembly and by a vote of any seven members of the Security Council.

Chapter XIX
Ratification and Signature

Article 110

1. The present Charter shall be ratified by the signatory states in accordance with their respective constitutional processes.
2. The ratifications shall be deposited with the Government of the United States of America, which shall notify all the signatory states of each deposit as well as the Secretary-General of the Organization when he has been appointed.
3. The present Charter shall come into force upon the deposit of ratifications by the Republic of China, France, the Union of Soviet Socialist Republics, the United Kingdom of Great Britain and Northern Ireland, and the United States of America, and by a majority of the other signatory states. A protocol of the ratification deposited shall thereupon be drawn up by the Government of the United States of America which shall communicate copies thereof to all the signatory states.
4. The states signatory to the present Charter which ratify it after it has come into force will become original Members of the United Nations on the date of deposit of their respective ratifications.

Article 111

The present Charter of which the Chinese, French, Russian, English, and Spanish texts are equally authentic, shall remain deposited in the archives of the Government of the United States of America. Duly certified copies thereof shall be transmitted by that Government to the Governments of the other signatory states.

IN FAITH WHEREOF the representatives of the Governments of the United Nations have signed the present Charter.

DONE at the city of San Francisco the twenty-sixth day of June, one thousand nine hundred and forty-five.

APPENDIX 2
THE UNIVERSAL DECLARATION
OF HUMAN RIGHTS

(Adopted by UN General Assembly, December 10, 1948)

Preamble

Whereas recognition of the inherent dignity and of the equal and inalienable rights of all members of the human family is the foundation of freedom, justice and peace in the world,

Whereas disregard and contempt for human rights have resulted in barbarous acts which have outraged the conscience of mankind, and the advent of a world in which human beings shall enjoy freedom of speech and belief and freedom from fear and want has been proclaimed as the highest aspiration of the common people,

Whereas it is essential, if man is not to be compelled to have recourse, as a last resort, to rebellion against tyranny and oppression, that human rights should be protected by the rule of law,

Whereas it is essential to promote the development of friendly relations between nations,

Whereas the peoples of the United Nations have in the Charter reaffirmed their faith in fundamental human rights, in the dignity and worth of the human person and in the equal rights of men and women and have determined to promote social progress and better standards of life in larger freedom,

Whereas Member States have pledged themselves to achieve, in co-operation with the United Nations, the promotion of universal respect for and observance of human rights and fundamental freedoms,

Whereas a common understanding of these rights and freedoms is of the greatest importance for the full realization of this pledge,

Now, therefore,
The General Assembly
Proclaims this Universal Declaration of Human Rights as a common standard of achievement for all peoples and all nations, to the end that every individual and every organ of society, keeping this Declaration constantly in mind, shall strive by teaching and education to promote respect for these rights and freedoms and by progressive measures, national and international, to secure their universal and effective recognition and observance, both among the peoples of Member States themselves and among the peoples of territories under their jurisdiction.

Article 1

All human beings are born free and equal in dignity and rights. They are endowed with reason and conscience and should act towards one another in a spirit of brotherhood.

Article 2

Everyone is entitled to all the rights and freedoms set forth in this Declaration, without distinction of any kind, such as race, colour, sex, language, religion, political or other opinion, national or social origin, property, birth or other status.

Furthermore, no distinction shall be made on the basis of the political, jurisdictional or international status of the country or territory to which a person belongs, whether it be independent, trust, non-self-governing or under any other limitation of sovereignty.

Article 3

Everyone has the right to life, liberty and the security of person.

Article 4

No one shall be held in slavery or servitude; slavery and the slave trade shall be prohibited in all their forms.

Article 5

No one shall be subjected to torture or to cruel, inhuman or degrading treatment or punishment.

Article 6

Everyone has the right to recognition everywhere as a person before the law.

Article 7

All are equal before the law and are entitled without any discrimination to equal protection of the law. All are entitled to equal protection against any discrimination in violation of this Declaration and against any incitement to such discrimination.

Article 8

Everyone has the right to an effective remedy by the competent national tribunals for acts violating the fundamental rights granted him by the constitution or by law.

Article 9

No one shall be subjected to arbitrary arrest, detention or exile.

Article 10

Everyone is entitled in full equality to a fair and public hearing by an independent and impartial tribunal, in the determination of his rights and obligations and of any criminal charge against him.

Article 11

1. Everyone charged with a penal offence has the right to be presumed innocent until proved guilty according to law in a public trial at which he has had all the guarantees necessary for his defence.
2. No one shall be held guilty of any penal offence on account of any act or omission which did not constitute a penal offence, under national or international law, at the time when it was committed. Nor shall a heavier penalty be imposed than the one that was applicable at the time the penal offence was committed.

Article 12

No one shall be subjected to arbitrary interference with his privacy, family, home or correspondence, nor to attacks upon his honor and reputation. Everyone has the right to the protection of the law against such interference or attacks.

Article 13

1. Everyone has the right to freedom of movement and residence within the borders of each State.
2. Everyone has the right to leave any country, including his own, and to return to his country.

Article 14

1. Everyone has the right to seek and to enjoy in other countries asylum from persecution.
2. This right may not be invoked in the case of prosecutions genuinely arising from non-political crimes or from acts contrary to the purposes and principles of the United Nations.

Article 15

1. Everyone has the right to a nationality.
2. No one shall be arbitrarily deprived of his nationality nor denied the right to change his nationality.

Article 16

1. Men and women of full age, without any limitation due to race, nationality or religion, have the right to marry and to found a family. They are entitled to equal rights as to marriage, during marriage and at its dissolution.
2. Marriage shall be entered into only with the free and full consent of the intending spouses.
3. The family is the natural and fundamental group unit of society and is entitled to protection by society and the State.

Article 17

1. Everyone has the right to own property alone as well as in association with others.
2. No one shall be arbitrarily deprived of his property.

Article 18

Everyone has the right to freedom of thought, conscience and religion; this right includes freedom to change his religion or belief, and freedom, either alone or in community with others and in public or private, to manifest his religion or belief in teaching, practice, worship and observance.

Article 19

Everyone has the right to freedom of opinion and expression; this right includes freedom to hold opinions without interference and to seek, receive and impart information and ideas through any media and regardless of frontiers.

Article 20

1. Everyone has the right to freedom of peaceful assembly and association.
2. No one may be compelled to belong to an association.

Article 21

1. Everyone has the right to take part in the government of his country, directly or through freely chosen representatives.
2. Everyone has the right of equal access to public service in his country.
3. The will of the people shall be the basis of the authority of government; this will shall be expressed in periodic and genuine elections which shall be by universal and equal suffrage and shall be held by secret vote or by equivalent free voting procedures.

Article 22

Everyone, as a member of society, has the right to social security and is entitled to realization, through national effort and international co-operation and in accordance with the organization and resources of each State, of the economic, social and cultural rights indispensable for his dignity and the free development of his personality.

Article 23

1. Everyone has the right to work, to free choice of employment, to just and favorable conditions of work and to protection against unemployment.
2. Everyone, without any discrimination, has the right to equal pay for equal work.
3. Everyone who works has the right to just and favorable remuneration ensuring for himself and his family an existence worthy of human dignity, and supplemented, if necessary, by other means of social protection.
4. Everyone has the right to form and to join trade unions for the protection of his interests.

Article 24

Everyone has the right to rest and leisure, including reasonable limitation of working hours and periodic holidays with pay.

Article 25

1. Everyone has the right to a standard of living adequate for the health and well-being of himself and of his family, including food, clothing, housing and medical care and necessary social services, and the right to security in the event of unemployment, sickness, disability, widowhood, old age or other lack of livelihood in circumstances beyond his control.
2. Motherhood and childhood are entitled to special care and

assistance. All children, whether born in or out of wedlock, shall enjoy the same social protection.

Article 26

1. Everyone has the right to education. Education shall be free, at least in the elementary and fundamental stages. Elementary education shall be compulsory. Technical and professional education shall be made generally available and higher education shall be equally accessible to all on the basis of merit.
2. Education shall be directed to the full development of the human personality and to the strengthening of respect for human rights and fundamental freedoms. It shall promote understanding, tolerance and friendship among all nations, racial or religious groups, and shall further the activities of the United Nations for the maintenance of peace.
3. Parents have a prior right to choose the kind of education that shall be given to their children.

Article 27

1. Everyone has the right freely to participate in the cultural life of the community, to enjoy the arts and to share in scientific advancement and its benefits.
2. Everyone has the right to the protection of the moral and material interests resulting from any scientific, literary or artistic production of which he is the author.

Article 28

Everyone is entitled to a social and international order in which the rights and freedoms set forth in this Declaration can be fully realized.

Article 29

1. Everyone has duties to the community in which alone the free and full development of his personality is possible.
2. In the exercise of his rights and freedoms, everyone shall be subject only to such limitations as are determined by law solely for the purpose of securing due recognition and respect for the rights and freedoms of others and of meeting the just requirements of morality, public order and the general welfare in a democratic society.
3. These rights and freedom may in no case be exercised contrary to the purposes and principles of the United Nations.

Article 30

Nothing in this Declaration may be interpreted as implying for any State, group or person any right to engage in any activity or to perform any act aimed at the destruction of any of the rights and freedoms set forth herein.

APPENDIX 3

Members of the United Nations: Date of Membership and Assessment

NAME OF COUNTRY	DATE OF ADMISSION	PERCENTAGE OF UN BUDGET ASSESSMENT
Afghanistan	19 Nov. 1946	0.01
Albania	14 Dec. 1955	0.01
Algeria	8 Oct. 1962	0.16
Andorra	8 July 1993	0.01
Angola	1 Dec. 1976	0.01
Antigua and Barbuda	11 Nov. 1981	0.01
Argentina	24 Oct. 1945	0.57
Armenia	2 Mar. 1992	0.13
Australia	1 Nov. 1945	1.51
Austria	14 Dec. 1955	0.75
Azerbaijan	2 Mar. 1992	0.22
Bahamas	18 Sep. 1973	0.02
Bahrain	21 Sep. 1971	0.03
Bangladesh	17 Sep. 1974	0.01
Barbados	9 Dec. 1966	0.01
Belarus	2 Mar. 1992	0.48
Belgium	27 Dec. 1945	1.06
Belize	25 Sep. 1981	0.01
Benin	20 Sep. 1960	0.01
Bhutan	21 Sep. 1971	0.01
Bolivia	14 Nov. 1945	0.01
Bosnia and Herzegovina	22 May 1992	0.04
Botswana	17 Oct. 1966	0.01
Brazil	24 Oct. 1945	1.59

Brunei Darussalam	21 Sep. 1984	0.03
Bulgaria	14 Dec. 1955	0.13
Burkina Faso	20 Sep. 1960	0.01
Burundi	18 Sep. 1962	0.01
Cambodia	14 Dec. 1955	0.01
Cameroon	20 Sep. 1960	0.01
Canada	9 Nov. 1945	3.11
Cape Verde	16 Sep. 1975	0.01
Central African Republic	20 Sep. 1960	0.01
Chad	20 Sep. 1960	0.01
Chile	24 Oct. 1945	0.08
China	24 Oct. 1945	0.77
Colombia	5 Nov. 1945	0.13
Comoros	12 Nov. 1975	0.01
Congo	20 Sep. 1960	0.01
Costa Rica	2 Nov. 1945	0.01
Côte d'Ivoire	20 Sep. 1960	0.02
Croatia	22 May 1992	0.13
Cuba	24 Oct. 1945	0.09
Cyprus	20 Sep. 1960	0.02
Czech Republic	19 Jan. 1993	0.42*
Democratic People's Republic of Korea	17 Sep. 1991	0.05
Denmark	24 Oct. 1945	0.65
Djibouti	20 Sep. 1977	0.01
Dominica	18 Dec. 1978	0.01
Dominican Republic	24 Oct. 1945	0.02
Ecuador	21 Dec. 1945	0.03
Egypt	24 Oct. 1945	0.07
El Salvador	24 Oct. 1945	0.01
Equatorial Guinea	12 Nov. 1968	0.01
Eritrea	28 May 1993	0.01
Estonia	17 Sep. 1991	0.07
Ethiopia	13 Nov. 1945	0.01
Fiji	13 Oct. 1970	0.01
Finland	14 Dec. 1955	0.57
France	24 Oct. 1945	6.00
Gabon	20 Sep. 1960	0.02
Gambia	21 Sep. 1965	0.01

Georgia	31 July 1992	0.21
Germany	18 Sep. 1973	8.93
Ghana	8 Mar. 1957	0.01
Greece	25 Oct. 1945	0.35
Grenada	17 Sep. 1974	0.01
Guatemala	21 Nov. 1945	0.02
Guinea	12 Dec. 1958	0.01
Guinea-Bissau	17 Sep. 1974	0.01
Guyana	20 Sep. 1966	0.01
Haiti	24 Oct. 1945	0.01
Honduras	17 Dec. 1945	0.01
Hungary	14 Dec. 1955	0.18
Iceland	19 Nov. 1946	0.03
India	30 Oct. 1945	0.36
Indonesia	28 Sep. 1950	0.16
Iran (Islamic Republic of)	24 Oct. 1945	0.77
Iraq	21 Dec. 1945	0.13
Ireland	14 Dec. 1955	0.18
Israel	11 May 1949	0.23
Italy	14 Dec. 1955	4.29
Jamaica	18 Sep. 1962	0.01
Japan	18 Dec. 1956	12.45
Jordan	14 Dec. 1955	0.01
Kazakhstan	2 Mar. 1992	0.35
Kenya	16 Dec. 1963	0.01
Kuwait	14 May 1963	0.25
Kyrgyzstan	2 Mar. 1992	0.06
Lao People's Democratic Republic	14 Dec. 1955	0.01
Latvia	17 Sep. 1991	0.13
Lebanon	24 Oct. 1945	0.01
Lesotho	17 Oct. 1966	0.01
Liberia	2 Nov. 1945	0.01
Libyan Arab Jamahiriya	14 Dec. 1955	0.24
Liechtenstein	18 Sep. 1990	0.01
Lithuania	17 Sep. 1991	0.15
Luxembourg	24 Oct. 1945	0.06
Madagascar	20 Sep. 1960	0.01
Malawi	1 Dec. 1964	0.01

Malaysia	17 Sep. 1957	0.12
Maldives	21 Sep. 1965	0.01
Mali	28 Sep. 1960	0.01
Malta	1 Dec. 1964	0.01
Marshall Islands	17 Sep. 1991	0.01
Mauritania	27 Oct. 1961	0.01
Mauritius	24 Apr. 1968	0.01
Mexico	7 Nov. 1945	0.88
Micronesia (Federated		
States of)	17 Sep. 1991	0.01
Monaco	28 May 1993	0.01*
Mongolia	27 Oct. 1961	0.01
Morocco	12 Nov. 1956	0.03
Mozambique	16 Sep. 1975	0.01
Myanmar	19 Apr. 1948	0.01
Namibia	23 Apr. 1990	0.01
Nepal	14 Dec. 1955	0.01
Netherlands	10 Dec. 1945	1.50
New Zealand	24 Oct. 1945	0.24
Nicaragua	24 Oct. 1945	0.01
Niger	20 Sep. 1960	0.01
Nigeria	7 Oct. 1960	0.20
Norway	27 Nov. 1945	0.55
Oman	7 Oct. 1971	0.03
Pakistan	30 Sep. 1947	0.06
Panama	13 Nov. 1945	0.02
Papua New Guinea	10 Oct. 1975	0.01
Paraguay	24 Oct. 1945	0.02
Peru	31 Oct. 1945	0.06
Philippines	24 Oct. 1945	0.07
Poland	24 Oct. 1945	0.47
Portugal	14 Dec. 1955	0.20
Qatar	21 Sep. 1971	0.05
Republic of Korea	17 Sep. 1991	0.69
Republic of Moldova	2 Mar. 1992	0.15
Romania	14 Dec. 1955	0.17
Russian Federation	24 Oct. 1945	6.71
Rwanda	18 Sep. 1962	0.01
Saint Kitts and Nevis	23 Sep. 1983	0.01
Saint Lucia	18 Sep. 1979	0.01

Saint Vincent and		
the Grenadines	16 Sep. 1980	0.01
Samoa	15 Dec. 1976	0.01
San Marino	2 Mar. 1992	0.01
São Tome and Principe	16 Sep. 1975	0.01
Saudi Arabia	24 Oct. 1945	0.96
Senegal	28 Sep. 1960	0.01
Seychelles	21 Sep. 1976	0.01
Sierra Leone	27 Sep. 1961	0.01
Singapore	21 Sep. 1965	0.12
Slovak Republic	19 Jan. 1993	0.13*
Slovenia	22 May 1992	0.09
Solomon Islands	19 Sep. 1978	0.01
Somalia	20 Sep. 1960	0.01
South Africa	7 Nov. 1945	0.41
Spain	14 Dec. 1955	1.98
Sri Lanka	14 Dec. 1955	0.01
Sudan	12 Nov. 1956	0.01
Suriname	4 Dec. 1975	0.01
Swaziland	24 Sep. 1968	0.01
Sweden	19 Nov. 1946	1.11
Syrian Arab Republic	24 Oct. 1945	0.04
Tajikistan	2 Mar. 1992	0.05
Thailand	16 Dec. 1946	0.11
The Former Yugoslav		
Republic of		
Macedonia	8 Apr. 1993	0.02*
Togo	20 Sep. 1960	0.01
Trinidad and Tobago	18 Sep. 1962	0.05
Tunisia	12 Nov. 1956	0.03
Turkey	24 Oct. 1945	0.27
Turkmenistan	2 Mar. 1992	0.06
Uganda	25 Oct. 1962	0.01
Ukraine	24 Oct. 1945	1.87
United Arab Emirates	9 Dec. 1971	0.21
United Kingdom	24 Oct. 1945	5.02
United Republic		
of Tanzania	14 Dec. 1961	0.01
United States		
of America	24 Oct. 1945	25.00

Uruguay	18 Dec. 1945	0.04
Uzbekistan	2 Mar. 1992	0.26
Vanuatu	15 Sep. 1981	0.01
Venezuela	15 Nov. 1945	0.49
Vietnam	20 Sep. 1977	0.01
Yemen	30 Sep. 1947	0.01
Yugoslavia	24 Oct. 1945	0.14*
Zaire	20 Sep. 1960	0.01
Zambia	1 Dec. 1964	0.01
Zimbabwe	25 Aug. 1980	0.01

*Provisional

APPENDIX 4

Presidents of the General Assembly

NAME	COUNTRY	YEAR
1. Paul-Henri Spaak	Belgium	1946
2. Oswaldo Aranha	Brazil	1947
3. H. V. Evatt	Australia	1948
4. Carlos P. Romulo	Philippines	1949
5. Nasrollah Entezam	Iran	1950
6. Luis Padilla Nervo	Mexico	1951
7. Lester B. Pearson	Canada	1952
8. Vijaya Lakshmi Pandit	India	1953
9. Eelco N. van Kleffens	Netherlands	1954
10. José Maza	Chile	1955
11. Prince Wan Waithayakon	Thailand	1956
12. Sir Leslie Munro	New Zealand	1957
13. Charles Malik	Lebanon	1958
14. Victor Andrés Belaúnde	Peru	1959
15. Frederick H. Boland	Ireland	1960
16. Mongi Slim	Tunisia	1961
17. Sir Muhammad Zafrulla Khan	Pakistan	1962
18. Carlos Sosa Rodríguez	Venezuela	1963
19. Alex Quaison-Sackey	Ghana	1964
20. Amintore Fanfani	Italy	1965
21. Abdul Rahman Pazhwak	Afghanistan	1966
22. Corneliu Manescu	Romania	1967
23. Emilio Arenales Catalán	Guatemala	1968
24. Angie E. Brooks	Liberia	1969
25. Edvard Hambro	Norway	1970
26. Adam Malik	Indonesia	1971
27. Stanislaw Trepczynski	Poland	1972

28. Leopoldo Benites	Ecuador	1973
29. Abdelaziz Bouteflika	Algeria	1974
30. Gaston Thorn	Luxembourg	1975
31. H. S. Amerasinghe	Sri Lanka	1976
32. Lazar Mojsov	Yugoslavia	1977
33. Indalecio Liévano	Colombia	1978
34. Salim A. Salim	United Republic of Tanzania	1979
35. Rüdiger von Wechmar	Federal Republic of Germany	1980
36. Ismat T. Kittani	Iraq	1981
37. Imre Hollai	Hungary	1982
38. Jorge E. Illueca	Panama	1983
39. Paul J. F. Lusaka	Zambia	1984
40. Jaime de Piniés	Spain	1985
41. Humayun Rasheed Choudhury	Bangladesh	1986
42. Peter Florin	German Democratic Republic	1987
43. Dante M. Caputo	Argentina	1988
44. Joseph Nanven Garba	Nigeria	1989
45. Guido de Marco	Malta	1990
46. Samir S. Shihabi	Saudi Arabia	1991
47. Stoyan Ganev	Bulgaria	1992
48. Samuel R. Insanally	Guyana	1993
49. Amara Essy	Ivory Coast	1994

APPENDIX 5
SECRETARIES-GENERAL OF THE
UNITED NATIONS

Although the term of office is not specified in the Charter of the United Nations, Secretaries-General are elected for five-year terms.

Trygve Lie (Norway) 1946–1953. Previously led Norwegian delegation to San Francisco Conference which drafted the Charter. In 1951 the Soviet Union vetoed his appointment to a second five-year term whereupon the General Assembly extended his term. He resigned effective April 1953.

Dag Hammarskjöld (Sweden) 1953–1961. Previously served as Swedish delegate to the Organization for European Economic Cooperation and to the Commission of Ministers of the Council of Europe. Pioneered in developing the principles of peacekeeping for forces sent to the Middle East and the Congo. Killed in plane crash en route to mediate the Congo crisis.

U Thant (Burma, now Myanmar) 1961–1971. Previously Permanent Representative of Burma to the United Nations. First third-world UN Secretary-General. Arranged withdrawal of UN peacekeeping forces from the Congo (1964) and the Middle East (1967). Presided over first UN financial crisis resulting from unpaid peacekeeping assessments.

Kurt Waldheim (Austria) 1972–1981. Previously head of Austrian delegation to the United Nations. Took charge of the establishment of three new peacekeeping forces in the Middle East. Was generally supportive of third-world aspirations in

North-South economic issues. Charges of World War II involvement in German war crimes did not surface until five years after his term of office.

Javier Pérez de Cuéllar (Peru) 1982–1991. Previously served as Permanent Representative of Peru to the United Nations and as UN Undersecretary-General for Special Political Affairs. Presided over the intensified UN financial crisis and strong demands, led by the United States, for administrative and budgetary reforms. Also involved in growing UN peacekeeping operations and the UN role in the Iraqi invasion of Kuwait.

Boutros Boutros-Ghali (Egypt) 1992– . First Secretary-General from Africa and the Arab world. Prolific scholar and previous Deputy Prime Minister of Egypt. Faced problem of financing expanded UN peacekeeping activities as numerous new and large missions were established, often involving enforcement measures in civil disorders. Also continued responses to demands for further administrative reforms.

ABOUT THE AUTHOR

A. LEROY BENNETT (B.Ed., Western Illinois University; M.A., Ph.D., University of Illinois) is Professor Emeritus of Political Science and International Relations at the University of Delaware. He has been a student of United Nations and international organization affairs since 1946, and has regularly taught courses on these subjects. His textbook, *International Organizations: Principles and Issues* (Prentice-Hall) has recently appeared in its 6th edition. In 1951–52 he spent the academic year in New York as an observer of United Nations activities as a recipient of a Ford Foundation fellowship. In 1980 he took a sabbatical leave to study United Nations operations in Geneva and Vienna. From 1962 until 1984 he was coordinator of the interdisciplinary program in international relations at the University of Delaware. His previous collegiate appointments were at Michigan State University and Drake University. He serves on the Board of Directors of the Delaware Chapter of the United Nations Association and of the World Affairs Council of Wilmington. He is a member of the American Political Science Association, the International Studies Association, and the Academic Council on the United Nations System.